A Cook's Tour
of the
Azalea
Coast

including recipes from
famous Auxiliary Taste & Tell Luncheons
Local physicians, Area Restaurants, Celebrities
and a Special Diet Section

published By

The Auxiliary to the

New Hanover, Pender, Brunswick

County Medical Society

Wilmington, North Carolina

Cover: Orton Plantation, Wilmington, North Carolina
    Photographed by Freda and Lucien Wilkins

International Standard Book Number: 939114-36-4

Printed in the United States of America
Wimmer Brothers Fine Printing and Lithography
Memphis, Tennessee 38118
"Cookbooks of Distinction" ™

COMMITTEES

Chairwomen: Katherine Matthews
Emily McCoy
Freda Wilkins

Calligraphy: Harriette Taylor
Photography: Freda Wilkins

SECTION EDITORS:
Appetizers and beverages: Barbara Gonzales
Soups and salads: Nancy Musselwhite
Meats: Libby Lewis
Seafoods: Maryann Robison
Poultry, cheese and egg dishes: Marion Morrison
Vegetables: Carolyn Morris
Breads: Harriette Taylor
Desserts and pies: Teri Donahue
Cakes, cookies and candies: Martha Wortman
Preserves, pickles and sauces: Betsy Codington
Special diets: Robbie Weinel

Celebrity recipes editors: Karen Roberts and Sherry Lovette
Taste and Tell recipes editors: Drukie Cathell and Pat Marshburn
Physician recipes editor: Betsy Ormand
Restaurant recipes editor: Joan Pence

Index editor: Betty Tinsley
Artists: Diane Cashman, Lynn MacQueen, Sue Mobley and
Becky Shuford

Historian: Miriam Warshauer

Recipe testing committee: Auxiliary members and friends too numerous to mention. Special credits to the Home Economic Departments from John T. Hoggard High School and Emsley A. Laney High School, Wilmington, North Carolina
Publicity: Eleanor Hunt and Jane Morse
Distribution and marketing: Jane Maloy and Sue Mobley

3

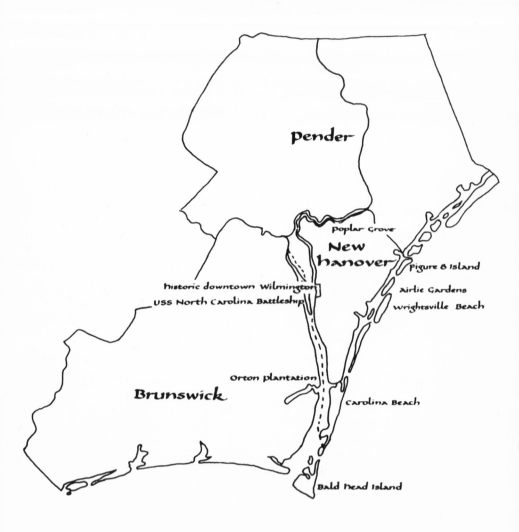

Pender

New hanover

Poplar Grove

Figure 8 Island

historic downtown Wilmington

Airlie Gardens

USS North Carolina Battleship

wrightsville Beach

Orton plantation

Brunswick

Carolina Beach

Bald head Island

azalea Coast

Table of Contents

HISTORY OF ORGANIZATION

The Auxiliary to the Medical Society was organized in 1928. Its primary purpose was to promote fellowship for families of physicians. Over the years, the organization has grown into a service oriented group which channels its talents and financial resources into a wide range of projects to benefit the health education of the community.

Many hours of volunteer service to the hospitals, schools and community health organizations have been logged. The Auxiliary has provided nursing scholarships, sponsored a para-medical careers day in the schools, established a bicycle safety program and sponsored a workshop for baby-sitters and a health fair for fifth graders. It established *The Incredible You* exhibit for the New Hanover County Museum and raised funds for hospital equipment, teaching aids for the nursing programs and for a drug abuse program. A history of medicine of the Lower Cape Fear area, *The Lonely Road,* was published in 1976.

The proceeds from this cookbook will be used to continue to support health education and other related projects in the community.

appetizers
&
Beverages

Dawn . . . Pelicans search out a breakfast catch while early fishermen follow suit on Johnny Mercer's Pier.

SPECIAL BROILED SHRIMP

2 pounds raw shrimp
1 cup oil
1½ tablespoons chili powder
1 tablespoon vinegar
3 cloves of garlic, minced
1 teaspoon salt

¼ teaspoon black pepper
1 tablespoon mint leaves,
  chopped
1½ teaspoons basil
Lemon slices

Shell and dry shrimp. Make a marinade of oil, chili powder, vinegar, garlic, salt, black pepper, mint leaves and basil. Place shrimp in the marinade in a Zip-lock bag and marinate overnight or at least 4 hours. Partially drain shrimp and put in a broiling pan under high heat for 6-10 minutes, turning once. Garnish with lemon slices.

Note: Marinade can be stored in refrigerator to be used again within 1 week. Can be served as a main dish with rice. Serves 4.

Mrs. Emil Werk (Dottie)

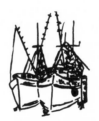

PICKLED SHRIMP

4½ pounds shrimp
4 onions, sliced
4 lemons, sliced thin
2 bottles Kraft Italian dressing
½ cup white vinegar
4 bay leaves, broken
1 tablespoon horseradish

1 tablespoon Worcestershire
  sauce
2 tablespoons sugar
¼ teaspoon celery seed
1 tablespoon Tabasco sauce
1 teaspoon salt
1 jar capers

Cook and clean shrimp. In a bowl, layer shrimp, onions, and lemons. Make a dressing by pouring off oil of one bottle of Italian dressing and combining the remainder with the second bottle of dressing. Add vinegar, bay leaves, horseradish, Worcestershire sauce, sugar, celery seeds, Tabasco sauce, salt and capers. Pour dressing over layers and chill 24 hours. Remove from marinade and serve. Serves 10 to 12.

Mrs. Ben Yue (Haeyoon)

CHICKEN NUGGETS

3 chicken breasts, skinned
  and boned
¾ cup unseasoned bread
  crumbs
½ cup Parmesan cheese

½ teaspoon Accént
½ teaspoon salt
¼ teaspoon thyme
1 teaspoon basil
2 sticks margarine, melted

Cut chicken into bite size pieces. Combine bread crumbs, Parmesan cheese, Accént, salt, thyme and basil and mix well. Dip chicken in margarine, then into bread crumb mixture. Place in single layer on foil lined cookie sheet. Bake at 400 degrees for 20 minutes.

Note: Can be frozen in single layer, then placed in plastic bags. To serve, thaw to room temperature and reheat at 350 degrees for 15 minutes.

Mrs. Martin B. Meyerson (Margery)

CRAB BALL HORS D'OEUVRE

1 (6-ounce) package snow crab
1 (8-ounce) package cream
  cheese, softened
2 teaspoons chives

¼ teaspoon garlic powder
¼ teaspoon salt
½ cup pecans, chopped

Blend together snow crab, cream cheese, chives, garlic powder and salt. Shape mixture into a ball. Roll in pecans. Serve with crackers.

Mrs. Terry Stewart (Susan)

HOT CRAB MEAT PUFFS

2 egg whites, stiffly beaten
1 cup mayonnaise
1 cup crab meat, flaked
1 teaspoon lemon juice
½ teaspoon Worcestershire
  sauce

¼ teaspoon Tabasco sauce
Toast rounds
Paprika

Combine egg whites, mayonnaise, and crab meat. Add lemon juice, Worcestershire sauce, Tabasco sauce. Spoon onto toast rounds. Sprinkle with paprika, and broil until bubbly. Makes 3 to 4 dozen.

Mrs. Thomas B. Mobley, III (Sue)

STUFFED MUSHROOMS

8 ounces fresh mushrooms
(approximately 30-35)
Butter to dot
1½ tablespoons onions,
chopped
½ stick margarine
1 egg, beaten
1½ teaspoons lemon juice
1 teaspoon parsley
5 slices bacon, fried
and crushed
½ cup herb croutons,
finely crushed
Salt and pepper

Preheat oven to 400 degrees. Remove stems from mushrooms. Place caps in baking dish, dot with butter, and bake in a 400 degree oven for 10 minutes. Chop stems finely. Sauté stems and onion in margarine. Add egg, lemon juice and parsley. Add bacon and enough crumbs to absorb liquid. Add salt and pepper to taste. Fill caps with mixture in mound shape. Bake in 350 degree oven until warmed.

Note: May be done ahead and refrigerated, then baked before serving.

Mrs. Kenny Morris (Carolyn)

STUFFED MUSHROOMS WITH HAM

36 fresh mushrooms, washed
and stemmed
1 cup fine dry bread crumbs
1 (3-ounce) jar Deviled
Smithfield Ham spread
Cream or milk to moisten
Parmesan cheese, finely grated

Preheat oven to 350 degrees. Chop mushroom stems and mix with the bread crumbs, ham, and a little cream or milk to moisten. Stuff mushrooms with mixture. Sprinkle with Parmesan cheese. Bake for 15 minutes. Serve hot on toothpicks as an hors d'oeuvre or as a garnish for meat. Serves 6.

Note: These may be prepared ahead and baked just before serving.

Mrs. Landon B. Anderson (Connie)

MEAT BALLS IN SHERRY SAUCE

3 pounds ground chuck
6 eggs, beaten
1½ teaspoons salt
Pepper, finely ground
¼ cup flour
¼-½ cup salad oil

4 beef bouillon cubes
3 cups water, hot
4 tablespoons flour
1 tablespoon Kitchen Bouquet
1 cup sherry

Mix together chuck, eggs, salt, pepper, and ¼ cup flour. Shape into balls. Brown a few at a time in hot salad oil. After browning, reserve 4 tablespoons of oil. Dissolve bouillon cubes in water. Add 4 tablespoons flour to reserved oil. Stir and add bouillon and Kitchen Bouquet. Cook, stirring constantly, until thickened. Add sherry.

Note: Freezes well. May also be used as an entrée. Serve over rice or noodles.

Mrs. Henry Singletary (Gorda)

TRAIL'S END MEATBALLS

2 pounds ground sirloin
½ cup grated onion
1 (7½-ounce) can jalapeño
  relish
2 eggs

½ teaspoon monosodium
  glutamate
2 dashes Worcestershire sauce
1 teaspoon ground black
  pepper

Mix all ingredients, being careful not to overmix. Shape into bite size balls. Place evenly on sheetpan. Bake in 375 degree oven 10 minutes. Serves 16-20 people.

Sarah Hedgpeth
Trail's End
Wilmington, North Carolina

MOCK BOURSIN CHEESE SPREAD

2 (8-ounce) packages cream
cheese
2 sticks butter or oleo
1 scant teaspoon ground garlic
1 teaspoon dill weed
½ teaspoon thyme
½ teaspoon marjoram

½ teaspoon sweet basil
1 teaspoon oregano
Salt and pepper to taste
Optional: fresh parsley,
chopped and/or chives
to taste

Soften cream cheese and butter and mix together until it is free of lumps and well blended. Add the garlic, dill weed, thyme, marjoram, sweet basil, oregano, salt, and pepper, fresh parsley, and/or chives. Fill a crock or wrap in Saran Wrap in a ball shape. Refrigerate. Serve with favorite cracker or Melba toast rounds. After the ball is firm, it can be rolled in cracked peppercorns for those who like pepper boursin.

Mrs. John Cashman (Diane)

GROUND SHRIMP

2 quarts water
1 tablespoon McCormick's
Seafood Boil
1 pound shrimp
1 (5-ounce) jar prepared
horseradish

1 lemon, squeezed,
or juice to taste
Mayonnaise to bind
Salt
Pepper, freshly ground

Add Seafood Boil to water and boil shrimp. Devein shrimp and grind through a food mill. Mix together shrimp, horseradish, lemon juice, mayonnaise, salt and pepper to taste, and place in a buttered mold. Refrigerate. Serve on crackers.

Mrs. Joseph James (Eleanor)

PATÉ DE CREVETTE

1 (3-ounce) package cream
   cheese, cut up
½ stick of butter
½ pound firm-fleshed fish,
   poached, skinned, boned,
   and flaked
Pinch of mace

Pinch of cayenne pepper
1 tablespoon lemon juice
Salt to taste
½ pound shrimp, cooked,
   shelled and deveined
2-3 tablespoons fresh cream

In a food processor, cream together the cream cheese and butter. Add fish to creamed mixture and process until combined. Season with mace, cayenne pepper, lemon juice and salt. Add shrimp and cream. Process until mixture is light and fluffy. Add more cream if necessary to achieve a light consistency. Line a bowl with plastic wrap. Fill with mixture. Cover and chill at least 4 hours or overnight. To serve, uncover and turn serving plate upside down over bowl. Turn plate and bowl over together. Remove bowl. Peel plastic wrap away from paté. Smooth over with a knife. Garnish with lemon wedges and green olives. Serve with crackers.

Note: You may use frozen fish, such as flounder, sole, etc.

Mrs. John Morse (Jane)

LIVER SPREAD

1 pound chicken livers
⅛ cup oil
1 egg, hard boiled

1 small onion, finely chopped
½ cup mayonnaise

Rinse chicken livers and pat dry with paper toweling. Brown chicken livers in oil in a frying pan. Cover and cook 10 minutes. Mash livers in frying pan. Remove to bowl and mix with egg, onion, and mayonnaise. Serve on crackers. Serves 8-10 people.

Note: Doubles easily.

Mrs. Charles Nance (Linda)

JEZEBEL (HOT AND SWEET)

1 (18-ounce) jar of pineapple
  preserves
1 (10-ounce) jar apple jelly
¼ cup vinegar
1 tablespoon black
  peppercorns, coarsely ground

1 teaspoon dry mustard
1 teaspoon cayenne pepper
⅛ teaspoon salt

Mix pineapple preserves and apple jelly with vinegar. Add black pepper-corns, coarsely ground or cracked with a hammer. Add mustard, cayenne pepper, and salt. Serve over cream cheese with crackers or melba toast.

Note: Keeps indefinitely in refrigerator.

Mrs. Charles Wilkinson (Anne)

ARTICHOKE SOUFFLÉ

2 (8½-ounce) cans artichoke
  hearts, drained and mashed
1 cup Parmesan cheese, grated

1 cup Hellman's mayonnaise
Sprinkle of garlic salt

Preheat oven to 350 degrees. Mix artichoke hearts, Parmesan cheese, mayonnaise, and garlic salt. Put mixture into a greased 1½-quart casserole dish. Bake for 20 to 25 minutes. Serve with crackers or Melba rounds.

Mrs. William H. Weinel, Jr. (Robbie)

CHEESE BROCCOLI DIP

1 (12-ounce) jar Cheese Whiz
½ teaspoon garlic powder
1 (10¾-ounce) can cream of
  mushroom soup
1 (10-ounce) package frozen
  chopped broccoli, cooked
  and drained

1 teaspoon Worcestershire
  sauce
¼ teaspoon Tabasco sauce
2 (8-ounce) cans chopped
  mushrooms, drained

Combine Cheez Whiz and garlic powder. Melt cheese in double boiler. Add mushroom soup, broccoli, Worcestershire sauce, Tabasco sauce, and mushrooms. Heat until piping hot. Serve hot in a chafing dish with Bugles or Melba rounds.

Mrs. James Sloan (Blair)

FRESH VEGETABLE DIP

1 cup mayonnaise
½ tablespoon lemon juice
½ cup parsley, chopped or
   1 tablespoon parsley flakes
1 tablespoon onion, grated
2 tablespoons chives, chopped

½ cup sour cream
¼ teaspoon salt
¼ teaspoon paprika
⅛ teaspoon curry powder
¼ teaspoon garlic powder

Combine all ingredients. Let set overnight in the refrigerator. Fresh vegetables to use with dip include: carrots, celery, green peppers, broccoli, cauliflower, mushrooms, and radishes.

Mrs. Michael Rallis (Debra)
Burgaw, North Carolina

CHILI CON QUESO

2 pound box Velveeta cheese
2 (10-ounce) cans tomatoes and
   chilies
1 cup onion, chopped

1 (6-ounce) package mozzarella
   cheese
4 ounces Picante sauce or hot
   taco sauce

Cut Velveeta cheese into chunks. Heat all ingredients in double boiler until well mixed. Transfer to chafing dish. Serve with Doritos. Makes 1½ quarts.

Note: Can add more Picante sauce to taste.

Mrs. Carl Rust (Polly)

PECAN BEEF DIP

1 cup pecans, chopped
2 tablespoons butter, melted
2 (8-ounce) packages cream
   cheese
4 tablespoons milk

1 teaspoon garlic salt
4 teaspoons onion, minced
1 cup sour cream
4 ounces dried beef

Sauté pecans in butter. Mix cream cheese, milk, garlic salt, onion, and sour cream. Shred beef and add into mixture. Mix ¼ cup nuts into mixture. Place in small baking dish and top with remaining nuts. Bake at 350 degrees for 20 minutes. Serve with Corn Diggers or Bugles.

Mrs. James D. Hundley (Linda)

SMOKED OYSTER DIP

1 (3-ounce) package cream
  cheese, softened
½ cup sour cream
1 (3½-ounce) can smoked
  oysters, drained and chopped
½ cup ripe olives, minced
1 teaspoon onion, grated

Thoroughly blend cream cheese, sour cream, oysters, olives and onion. Serve with chips or crackers. Makes 1 cup.

Mrs. Landon B. Anderson (Connie)

HOT CRAB CHEESE DIP

1 (8-ounce) package
  Philadelphia cream cheese
1 pound fresh crab meat
1 teaspoon onion salt
½ teaspoon garlic powder
Red pepper to taste
1 tablespoon Worcestershire
  sauce
1 (4-ounce) can mushrooms,
  chopped and drained
Dash of sherry wine
1 cup mayonnaise

Melt the cream cheese in double boiler. Add crab meat, onion salt, garlic powder, red pepper, Worcestershire sauce, mushrooms, sherry, and mayonnaise. Reheat in a chafing dish at serving time. Serve with Melba rounds or toast points.

Mrs. Conway Ficklen (Rose)

HOT CHILE QUICHE

2 (4-ounce) cans hot Mexican
  green chiles
8 ounces Cheddar cheese,
  grated
2 eggs, beaten
2 tablespoons milk

Preheat oven to 350 degrees. Put chilies in bottom of aluminum or ceramic pie plate. Sprinkle with Cheddar cheese. Add beaten eggs and milk. Bake for 30 minutes. Serve on crackers.

Note: This can be frozen and reheated.

Mrs. David P. Thomas (Ginny)

ATLANTA CHEESE BALL

2 (8-ounce) packages cream
  cheese, softened
½ pound sharp Cheddar
  cheese, grated
2 teaspoons onion, grated
2 teaspoons Worcestershire
  sauce
1 teaspoon lemon juice
1 teaspoon dry mustard

½ teaspoon paprika
½ teaspoon seasoning salt
¼ teaspoon salt
1 (2¼-ounce) can deviled ham
2 teaspoons parsley, chopped
2 teaspoons pimento, chopped
  and well drained
½ cup pecans, chopped

Mix cream cheese, Cheddar cheese, onion, Worcestershire sauce, lemon juice, dry mustard, paprika, seasoning salt, salt, deviled ham, parsley, and pimento. Chill. Form into one large or two small balls. Roll in nuts. Refrigerate. Remove from refrigerator 15 minutes before serving.

Mrs. James B. Sloan (Blair)

CLAMS CASINO

2 dozen clams
  (small littlenecks)

Casino Topping:
½ cup finely chopped onions
½ cup finely chopped green
  peppers
½ cup finely chopped
  pimentos
¼ teaspoon seafood seasoning

¼ tablespoon red pepper—
  less if desired
½ stick butter
2 tablespoons chicken paste
¼ pound bacon (uncooked),
  chopped

Shuck clams into one half of shell (keep chilled). Combine the onions, peppers, pimento, seafood seasoning, red pepper, butter, and chicken paste into a saucepan. Cook over medium heat until thoroughly heated. Dish out about one tablespoon of this dressing onto each clam. Top with the chopped bacon. Broil for 6-10 minutes or until bacon is well cooked. Serve hot with lemon wedges.

Fish Market Restaurant
Wilmington, North Carolina

CAVIAR MOUSSE

6 ounces of red or black caviar
¼ cup fresh parsley, chopped
1 tablespoon onion, grated
1 tablespoon lemon rind, grated
1 pint sour cream

1 envelope gelatin
1 cup heavy cream
¼ cup water
Fresh pepper
Egg, boiled (optional)

Combine caviar, parsley, onion, and lemon rind. Stir in sour cream. Sprinkle gelatin over water in a saucepan. Whip heavy cream. Cook gelatin over low heat stirring constantly until gelatin is dissolved. Stir gelatin mixture into caviar and sour cream mix. Fold in whipped cream. Add pepper to taste. Chill until set in buttered mold. Serve on a bed of lettuce and garnish with slices of boiled egg. Spread on crackers or buttered pumpernickel bread.

Note: Use simple mold, as it is easier to remove.

Mrs. William Parker (Connie)

HOT SHERRIED V-8

1 (46-ounce) can V-8 juice
2 tablespoons brown sugar
¼ teaspoon basil, crushed

Dash of cinnamon
Dash of cloves
¼ cup sherry

Combine V-8 juice, sugar, basil, cinnamon and cloves. Heat thoroughly. Add sherry just before serving. Makes 10 (5-ounce) servings.

Mrs. Wilbur P. Matthews (Katherine)

PAPPY'S BLOODY MARYS

1 (46-ounce) can V-8 juice
6 ounces vodka
¼ cup lemon juice, freshly
   squeezed
8 or 9 grinds of the pepper mill

¾ teaspoon celery salt
9 teaspoons Worcestershire
   sauce
6 dashes Tabasco sauce

Mix all ingredients in a big glass pitcher. Serve over ice cubes and enjoy! Makes 13-14 (four-ounce) drinks.

Wesley W. Hall, M.D.

SEAFOOD MOUSSE

4 envelopes gelatin
1 cup water
1 cup mayonnaise
1 cup sour cream
1 (7-ounce) can tuna fish
with juice
½ pound shrimp, cooked
and chopped
2 jars chow chow or
hot pepper relish
1 small onion, grated
1 medium cucumber, chopped
1 cup cauliflower,
finely chopped
⅓ cup vinegar
¼ cup sugar
1 teaspoon salt
4 or 5 dashes Tabasco
1 tablespoon Worcestershire
sauce
½ cup sweet pickle relish
1 (2-ounce) jar chopped
pimentos

Mix gelatin in cold water. Place over low heat until dissolved. Cream mayonnaise and sour cream. Combine all other ingredients with mayonnaise and sour cream. Stir in gelatin. Pour into mold. Makes 3 quarts. 12 servings.

Jerry Rouse
Figure 8 Yacht Club
Wilmington, North Carolina

SALMON MOUSSE

1 (16-ounce) can salmon
1 envelope unflavored gelatin
1 small onion, chopped
2 tablespoons lemon juice
½ cup water, boiling
½ cup mayonnaise
⅓ teaspoon paprika
1 teaspoon dill
1 cup heavy cream

Drain and clean salmon and set aside. Empty unflavored gelatin into blender with onion, lemon juice, and boiling water. Blend 1 minute. Add mayonnaise, paprika, dill and salmon. Blend at high speed 30 seconds. Add ⅓ of cream. Blend several seconds. Add remaining cream. Blend 30 seconds. Pour mixture into lightly oiled 4-cup mold. Chill. Serve with crackers or rye bread slices.

Mrs. James E. Wortman (Martha)

BETSY'S ICED COFFEE

6 teaspoons decaffeinated
  instant coffee
1 cup water, boiling

9 (¼-grain) saccharin tablets
1 quart cold milk
¼ teaspoon cloves, ground

Dissolve six teaspoons decaffeinated coffee in boiling water. Add saccharin tablets and stir until dissolved. Let stand until cool. Add 1 quart cold milk and ¼ teaspoon ground cloves. Serve over ice.

Mrs. David Sloan, Jr. (Emily)

COFFEE PUNCH

1 gallon double strength coffee
½ cup sugar
1 quart whipping cream,
  whipped

1 gallon vanilla ice cream
2 tablespoons brandy extract
1 bottle (750 ml) brandy

Add sugar to coffee and chill. Add brandy extract and brandy. Fold in whipping cream and pour in punch bowl. Float scoops of ice cream on top. Serves 50-60 people.

Gray Gables Restaurant
Wrightsville Beach, North Carolina

SPICED HOT GRAPE JUICE

3 cups water
12 whole cloves
12 whole allspice
2 sticks cinnamon

1 cup grape juice
1 medium lemon
Sugar to taste

Boil water and spices 10 minutes. Remove spices and add grape juice and juice of 1 lemon. Sweeten to taste. Makes 1 quart.

Mrs. Ralph McCoy (Emily)

QUEEN'S GARDEN PARTY PUNCH

½ cup sugar
1½ cups water
4 sticks cinnamon
12 cloves
1 (46-ounce) can pineapple
   juice
1 (12-ounce) can frozen orange
   juice

3 (12-ounce) cans water
1 (12-ounce) can frozen
   lemonade
3 (12-ounce) cans water
1 (28-ounce) bottle ginger ale

In a saucepan, bring to a boil the sugar, water, cinnamon, and cloves and simmer for 30 minutes. Strain out the cinnamon and cloves. In a large container mix together the sugar syrup, the pineapple juice, the orange juice, water, lemonade and water. Add the ginger ale just before serving. Makes a little over 1 gallon.

Note: For very cold punch, I substitute an equal amount of ice for part of the water.

Mrs. Lucien S. Wilkins (Freda)

RUM CRANBERRY PUNCH

2 cups light rum
½ cup white sugar
1 (12-ounce) can frozen orange
   juice, thawed and undiluted
1 (32-ounce) bottle cranberry
   juice, chilled

1 (28-ounce) bottle ginger ale,
   chilled
Orange slices or strawberries
Ice cubes

Combine rum, sugar, orange juice, and cranberry juice. Refrigerate. Just before serving, add the ginger ale and ice cubes. Garnish with orange slices or strawberries. Makes 2½ quarts.

Mrs. Stephen Kash (Anne)

WASSAIL BOWL

3 whole oranges
Whole cloves
6 cups apple juice
1 (2-inch) stick cinnamon
¼ teaspoon nutmeg
¼ cup honey

3 tablespoons lemon juice
1 teaspoon lemon rind,
 freshly grated
2½ cups unsweetened
 pineapple juice

Stud oranges with cloves. Place in a baking pan with half an inch of water (cover bottom of pan). Bake in a 350 degree oven for 30 minutes. Heat apple juice and cinnamon stick in a large pan. Bring to a boil and simmer, covered, for 5 minutes. Add nutmeg, honey, lemon juice, lemon rind and pineapple juice. Simmer uncovered for 5 minutes more. Place in punch bowl and float baked oranges on top. Keep warm over low flame.

Note: You may add 1 jigger of rum per cup. Makes about 20 cups.

Mrs. Oliver Raymond Hunt (Eleanor)

MAMMA'S EGGNOG

12 large eggs
1 pint whipping cream
Pinch of salt

12 tablespoons sugar
12 tablespoons bourbon

Separate white and yolks of eggs. With electric mixer beat egg whites in large bowl until very stiff. In separate large bowl, beat whipping cream until thick. Beat egg yolks in separate large bowl and add salt. Next, while still beating, add sugar one tablespoon at a time to egg yolks. Last add the bourbon to egg yolks, while still beating, one tablespoon at a time *very slowly*. If the bourbon is added too rapidly you will cook the egg yolks. Pour egg yolk mixture into a punch bowl. Fold in egg whites. Last fold in cream. Chill. Serves 12.

Mrs. William P. Robison (Maryann)

EDGEWATER CHRISTMAS PUNCH

2 cups orange juice
2 cups tea
1 cup simple syrup
1 cup lemon juice

1 cup pineapple juice
2 quarts Club Soda
1 quart Applejack brandy

Chill all ingredients before mixing. In a punch bowl, mix orange juice, tea, simple syrup, lemon juice, and pineapple juice. Just before arrival of guests, mix in Club Soda and brandy.

Note: Keeps cooler longer if ice mold added.

Mrs. Donald Getz (Judy)

SNOW-WHITE GRANITA

1 (6-ounce) can frozen
   concentrate for lemonade
3 cups ice, crushed

½ cup superfine sugar
2 egg whites
¾ cup light rum

Place all ingredients in blender container. Blend at high speed until mixture is snowy (about 45 seconds). Makes 3 cups.

Mrs. Ralph McCoy (Emily)

BOURBON SLUSH

2 individual-sized tea bags
1 cup water, boiling
1 cup sugar
½ of a (6-ounce) can frozen
   lemonade concentrate,
   thawed

3½ cups water
¾ cup bourbon
1 (6-ounce) can frozen orange
   juice concentrate, thawed

Steep tea in 1 cup boiling water for 2 to 3 minutes. Stir in sugar until dissolved. Add lemonade concentrate, water, bourbon, and orange juice concentrate. Blend well. Pour into freezer containers and freeze. Remove from freezer about 10 minutes before serving. Spoon into glasses. Makes 1½ quarts.

Mrs. Thomas B. Mobley, III (Sue)

soups & salads

Cape Fear River Front—Tugs await a ship's arrival across from the permanently berthed U.S.S. North Carolina.

SWEET AND SOUR ASPIC

⅓ cup sugar
½ cup tomato juice
¼ teaspoon wine or tarragon
  vinegar
⅛ teaspoon salt
1 envelope unflavored gelatin
¼ cup water
½ cup celery, chopped

1 (2-ounce) jar pimento,
  chopped
¼ cup lemon juice
1 teaspoon onion, grated
½ cup asparagus, cut into
  1-inch lengths
1½ cups pecans, chopped

Blend sugar, juice, vinegar, and salt in saucepan and bring to a boil. Soften gelatin in cold water and add to mixture. Place celery, pimento, asparagus, lemon juice, and onion in a 1-quart shallow greased pan. Add heated mixture and chill in refrigerator until set. Serve on lettuce. Serves 4 to 6.

Mrs. Stephen Kash (Ann)

ASPIC VEGETABLE SALAD

2 (3-ounce) packages lemon
  Jello
4 cups V-8 juice or tomato juice
½ teaspoon seasoned salt
2 tablespoons lemon juice
2 tablespoons brown sugar

2 or 3 cups raw vegetables, any
  combination of the following:
  cucumbers, spring onions,
  celery, carrots, cauliflower,
  mushrooms, canned
  artichokes, and pimento-
  stuffed olives
Lettuce

Bring V-8 juice to a boil. Add Jello, seasoned salt, lemon juice, and brown sugar. Allow to completely dissolve. Cool. Arrange vegetables in a 2-quart pyrex dish; pour liquid gelatin over vegetables and chill until firm. Serve on lettuce with mayonnaise topping, if desired. Serves 6 to 8.

Mrs. John Cashman (Diane)

CONGEALED CHICKEN

1 (4-pound) chicken
2 envelopes unflavored gelatin
1 cup hot water
1 pint mayonnaise
1 cup chicken stock
1 (8½-ounce) can green peas, drained
1 cup slivered almonds
2 cups celery, chopped
4 tablespoons pimento, chopped
4 tablespoons India relish

Boil, bone, and cut up chicken. Save chicken stock. Dissolve gelatin in one cup hot water. Mix mayonnaise with gelatin mixture. Add chicken stock and mix. Add chicken, peas, almonds, celery, pimento, and relish. Pour into a 9x13 dish and cover. Chill overnight. Cut into squares and serve on lettuce. Makes 14 servings.

Mrs. Clifford Lewis (Libby)

CONGEALED TUNA

1 envelope unflavored gelatin
½ cup cold water
2 (9¼-ounce) cans tuna, flaked
1 cup salad dressing
1 cup celery, chopped
1 (5¾-ounce) jar stuffed olives, sliced
5 hard boiled eggs, chopped
¼ cup pecans, chopped
Juice of one lemon

Soak gelatin in cold water for five minutes. Place container in boiling water to dissolve the gelatin. Mix tuna, salad dressing, celery, olives, eggs, lemon juice, and pecans together. Add to gelatin solution. Pour into 1-quart container and chill. Serves 6 to 8.

Mrs. Charles Nance, Jr. (Linda)

TOMATO PINEAPPLE SURPRISE

3 (16-ounce) cans stewed
  tomatoes
3 (3-ounce) packages lemon
  Jello
1½ teaspoons salt
4½ tablespoons vinegar

3 (8¾-ounce) cans crushed
  pineapple, drained
⅜ teaspoon ground allspice
1 tablespoon sugar
¼ teaspoon dried basil

Bring tomatoes to a boil. Add allspice, basil, Jello, sugar, and salt. Stir until dissolved. Add vinegar and drained pineapple. Pour into 2-quart pyrex flat dish and chill until set. Serves 12.

Mrs. Neill Musselwhite (Nancy)

VEGETABLE RIBBON SALAD

9 (3-ounce) packages lemon
  Jello
2 quarts water, boiling
1¾ quarts cold water
⅔ cup vinegar
2 tablespoons salt
1½ quarts cabbage, finely
  chopped

1½ quarts carrots, grated
1½ quarts raw spinach, finely
  chopped
3 tablespoons green onions,
  finely cut
Crisp lettuce

Dissolve gelatin in boiling water. Add cold water, vinegar, and salt. Divide into 3 parts. Chill each until slightly thickened. Add cabbage to first part of gelatin. Turn into 6 loaf pans 4x9x2½ to depth of one inch. Chill until firm. Add carrots to second part of thickened gelatin. Pour over firm cabbage layers. Chill until firm. Add spinach and onion to remaining gelatin. Pour over carrot layers. Chill until firm. Unmold; cut each loaf into 8 slices. Serve on crisp lettuce. Makes 48 servings.

Mrs. Charles P. Graham (Jean)

GLORIA'S CUCUMBER LIME SALAD

2 (3-ounce) packages lime Jello
1¾ cups water, boiling
2 cups cottage cheese, (small curd)
1 cup mayonnaise

2 medium cucumbers peeled and finely chopped
1 medium onion, finely chopped
¼ cup celery, chopped
¼ cup green pepper, chopped

Dissolve Jello in boiling water. Cool. Blend in cottage cheese and mayonnaise. Chill until slightly thickened. Fold in cucumbers, onion, celery, and green pepper. Pour into 8-cup mold. Chill until firm. Serves 8.

Mrs. Stephen Kash (Ann)

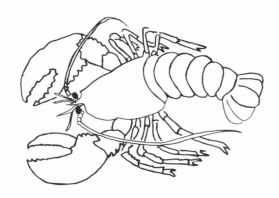

LORNA'S WONDERFUL SALAD

1 (3-ounce) package lemon Jello
1 (3-ounce) package lime Jello
2 cups water, boiling
3 teaspoons prepared horseradish
1 cup mayonnaise

1 cup cottage cheese (small curd)
2 cups crushed pineapple, drained
1 (14-ounce) can Eagle Brand condensed milk
1 cup nuts, chopped

Combine Jello packages in boiling water until Jello is dissolved. Add horseradish and stir. Blend in mayonnaise well. Then add cottage cheese, crushed pineapple, condensed milk, and nuts. Pour into 8x12x2 pyrex dish. Chill in refrigerator until firm. Serves 6 to 8.

Mrs. Henry Jordan (Jean)

APRICOT PINEAPPLE SALAD

2 (3-ounce) packages orange
   Jello
2 cups water, boiling
1 (1-pound, 13-ounce) can
   apricots, chopped (save juice)
1 (16-ounce) can crushed
   pineapple (save juice)
2 cups combined apricot and
   pineapple juice

1½ cups miniature
   marshmallows
½ cup sugar
3 tablespoons all-purpose flour
1 egg
2 tablespoons butter
1 cup cream, whipped
1 cup cheese, grated

Drain apricots and pineapple and chill. Combine juices and reserve. Dissolve Jello in boiling water; add 1 cup of combined juices. Let chill and partially set. Fold in apricots, chopped fine, crushed pineapple, and marshmallows. Pour into 9x13 dish. Let chill until set. For top layer, combine in double boiler sugar, flour, egg, butter, and 1 cup combined juices. Cook until thick, stirring constantly. Cool. Fold in whipped cream. Spoon over congealed salad. Top with grated cheese. Serves 8 to 10.

Mrs. Frederick Butler, Jr. (Ann)

STRAWBERRY JELLO MOLD

1 large package strawberry
   Jello (6 ounce)
1 cup boiling water
1 (13½-ounce) can crushed
   pineapple in unsweetened
   pineapple juice

2 (10-ounce) packages frozen
   strawberries in sugar
   (thawed)
3 mashed bananas
½ cup chopped nuts
1 pint sour cream

Dissolve Jello with 1 cup boiling water. Add thawed strawberries, pineapple, nuts and bananas. Mix well. Pour half of the mixture into jello mold. Freeze 15 minutes. Spread sour cream over it. Pour remaining mixture on top and chill.

Mrs. Michael Rallis (Debra)
Burgaw, North Carolina

RED AND GREEN RIBBON RING

3½ cups water, boiling
1 (3-ounce) package strawberry
  Jello
1 (16-ounce) can whole
  cranberry sauce
1 (3-ounce) package lemon
  Jello
1 (8-ounce) package cream
  cheese, softened

1 (9-ounce) can crushed
  pineapple
¼ cup pecans, chopped and
  salted
1 (3-ounce) package lime Jello
2 tablespoons sugar
1 (16-ounce) can grapefruit
  sections (2 cups)

Cranberry Layer:
Dissolve strawberry Jello in 1¼ cups boiling water. Add cranberry sauce, mixing well. Chill until partially set. Pour into an 8-cup ring mold. Chill until partially set and top with cheese layer.

Cheese Layer:
Dissolve lemon Jello in 1¼ cups boiling water. Add cheese, beating smooth with electric or rotary beater. Add pineapple with syrup. Chill until partially set. Stir in pecans and pour over cranberry layer in mold. Chill until almost firm. Top with grapefruit layer.

Grapefruit Layer:
Dissolve lime Jello and sugar in one cup boiling water. Add grapefruit with syrup. Chill until partially set. Pour over cheese layer. Chill overnight. Serves 8 to 12.

Mrs. Robert Moore, Jr. (Wanda)

BUTTERMILK SALAD

1 (20-ounce) can crushed
  pineapple, undrained
1 (6-ounce) package lime or
  strawberry Jello

2 cups buttermilk
1 (12-ounce) carton Cool Whip,
  thawed
1 cup pecans, chopped

Combine pineapple, undrained, and Jello in large saucepan over low heat. Stir until Jello dissolves. Remove from heat. Add buttermilk and nuts. Fold in Cool Whip and pour into 9x13 pan. Refrigerate until completely congealed. Serves 10.

Mrs. Thomas Mobley (Sue)

GOLDEN DELIGHT

2 (3-ounce) packages lemon
Jello
1 (20-ounce) can crushed
pineapple, drained (save
juice)

4 bananas, sliced
1½ cups marshmallows, cut in
fourths
½ cup nuts, chopped (optional)

Dissolve lemon Jello according to package directions. Cool until partially set. Add pineapple, bananas, nuts, and marshmallows. Pour into 3-quart dish. Chill until firm.

Topping:
½ cup sugar
2 tablespoons flour
2 eggs, well beaten
¼ teaspoon salt
1 cup pineapple juice from can
with water to make 1 cup

1 tablespoon unflavored gelatin
¼ cup cold water
1 cup whipping cream, whipped
1 cup sharp cheese, grated

Mix sugar, salt, flour, and pineapple juice-water mixture. Stir in eggs. Cook over low heat until thick, stirring constantly. Soften gelatin in cold water and dissolve in hot mixture. Chill until partially thickened. Fold in cream, pile on firm lemon gelatin layer. Sprinkle with cheese, if desired. Chill until firm. Cut salad in squares. Serves 15.

Mrs. J. J. Pence, Jr. (Joan)

SPICED PEACH SALAD

¾ cup water, boiling
1 (3-ounce) package lemon
Jello
1 cup peach pickle juice
1 (3-ounce) package cream
cheese

3 or 4 spiced pickled peaches,
chopped
½ cup pecans, chopped

Dissolve Jello in boiling water. Add pickle juice. Cool; refrigerate mixture until it begins to thicken. Whip with rotary beater until light and fluffy. Cream the cheese in with chopped peaches and nuts. Mix in with Jello. Pour into a 1-quart container; chill until firm. Serves 6.

Note: Excellent with fried chicken or ham.

Mrs. Frederick Butler, Jr. (Ann)

FRUIT SALAD WITH PINEAPPLE DRESSING

6 oranges, peeled and
  sectioned
2 grapefruit, peeled and
  sectioned
4 bananas, sliced
1 (16-ounce) can pineapple
  chunks, drained (save syrup)

Small bunch Tokay grapes,
  halved and seeded
1 cup miniature marshmallows
1 cup pecan halves

Combine oranges, grapefruit, bananas, grapes, marshmallows, pineapple, and pecans in bowl.

Dressing:
3 tablespoons flour
½ teaspoon salt
⅔ cup sugar
1 egg

¼ cup lemon juice
1½ cups juice from canned
  pineapple

Combine flour, salt, and sugar in top of a double boiler. Add egg, lemon juice, and pineapple juice. Beat well. Cook mixture, stirring constantly until mixture thickens. Cool before using. Gently mix pineapple dressing over all. Serves 8 to 10.

Mrs. J. Gibb Combs, Jr. (Ann)

FIVE CUP SALAD

1 cup Mandarin oranges,
  drained
1 cup pineapple chunks,
  drained

1 cup miniature marshmallows
1 cup coconut, flaked
1 cup sour cream

Drain oranges and pineapple. Fold oranges, pineapple, marshmallows, and coconut into sour cream. Refrigerate overnight. Serves 6.

Mrs. Charles Almond (Aimee)

CRANBERRY CREAM SALAD

4 cups cranberries, raw
1 cup crushed pineapple,
 drained
16 ounces miniature
 marshmallows
1½ cups sugar

Salt to taste
½ pint whipping cream,
 whipped
¾ cup walnuts, chopped
 (optional)

Grind cranberries and combine with drained pineapple. Mix with sugar, salt, marshmallows, and nuts. Whip cream and fold into other ingredients. Refrigerate overnight in covered bowl. Serves 12 to 15.

Mrs. William Parker (Connie)

BONNIE'S TWENTY FOUR HOUR COLE SLAW

1 large cabbage, shredded fine
1 green pepper, cut fine
1 cup celery, cut fine
2 teaspoons salt
1 teaspoon celery seed

1 teaspoon mustard seed
1 onion, diced very fine
1½ cups sugar
½ cup white vinegar

Mix cabbage, green pepper, celery, salt, celery seed, mustard seed, onion, sugar, and white vinegar together well and refrigerate in an airtight container overnight. Slaw will keep for several days in the refrigerator.

Note: If you do not like a lot of onion, you may use a very small one and it does not detract from the flavor.

Mrs. Charles L. Nance, Jr. (Linda)

PECAN ORANGE SLAW

4 small oranges, peeled and
 cut in small pieces
1 small head cabbage,
 shredded
½ cup pecans, chopped

¾ cup mayonnaise (home-
 made if possible)
1 tablespoon lemon juice
1 tablespoon honey
½ teaspoon salt

Combine shredded cabbage, chopped pecans, and orange pieces. Combine mayonnaise, lemon juice, honey, and salt. Pour mixture over vegetables. Toss lightly. Cover and refrigerate one hour. Serves 6 to 8.

Mrs. Wilbur P. Matthews (Katherine)

LAYERED SALAD

2 to 3 cups fresh spinach, chopped
2 teaspoons salt
½ teaspoon pepper
2 tablespoons sugar
1 pound bacon, fried, drained, and crumbled
6 hard boiled eggs, sliced
1 (8-ounce) can water chestnuts, sliced
1 (10-ounce) package frozen peas, thawed not cooked
½ cup onions or scallions, sliced
2 to 3 cups lettuce, shredded
1 cup mayonnaise
1 cup Miracle Whip
1 cup Swiss cheese, grated

Use large flat-bottomed container to preserve layers. Place spinach on bottom. Sprinkle with one teaspoon salt, ¼ teaspoon pepper, and one tablespoon sugar. Next add cooked bacon, eggs, and lettuce. Sprinkle with one teaspoon salt, ¼ teaspoon pepper, and one tablespoon sugar. Cover top with water chestnuts, peas, and onions. Combine mayonnaise and Miracle Whip. Seal vegetable layers with this mixture. Sprinkle with cheese. Serves 8 to 12.

Note: Refrigerate for at least 12 hours.

Mrs. Albert B. Brown (Margaret)

SLAW

2 small carrots, shredded
6 cups cabbage, shredded
½ cup sugar
¼ cup vinegar
½ teaspoon salt
¼ cup onion, chopped
1 cup mayonnaise

Mix carrots, cabbage, sugar, vinegar, salt, onion, and mayonnaise. Refrigerate well before serving.

Cape Fear Country Club
Wilmington, North Carolina

CAULIFLOWER SALAD BOWL

4 cups cauliflower, thinly sliced
1 cup pitted ripe olives, halved
⅔ cup green pepper, coarsely
  chopped
½ cup pimento, coarsely
  chopped
½ cup onion, chopped
Crisp salad greens

In medium bowl, combine cauliflower, olives, green pepper, pimento, and onion. Chill.

Dressing:
½ cup oil
3 tablespoons lemon juice
3 tablespoons wine vinegar
2 teaspoons salt
½ teaspoon sugar
¼ teaspoon pepper

In small bowl, combine salad oil, lemon juice, vinegar, salt, sugar, and pepper. Beat with rotary beater until well blended. Pour over cauliflower mixture. Refrigerate, covered, until well chilled (four hours or overnight). To serve: Spoon salad into bowl lined with salad greens; toss just before serving. Makes 8 to 10 servings.

Mrs. Ralph McCoy (Emily)

FRESH VEGETABLE MARINATE

4 stalks fresh broccoli, florets
  removed and chopped
8 large fresh mushrooms, sliced
1 medium green pepper,
  chopped
3 stalks celery, chopped
1 small head cauliflower, broken
  into florets
8 radishes, sliced
2 spring onions, chopped
1 cup sugar
2 teaspoons dry mustard
1 teaspoon salt
½ cup vinegar
1½ cups vegetable oil
1 small onion, grated
2 tablespoons poppy seeds

Combine broccoli florets, mushrooms, pepper, celery, cauliflower, radishes, and spring onion. Toss lightly. Combine sugar, mustard, salt, vinegar, vegetable oil, onions, and poppy seed. Mix well and pour over vegetables. Chill at least three hours, stirring often. Serves 10 to 12.

Mrs. Charles Almond (Aimee)

ORIENTAL BEAN SALAD

1 (16-ounce) can early English
  peas, drained
1 (16-ounce) can Blue Lake cut
  green beans, drained
1 (16-ounce) can Chinese fancy
  mixed vegetables, drained
1 cup celery, chopped

1 bell pepper, chopped
1 onion, chopped
1 (4-ounce) can pimento,
  chopped
1 cup white vinegar
1 cup sugar
½ cup Wesson oil

Mix peas, beans, Chinese vegetables, celery, bell pepper, onion, pimento, vinegar, sugar, and oil. Marinate 24 hours. Can be kept in a tightly covered container several days.

Mrs. Ellis Tinsley (Betty)

ASPARAGUS SALAD

Lettuce
3 (16-ounce) cans whole green
  asparagus
1 teaspoon tarragon leaves
1 teaspoon garlic salt

Fresh ground pepper to taste
1 (8-ounce) bottle Italian
  dressing
½ cup tarragon vinegar

Drain asparagus and layer in shallow glass dish. Sprinkle each layer with tarragon, pepper, and garlic salt. Mix Italian dressing with tarragon vinegar and pour over asparagus. Marinate at room temperature four hours. Refrigerate. Serve on lettuce leaves. Serves 8 to 10.

Mrs. Stephen Kash (Ann)

COLD FRESH TOMATO SOUP

12 large red ripe tomatoes
2 small onions, grated
2 teaspoons salt
2 teaspoons black pepper

1 tablespoon sugar
1 teaspoon dried basil
Sour cream or yogurt

Peel tomatoes by dropping them one at a time into boiling water for 30 seconds and then into chilled water. Remove core and the skin will peel off easily. Mash or grind the tomatoes through a medium grinder. Add grated onions. Stir in salt, pepper, sugar, and basil. Chill thoroughly. Taste for seasoning. Serve with a teaspoonful of sour cream or yogurt. Serves 8-12.

Mrs. Charles Graham (Jean)

CHILLED SPINACH SOUP

2 (10-ounce) packages frozen
  spinach, chopped (or 2 fresh
  packs)
½ cup onion, chopped
2 tablespoons butter
2 (10¾-ounce) cans chicken
  broth

1 teaspoon salt
⅛ teaspoon pepper
⅛ teaspoon ground mace
1 teaspoon lemon rind, grated
1 cup light cream

Thaw and drain spinach if frozen; trim and wash leaves if fresh. Sauté onion in butter in large saucepan until soft. Add spinach and cover. Cook over medium heat 10 minutes, or until just tender. Add chicken broth, salt, pepper, and mace. Simmer 5 minutes. Cool slightly. Pour soup a part at a time into electric blender; whirl until smooth. Stir in lemon rind and cream. Cover and chill several hours or overnight. Serves 8.

Mrs. Mike Donahue (Teri)

CLAM CHOWDER (MANHATTAN STYLE)

1 cup onion, chopped
1 cup celery, chopped
½ cup chives, chopped
46 ounces tomatoes, crushed
1 teaspoon monosodium
  glutamate
1 bay leaf

½ pound butter
4 tablespoons flour
1 quart chopped sea clams with
  juice—reserve juice
4 medium potatoes, diced and
  cooked in water (save water)
Salt and pepper to taste

Sauté onion, celery, and chives in ¼ pound butter. Add tomatoes, monosodium glutamate, bay leaf. Simmer this tomato mixture while making roux. Melt ¼ pound butter and add flour making roux with sea clam juice and potato water. Combine tomato mixture and roux. Add clams and potatoes. Simmer 25 minutes. Serve with oyster crackers. Serves 20-25.

Sarah Hedgpeth
The Neptune
Wrightsville Beach, North Carolina

CRAB SOUP

2 tablespoons butter
½ cup onion, chopped
½ cup celery, chopped
2 cups milk
1 (10¾-ounce) can green pea
  soup
1 (10¾-ounce) can tomato soup

2 bay leaves
1 teaspoon Worcestershire
  sauce
1 pound deluxe crabmeat
¼ cup sherry
Salt and pepper to taste

Cook butter, onion, celery in top of double boiler until tender. Add milk, green pea soup, tomato soup and bay leaves. Heat until hot. Discard bay leaves. Add Worcestershire sauce, crabmeat, salt and pepper. Heat thoroughly. Just before serving add sherry. Serve piping hot.

Mrs. Joseph Hooper, Sr. (Louise)

MANHATTAN FISH CHOWDER

1 pound fish filets or steak, skin and bones removed
¼ cup bacon or salt pork, chopped
½ cup onion, chopped
2 cups water, boiling
1 pound canned tomatoes
1 cup potatoes, diced
½ cup carrots, diced
½ cup celery, chopped
¼ cup catsup
1 tablespoon Worcestershire sauce
1 teaspoon salt
¼ teaspoon pepper
¼ teaspoon thyme
Parsley, chopped

Take frozen or thawed fish and remove skin and bones. Cut fish into 1-inch pieces. Fry bacon until crisp. Add onion and cook until tender. Add water, tomatoes, potatoes, carrots, celery, catsup, Worcestershire sauce, salt, pepper and thyme. Cover and simmer for 40-45 minutes or until vegetables are tender. Add fish. Cover and simmer about 10 minutes longer or until fish flakes. Sprinkle with parsley. Makes 6 servings.

Chef Robert W. Fetterolf
The Peppermill Restaurant
Wrightsville Beach, North Carolina

SHE-CRAB SOUP

1 (10½-ounce) can Harris She-Crab Soup
1 pound crabmeat (claw)
1 (10¾-ounce) can tomato soup
2 (10¾-ounce) cans cream of mushroom soup
1 cup sherry
3 soup cans milk

Mix she-crab soup, crabmeat, tomato soup, and cream of mushroom soup. Heat thoroughly. Remove from heat. Add sherry and milk. Return to low heat, but do not boil. Serves 15.

Mrs. E. Tilghman Poole (Jean)

CHICKEN ASPARAGUS SOUP (DIETER'S DELIGHT)

6 chicken thighs, legs, or 12 wings
1 (28-ounce) can asparagus spears, drained
3 cups water

Onion salt or onion flakes to taste
Garlic salt to taste
Ground black pepper to taste

Combine chicken, garlic salt, onion salt or flakes, pepper, and 3 cups water. Hard boil for 20 minutes and simmer for 20 minutes to assure that chicken is tender. Skin and bone chicken and return to broth. Add drained asparagus spears and simmer for 5 to 10 minutes. Serve with crackers or sandwiches. Serves 4.

Note: Asparagus should be rinsed in cold water if salted in cans.

R. M. Tan, M.D.

CANADIAN CHEDDAR CHOWDER

1 large potato, finely chopped
1 large onion, finely chopped
¼ cup carrots, finely chopped
¼ cup celery, finely chopped
1 cup water
1 (10½-ounce) can chicken broth

1 cup sharp Cheddar cheese, grated
½ cup cream or half and half
½ cup sour cream
2 tablespoons parsley, chopped

In covered saucepan simmer potato, onion, carrots, and celery in water until tender, about 10 or 15 minutes. Add chicken broth, cream, sour cream, and grated cheese. Heat and serve garnished with parsley. Serves 4 to 6.

Mrs. W. Ferrell Shuford (Becky)

EGG-LEMON SOUP

8 cups chicken broth
Salt to taste
1 cup rice

4 eggs
Juice of 2 lemons

Salt to taste chicken broth and bring to a boil in saucepan. Add rice and simmer, covered for 20 minutes. Remove from heat. In a large bowl or blender, beat eggs. Slowly add lemon juice, beating continuously. Add part of the hot broth to the egg mixture, beating constantly. When the eggs and broth are well mixed, pour this mixture back into the remaining broth and rice. Stir well over medium heat, but do not boil. Serve immediately. Serves 4 to 6.

Note: Always add hot broth to eggs, not eggs to broth.

Peter G. Zack, M.D.

HOLIDAY BUTTERNUT SQUASH SOUP

4 cups water
5 chicken bouillon cubes
3 medium onions, peeled and
**   halved**
3 cups butternut squash,
**   peeled, seeded, and chopped**

5 whole cloves
1 teaspoon curry powder
½ pint heavy cream

Dissolve bouillon cubes in warm water. Add onions, squash, and cloves; cook until just soft. Remove cloves. Blend mixture for 2 to 3 minutes. Add curry powder and cream. Mix well. May be served ice cold. Serves 8.

Note: Delicious served with holiday dinner.

Mrs. David Thomas (Ginny)

MUSHROOM ONION SOUP

1 pound fresh mushrooms,
  sliced
1 very large onion, sliced
1 clove garlic, minced
¼ cup margarine
3 tablespoons tomato paste
8 cups water, boiling

8 chicken bouillon cubes
¼ cup Parmesan cheese, grated
1 cup dry white wine
Salt and pepper to taste
Grated Parmesan cheese for
  garnish

Sauté mushrooms, onions, and garlic in margarine in heavy saucepan until onions are tender. Stir in tomato paste. Dissolve bouillon cubes in boiling water. Add broth, ¼ cup Parmesan cheese, wine, salt, and pepper to saucepan. Simmer 1 hour. Serve with additional Parmesan cheese. Serves 10 to 12.

Mrs. Martin Meyerson (Margery)

ONION WINE SOUP

¼ cup butter
5 large onions, chopped
5 cups beef broth
½ cup celery leaves
1 large potato, sliced
1 cup dry white wine

1 tablespoon vinegar
2 teaspoons sugar
1 cup light cream
1 tablespoon parsley, minced
Salt to taste
Pepper to taste

Melt butter in large saucepan. Add chopped onion and mix well. Add beef broth, celery leaves and potato. Bring to boiling. Cover and simmer for 30 minutes. Purée mixture in a blender. Return to saucepan and blend in wine, vinegar and sugar. Bring to boiling and simmer 5 minutes. Stir in cream, parsley, salt and pepper. Heat thoroughly, but do not boil. Yield: 6 to 8 servings.

Nancy Reagan
Washington D.C.

Participated in Azalea Festival—1969 (Ronald Reagan)

PUMPKIN SOUP

2 tablespoons butter
4 scallions, chopped
1 small onion, sliced
1½ pounds pumpkin, peeled
  and diced (may use canned
  pumpkin)
4 cups chicken stock

½ teaspoon salt
2 tablespoons flour
1 tablespoon butter
¾ cup hot light cream
Croutons and whipped cream
  for garnish

Melt 2 tablespoons butter in large saucepan; add scallions and onions and cook until soft. Add pumpkin, chicken stock, and salt. Simmer until pumpkin is soft. Knead flour with 1 tablespoon butter; stir into saucepan and bring to boil. Purée soup in blender or food processor. Correct seasoning and add hot cream. Heat soup and garnish with tiny croutons and whipped cream. Soup may also be served cold. Serves 8.

Mrs. Samuel E. Warshauer (Miriam)

TOMATO SOUP, PIQUANT

2 (8-ounce) cans tomato sauce
2 (10½-ounce) cans
  concentrated beef bouillon
5¼ cups water
1 quart tomato juice
½ teaspoon prepared
  horseradish

4 drops Tabasco
1½ teaspoons salt
¼ teaspoon dried basil
12 thin slices lemon

Combine tomato sauce, beef bouillon, water, tomato juice, horseradish, Tabasco, salt, and dried basil. Simmer, uncovered, for 10 minutes. Pour into hot cups or mugs, and add a slice of lemon to each. Serves 12.

Mrs. Oliver Raymond Hunt (Eleanor)

VEGETABLE SOUP

1½ pounds beef bones
1 gallon boiling water
1 (10-ounce) package frozen
  lima beans
1 (16-ounce) can V-8 vegetable
  juice
1 (3-pound) can mixed
  vegetables

1 pound can tomatoes, diced
3 large onions, sliced
1 pound can whole kernel corn
1 (10-ounce) package frozen
  okra
1 small cabbage, shredded
Dash of oregano
Salt and pepper to taste

Boil beef bones in water with limas and V-8 juice for about 20 minutes or until limas are tender. Add mixed vegetables, tomatoes, onions, corn, okra and cabbage. Bring to a boil, season with salt, pepper and oregano; then reduce heat to simmer for 25-30 minutes. Yield: approximately 2½ gallons.

Cape Fear Country Club
Wilmington, North Carolina

ZUCCHINI SQUASH SOUP

2 pounds zucchini, sliced
2 medium onions, sliced
3 tablespoons parsley, freshly
  chopped
3 tablespoons butter
1½ cups milk

3 cups chicken broth
Salt to taste
Pepper to taste
Chives (optional)
Unsweetened cream, whipped
  (optional)

Sauté onions in 3 tablespoons butter until translucent. Add sliced zucchini to onions. Pour ¼ cup chicken broth over onion-zucchini mixture. Cover tightly and cook over medium heat for 10 minutes. Remove from heat and place in blender. Add remaining chicken broth, milk, and parsley. Blend thoroughly. Pour into warmed soup bowls; sprinkle with chives or additional parsley. For richer soup, top with a teaspoon of unsweetened whipped cream. Serves 10 to 12.

Mrs. R. V. Fulk, Jr. (Judy)

Meats

Greenfield Lake waterfall, and Poplar Grove Plantation in Scott's Hill.

TOP SIRLOIN ROAST

8 to 12 pound top sirloin roast   Mr. and Mrs. "T" Krazy Salt

Preheat oven to 500 degrees. Have roast at room temperature. Season with Krazy Salt. Cook roast 5 minutes per pound (never more than 50 minutes). Turn oven off, do not open door, and leave roast in oven for 2 hours. If you prefer done to well done beef, slice roast and place in 350 degree oven for desired doneness. Serves 15 to 20.

Mrs. William P. Robison (Maryann)

STUFFED EYE OF ROUND ROAST

**Eye of round roast,
approximately 5 pounds
1 cup red wine
1 cup water
2 bunches of green onions,
finely chopped
4 fresh tomatoes, finely
chopped**

**1 cup ripe olives, finely
chopped
2 green peppers, finely chopped
3 teaspoons salt
2 tablespoons wine vinegar
1 stick margarine**

Simmer roast in wine and water for 3 to 4 hours, covered, until tender. Mix together onions, tomatoes, olives and peppers with salt and vinegar; cover and refrigerate. When roast is tender, cut in ¾ to 1-inch slices while hot. Place on foil and spoon chopped vegetables between slices. Melt margarine and pour over meat. Wrap tightly in foil and let stand for 1 hour. Place in warm oven to reheat, if necessary, before removing foil. Serves 8 to 10.

Mrs. Clifford T. Lewis (Libby)

BARBECUED BEEF BRISKET

2 tablespoons liquid smoke
3 teaspoons Worcestershire
   sauce
1 teaspoon garlic powder
1 teaspoon onion salt
3 teaspoons celery salt

3 to 4 pound fresh beef brisket
¼ teaspoon pepper
½ cup Carolina Treet barbecue
   sauce
½ cup Kraft barbecue sauce

Marinade: mix together liquid smoke, Worcestershire sauce, celery salt, garlic powder, and onion salt. Pour marinade over beef brisket, making sure both sides are coated; cover and let marinate overnight in refrigerator. Drain marinade and season beef brisket with pepper. Bake at 300 degrees for 1½ hours, covered. Uncover; pour Carolina Treet and Kraft barbecue sauces over meat. Cook 1 more hour at 300 degrees, uncovered. Slice thin. Serves 6 to 8.

Mrs. Rolf H. Fisscher (Marÿke)

SWEET AND SOUR BRISKET

4 pound lean beef brisket
2 tablespoons oil
2 onions, sliced
1 clove garlic, finely chopped
¾ cup brown sugar
½ cup vinegar

1 cup ketchup
1 cup water
1 teaspoon salt
¼ teaspoon pepper, freshly
   ground

Brown brisket on all sides in oil. Add onion and garlic, cook until golden. Add brown sugar, vinegar, ketchup, water, salt and pepper. Cover and cook over low heat for about 2½ hours or until meat is tender. Serves 6 to 8.

Mrs. Norman Robinson (Sonja)

INDIVIDUAL BEEF WELLINGTON

Beef:
4 (4-ounce) beef filets
1 clove garlic, halved
Salt to taste
Pepper to taste
¼ cup butter

4 tablespoons brandy
½ cup mushrooms, finely
  chopped
1 (4-ounce) can liver pâté

Mushroom Sauce:
¼ cup onion, finely chopped
6 large fresh mushrooms, sliced
3 tablespoons flour
½ cup red wine
1 (10¾-ounce) can beef broth

1 bay leaf
Salt to taste
Pepper to taste
1 teaspoon Worcestershire
  sauce

Pastry:
1⅓ cups all-purpose flour
1 teaspoon salt
1 tablespoon sugar
1 stick cold unsalted butter

¼ cup ice water
1 egg, beaten
2 tablespoons butter, melted

Beef: Rub each beef filet with garlic on both sides. Season with salt and pepper. Sauté filets in butter for 3 to 4 minutes on each side. Remove filets and refrigerate, reserving butter and meat juices in skillet. Add brandy to reserved juices and sauté mushrooms. Refrigerate mushrooms until chilled. Combine pâté with chilled mushrooms, spread over filets and refrigerate.

Mushroom Sauce: Using same skillet over medium heat, combine onion and mushrooms. Stir in flour and gradually add wine, broth and bay leaf. Stir until sauce bubbles and is thickened. Season with salt, pepper and Worcestershire sauce. Remove bay leaf.

Pastry: Mix flour, salt and sugar. Cut in butter with pastry blender until mixture has the consistency of coarse meal. Add ice water and mix well. (A food processor may be used to mix pastry dough.) Roll out dough on floured pastry cloth and trim into 4 6-inch squares. Brush with egg. Place each filet, pâté side down, on pastry square. Fold dough completely over filets and seal edges with melted butter. Place seam down on greased baking sheet and brush again with egg. Cut small flowers or leaves from extra dough and attach by using beaten egg or butter.

Bake at 425 degrees for 20 to 25 minutes or until crust is richly browned. Serve with heated mushroom sauce. Serves 4.

Note: Before baking, this may be refrigerated for up to 2 days or frozen for 1 month.

Mrs. Thomas Mobley (Sue)

GLAZED CORNED BEEF

6 to 7 pounds corned beef
½ cup bourbon
1 clove garlic

2 bay leaves
4 whole cloves
4 peppercorns

Glaze:
½ cup orange juice
¾ cup brown sugar
2 tablespoons corned beef
   stock

1 teaspoon mustard
¼ cup bourbon

Place corned beef in pot and cover with water. Add bourbon, garlic, bay leaves, cloves and peppercorns. Bring to a boil; simmer, covered, 3 to 6 hours until tender. Remove corned beef to roasting pan. Trim outer fat and score diagonally in diamond pattern.

Glaze: Mix all ingredients together in saucepan and cook until blended. Pour over corned beef and bake 30 minutes in 400 degree oven.

Keep corned beef on heated tray and slice as needed. Serve with mustard on rye bread.

Mrs. E. Thomas Marshburn, Jr. (Pat)

BEEF IN WINE SAUCE

4 pounds boneless beef chuck,
   cut into 1½-inch cubes
Garlic powder
2 (10½-ounce) cans condensed
   golden mushroom soup
1 (1⅜-ounce) envelope onion
   soup mix

¾ cup dry sherry
1 (8-ounce) can sliced
   mushrooms, drained
1 (20-ounce) bag frozen carrots

Preheat oven to 325 degrees. Sprinkle meat lightly with garlic powder. Put in heavy casserole or Dutch oven. Mix together soup, soup mix, sherry and mushrooms; pour over meat. Mix well, cover and bake for 2 hours, adding carrots during last 15 minutes of baking. Serves 8.

Mrs. Ralph McCoy (Emily)

STEAK AND BACON TOURNEDOS

½ pound bacon
1½ pounds flank steak
1½ teaspoons unseasoned
  meat tenderizer
1 teaspoon garlic salt
½ teaspoon pepper

2 tablespoons parsley, minced
1 (1¾-ounce) package
  Hollandaise sauce mix
¼ teaspoon tarragon leaves,
  crushed

Cook bacon until almost done. Drain and set aside. Sprinkle both sides of steak with tenderizer, pierce with fork and sprinkle both sides with garlic salt and pepper. Score diagonally, making diamond shaped cuts about ⅛-inch deep. Place bacon slices lengthwise on steak. Sprinkle with parsley. Roll steak up jelly-roll fashion and secure with string or wooden toothpicks at 1-inch intervals. Cut steak roll into 1-inch thick slices. Be sure each steak is securely fastened. Broil 3 to 5 minutes on each side in oven or grill over coals to desired doneness. To prepare sauce, combine Hollandaise mix with tarragon in a small saucepan, and prepare according to package directions. Spoon over tournedos and serve immediately. Serves 4 to 6.

Note: You need about 1 cup of sauce, if you prefer to make your own Hollandaise and add the tarragon.

Wilbur P. Matthews, M.D.

SHISH KABOBS

1 cup oil
¾ cup soy sauce
½ cup lemon juice
¼ cup Worcestershire sauce
¼ cup prepared mustard

2 tablespoons salt
1 tablespoon cracked pepper
3 pounds lean beef, cut into
  1-inch cubes

Mix oil, soy sauce, lemon juice, Worcestershire sauce, mustard, salt and pepper. Marinate beef in mixture all day in refrigerator. Alternate on skewers with your choice of green pepper, parboiled potatoes, onions, cherry tomatoes or mushrooms. Cook to desired doneness on outdoor grill or under broiler in oven. Serves 8.

Mrs. Robert B. Jones (Becky)

QUICK FRIED BEEF WITH SCALLIONS

½ teaspoon salt
½ tablespoon wine
1 tablespoon oil
¼ teaspoon pepper
1 tablespoon cold water
1 tablespoon corn starch
½ pound beef, sliced in thin,
  bite-sized pieces

4 tablespoons oil
3 tablespoons garlic, sliced
2 tablespoons soy sauce
2 cups scallions, shredded
1 teaspoon sesame oil

To prepare beef marinade, mix salt, wine, 1 tablespoon oil, pepper, water and corn starch in a bowl. Add sliced beef, mixing thoroughly with fingers. Set aside and soak for at least 10 minutes. Put 4 tablespoons oil in frying pan or wok, turning pan around so oil covers a 1 foot diameter. When oil is smoking hot, add garlic, then beef. Stir over high heat for 10 seconds. Splash soy sauce around sides of pan. Mix and remove to a bowl. Reserve the juice in pan. Reheat juice, add scallions, stirring only 5 seconds. Turn off heat; return beef to pan, combining with scallions; add sesame oil. Transfer to serving plate. Serves 2, generously.

Mrs. Alfred Chan (Judy)

SPICE BEEF SZECHWAN STYLE

1 pound beef round steak, cut
  in thin slices about 2 inches
  long
¼ cup Kikkoman soy sauce
1 tablespoon dry sherry
1 teaspoon sugar
1 teaspoon minced ginger root
6 tablespoons peanut oil,
  divided

1 carrot, cut in matchstick size
2 green onions, cut in 2-inch
  lengths
½ teaspoon sesame oil
¼ teaspoon crushed red chili
  pepper

Marinate beef in mixture of soy sauce, sherry, sugar and ginger root for 30 minutes. Heat wok over high heat. Add 3 tablespoons peanut oil to wok, wait 30 seconds and add carrot and green onions. Stir fry for 30 seconds. Remove to plate. Return wok to heat and stir fry beef in remaining oil over high heat until well browned. Return vegetables to wok and heat through. Add sesame oil and hot pepper. Stir fry well. Serves 4.

Egg Roll Factory
Wrightsville Beach, North Carolina

BURRITOS AMISTAD
(MEAT AND BEAN-FILLED TORTILLAS)

1 pound dried pinto beans,
  soaked overnight in water
2 cups water
1 pound chuck, cut into ¼-inch
  cubes
1 tablespoon chili powder

1 tablespoon salt
12 packaged flour tortillas
1 (1-pound) can enchilada
  sauce
½ pound sharp Cheddar
  cheese, grated

Sauce:
1 (28-ounce) can tomatoes
1 (4-ounce) can green chili
  peppers, finely chopped
1 cup onion, chopped
1 tablespoon lemon juice
1 teaspoon salt

½ teaspoon garlic,
  finely chopped
¼ teaspoon Tabasco
¼ cup fresh parsley,
  finely chopped

Drain pinto beans. In a pressure cooker, combine beans, water, chuck, chili powder, and salt. Cook mixture at 15 pounds pressure for 1 hour. Allow pressure to stabilize and drain the bean mixture, reserving liquid. In a food processor, fitted with the steel blade, blend bean mixture, adding some of reserved cooking liquid, if necessary, to make a moderately stiff mixture. Spread bean mixture on tortillas, roll them up and arrange them seam side down in one layer in two baking pans. Spoon enchilada sauce over tortillas, sprinkle grated cheese on top and bake at 350 degrees for 20 minutes or until mixture is hot and the cheese melted.

Sauce: In a blender, combine all the sauce ingredients and blend until tomatoes are chopped. Transfer the sauce to a sauce boat and serve with the burritos. Serves 6.

Mrs. John Parkinson (Vicki)

CAROL'S STEW BEEF WITH SOUR CREAM

2 pounds lean stew beef,
cut in ½-inch cubes
3 tablespoons oil
1 large onion, chopped
1 clove garlic, chopped
2 tablespoons flour
1 (3-ounce) can mushrooms
and broth

1 cup sour cream
½ cup celery, chopped
1 (8-ounce) can tomato sauce
⅛ teaspoon pepper
1 teaspoon salt
1 tablespoon Worcestershire
sauce

Brown beef in oil; add onion and garlic, cook until golden. Add flour, mushrooms with broth, sour cream, celery, tomato sauce, pepper, salt and Worcestershire sauce; mix well. Turn into a greased, 3-quart casserole; bake uncovered for 1½ hours, or until tender, at 325 degrees. Serves 5 to 6.

Mrs. John Parkinson (Vicki)

BEEF BURGUNDY

2 pounds stew beef
4 tablespoons oil
½ pound sweet onions,
chopped
½ pound fresh mushrooms,
sliced
¼ teaspoon thyme

¼ teaspoon marjoram
½ teaspoon salt
½ teaspoon pepper
1½ tablespoons flour
½ cup bouillon
1 cup red wine

Brown stew beef in oil. Add onions and mushrooms; sauté. Place these ingredients in a Dutch oven. Add thyme, marjoram, salt and pepper. In a separate bowl, mix flour and bouillon; add red wine. Pour liquid mixture over beef. Cover and bake at 300 degrees for 3 to 5 hours. Serve over rice. Serves 4 to 6.

Mrs. David B. Sloan, Jr. (Emily)

CHINESE BEEF CASSEROLE

1 pound ground beef, lean
2 cups onion, chopped
2 cups celery, chopped
½ cup uncooked rice
1 (10¾-ounce) can cream of
  mushroom soup

1 soup can of water
1 (16-ounce) can bean sprouts,
  drained
½ cup soy sauce
1 (4-ounce) can mushrooms,
  drained

Preheat oven to 325 degrees. Brown beef in a large skillet. Add onion, celery, rice, mushroom soup, water, bean sprouts, soy sauce and mushrooms. Mix and turn into a large casserole. Cover and bake for 2 hours. Serves 6 to 8.

Note: Do not add any salt, as soy sauce is salty.

Mrs. Donald MacQueen (Lynn)

ITALIAN SPAGHETTI

1 large onion, chopped
4 cloves garlic, finely chopped
3 tablespoons olive oil
1 pound lean ground beef
1 (28-ounce) can tomatoes,
  chopped but not drained
1 (6-ounce) can tomato paste
1 teaspoon salt

⅛ teaspoon pepper
1 bay leaf
1 teaspoon oregano
¼ teaspoon crushed red pepper
1 tablespoon fresh parsley,
  chopped
Dash allspice
1 tablespoon sugar (optional)

In a large pot, cook onions and garlic in olive oil until soft. Add meat and cook until brown, stirring constantly. Add tomatoes, tomato paste, salt, pepper, bay leaf, oregano, crushed red pepper, parsley, allspice and sugar (optional). Bring to a boil, reduce heat and simmer, partially covered, for 1½ hours, stirring occasionally. Remove bay leaf. Serve sauce over spaghetti and sprinkle with freshly grated Parmesan or Romano cheese. Serves 4.

Note: Sauce improves in flavor if made a day ahead and refrigerated overnight. Reheat slowly.

Mrs. John Codington (Betsy)

MY SPAGHETTI SAUCE

1 medium onion, chopped
2 tablespoons olive oil
1 pound ground beef
2 (12-ounce) cans tomato paste
3 (12-ounce) cans water
2 (1-pound) cans tomatoes
1 teaspoon salt

½ teaspoon pepper
2 teaspoons sugar
¼ teaspoon minced garlic or
  1 clove fresh garlic, crushed
1 teaspoon crushed red pepper
1 teaspoon basil

In a skillet, sauté onion in the olive oil until transparent. Add ground beef and cook until brown. Drain off fat. In a large pot combine tomato paste, water, tomatoes, salt, pepper, sugar, garlic, red pepper and basil. Add the beef mixture and simmer gently, uncovered, for 4 hours, stirring occasionally. Serves 10 to 12.

Note: For a smoother sauce, purée tomatoes in blender before adding to recipe. This is a very spicy hot sauce.

Mrs. Daniel Gottovi (Karen)

HIS SPAGHETTI SAUCE

1½ pounds pork neck bones
1 pound lean beef short ribs
2 tablespoons olive oil
2 (1-pound) cans tomatoes
2 (12-ounce) cans tomato paste
2 (12-ounce) cans water

1 bay leaf
½ teaspoon garlic powder or 2
  fresh garlic cloves, crushed
2½ teaspoons salt
¼ teaspoon pepper
⅛ teaspoon cinnamon

In a large pot, brown the pork neck bones and short ribs in the olive oil. Drain. Add tomatoes, tomato paste, water, bay leaf, garlic, salt, pepper and cinnamon. Simmer, covered, for at least 2 hours. Remove bones as the meat falls off. Makes 3 quarts of sauce.

Note: This is an authentic Italian recipe!

Daniel Gottovi, M.D.

MOUSSAKA

1½ pounds ground lamb or beef
1 medium onion, finely chopped
2 tablespoons margarine
Salt to taste
Freshly ground pepper to taste
1 teaspoon cinnamon

1 (8-ounce) can tomato paste
2 (8-ounce) cans water
1 large eggplant, unpeeled,
   chunked and salted
½ cup Cheddar or Swiss
   cheese, grated

Sauce:
4 tablespoons margarine
5 tablespoons flour
2 cups milk
Salt to taste

Freshly ground pepper to taste
1 egg, beaten
2 to 4 tablespoons Parmesan
   cheese, freshly grated

Brown meat and onion in margarine. Add salt, pepper, cinnamon and tomato paste diluted with water. Simmer for 15 minutes. Rinse and drain eggplant; simmer in boiling water for 10 minutes. Drain and arrange layer of eggplant in bottom of a shallow casserole, then add a layer of meat and a layer of cheese. Repeat layers.

Sauce: Melt margarine over medium heat in a saucepan. Add flour, cook until bubbly, stirring constantly. Add milk, salt and pepper; cook, stirring constantly, until slightly thickened. Remove sauce from heat; slowly stir ½ cup of sauce into beaten egg. Beat egg mixture into sauce. Pour half of egg sauce over eggplant casserole and bake at 350 degrees for 15 minutes. Cook remaining sauce over medium heat, stirring constantly, until very thick. Remove casserole from oven, top with remainder of sauce, sprinkle with Parmesan cheese and return to oven and bake for 45 to 50 minutes or until golden brown. Cut into squares to serve. Serves 8.

Note: Meat and eggplant casserole may be prepared ahead of time and refrigerated, but egg sauce should be prepared just before baking.

Mrs. Ralph B. Moore, Jr. (Vicki)

DEVILED HAMBURGERS

3 tablespoons butter
1½ cups celery, finely chopped
1 cup onion, finely chopped
1 medium green pepper,
  finely chopped
1½ pounds lean ground chuck
1 pound ground pork
½ teaspoon ground cloves
3 tablespoons vinegar

3 tablespoons sugar
1 (14-ounce) bottle ketchup
2 cups condensed tomato soup
1 tablespoon prepared mustard
1 cup water
½ teaspoon salt
½ teaspoon paprika
1 teaspoon chili powder

Melt butter in a large saucepan or electric frying pan. Add celery, onion, green pepper, ground chuck and ground pork. Cook until well browned. Drain excess grease. Add cloves, vinegar, sugar, ketchup, tomato soup, mustard, water, salt, paprika and chili powder. Cover and simmer for 1½ to 2 hours. Serve on hamburger buns with or without top. Serves 6 to 8.

Mrs. Oliver R. Hunt (Eleanor)

TAGLIARINI

1 medium onion, chopped
2 tablespoons oil
1 pound ground round beef
1 (17-ounce) can creamed corn
1 (15-ounce) can tomato sauce
1 (8-ounce) can tomato sauce
1 clove garlic, finely chopped

1 teaspoon chili powder
1 (12-ounce) package egg
  noodles
½ pound cheese, grated
1 (4-ounce) can ripe olives
  (optional)

Sauté onion in oil until golden. Add ground beef and cook over medium heat until brown. Add corn, tomato sauce, garlic and chili powder. Allow to simmer while preparing noodles. Cook noodles according to package directions and drain. Add sauce to noodles. Transfer to 1 3-quart casserole or 2 1½-quart casseroles. Sprinkle cheese over top; scatter olives over cheese. Bake for 1 hour at 300 to 325 degrees. Serves 8 to 10.

Note: Can be frozen before or after baking. It's a good idea to use one and freeze one.

Mrs. William P. Parker, Jr. (Connie)

SWEET AND SOUR STUFFED CABBAGE

1 pound lean beef round,
  ground twice
1 small onion, grated
½ cup fresh bread crumbs
¼ cup water
Salt to taste
Freshly ground pepper to taste
1 medium to large head of
  cabbage, cored
1 small onion, sliced

1 carrot, sliced
1 cup consommé
1 cup tomatoes or tomato
  sauce
Juice of ½ lemon
2 tablespoons brown sugar
Salt to taste
Pepper to taste
Paprika

Combine beef, grated onion, bread crumbs, water, salt and pepper. Mix well, until light and fluffy. Place cabbage in a large pot and cover with hot water. Simmer about 5 minutes, until leaves are flexible. Separate 12 leaves, fill each with meat mixture, roll and fasten with toothpicks. In a large pot, put sliced onion, carrot and stuffed cabbage leaves folded side down. Add consommé and simmer slowly 1 hour. Add tomatoes or sauce, lemon juice, brown sugar, salt, pepper and paprika. Simmer 2 more hours or until sauce is desired thickness.

Mrs. William R. Weinel, Jr. (Robbie)

BEST-EVER CHILI

1 pound ground beef
½ cup onions, chopped
½ cup green pepper,
  chopped
½ cup celery, chopped
1 (15-ounce) can kidney beans

1 (16-ounce) can tomatoes,
  cut up
1 (6-ounce) can tomato paste
1 tablespoon chili powder
¼ teaspoon salt
¼ teaspoon garlic powder

Brown ground beef, onions, green pepper and celery. Add the kidney beans, tomatoes, tomato paste, chili powder, salt and garlic powder. Cover and simmer for 2 hours. Serves 4, generously.

Mrs. John Krohn (Dorene)

GLAZED PORK ROAST

4 to 5 pound pork loin roast
Salt
Pepper
2/3 cup brown sugar, firmly
  packed

2½ teaspoons dry mustard
2 tablespoons cornstarch
2 cups apricot nectar
4 teaspoons cider vinegar

Preheat oven to 350 degrees. Rub roast well with salt and pepper; score fat on roast in a diamond pattern. Place roast, fat side up, on a rack in an open roasting pan. Insert meat thermometer into center of roast so that it does not rest on bone or in fat. Roast to an internal temperature of 170 degrees. About ½ hour before roast is done, mix brown sugar, mustard and cornstarch in a saucepan. Stir in apricot nectar and vinegar. Cook over medium heat, stirring constantly, until slightly thickened. Remove roast from oven and spoon about ½ cup of glaze over it, reserving remainder of glaze. Return meat to oven and bake until done. Remove roast from oven 20 minutes before serving for easier carving. To make apricot sauce to spoon over the roast, mix 3 tablespoons of meat drippings with remaining apricot glaze. Serves 8.

Note: Baking times vary with the type of loin cut. Center loin roast—30 to 35 minutes per pound. Blade loin or sirloin roast—40 to 45 minutes per pound.

Mrs. Howard L. Armistead (Linda)

MARINATED PORK CHOPS

1 (10-ounce) bottle soy sauce
1 (10-ounce) bottle of water
1 teaspoon ground ginger

1 large clove of garlic, crushed
6 to 8 center cut pork chops,
  ¾ to 1-inch thick

To prepare marinade, mix soy sauce, water, ginger and garlic; stir until well blended. Place pork chops in a shallow pan and pour marinade over them. Marinate in refrigerator for 6 to 8 hours. Grill chops over charcoal fire for 8 to 10 minutes on each side or broil in oven for 10-12 minutes on each side. Serves 6 to 8.

Note: Marinade may be used on chicken or steak, too.

Mrs. E. Thomas Marshburn, Jr. (Pat)

SWEET AND SOUR PORK

⅔ pound pork loin
1 teaspoon soy sauce
1 egg yolk
1 tablespoon cornstarch
6 cups oil
6 tablespoons cornstarch
3 tablespoons vinegar

3 tablespoons sugar
6 tablespoons crushed
  pineapple with juice
1 tablespoon soy sauce
1½ teaspoons cornstarch
1½ teaspoons water

Remove fat from pork loin and cut into bite-sized pieces ¼-inch thick. Mix together 1 teaspoon soy sauce, egg yolk and 1 tablespoon cornstarch; add pork, mix well and let meat soak for 20 minutes. Heat oil for frying. Spoon 6 tablespoons cornstarch into a small bowl and dip each piece of pork in cornstarch before frying. Deep fry pork pieces over medium heat for 3 minutes. Remove and reheat oil until very hot. Refry pork pieces another 30 seconds; remove and drain. To prepare sauce, mix vinegar, sugar, pineapple and 1 tablespoon soy sauce in a saucepan. Heat to boiling, stirring constantly. Combine 1½ teaspoons cornstarch and 1½ teaspoons water and add to sauce; continue cooking until thickened. Pour sauce over fried pork. Serves 3.

Mrs. Ben H. Yue (Haeyoon)

CREOLE PORK CHOPS

6 ¾-inch thick pork chops
1 (14-ounce) bottle ketchup
1 ketchup bottle of water
1 medium onion, sliced
1 (4-ounce) can mushroom
  stems and pieces, well
  drained
1 (10¾-ounce) can cream of
  mushroom soup

Salt to taste
Pepper to taste
Tabasco sauce to taste
1 teaspoon Worcestershire
  sauce
1 large green pepper,
  sliced to make rings

Place pork chops in a 9x13-inch casserole dish. Mix ketchup and water; pour over pork chops. Add onions, mushrooms and mushroom soup. Season with salt, pepper, Tabasco sauce and Worcestershire sauce. Place ½ pepper ring on each chop. Bake at 375 degrees for 1 hour or until chops are tender. Serves 6.

Mrs. Elbert C. Anderson (Martha)

PORK CHOPS WITH MUSTARD SAUCE

2 tablespoons butter
3 tablespoons oil
6 pork chops, 1½-inches thick
Salt
Pepper
Flour
1½ cups onions,
    thinly sliced

3 tablespoons white wine
    vinegar
Bouquet garni made of 2
    parsley sprigs and 1 bay leaf,
    tied together
¾ cup cream
2 teaspoons Dijon mustard
Few drops of lemon juice

Preheat oven to 325 degrees. Melt butter with oil over moderate heat in a heavy skillet. Sprinkle chops with salt and pepper, dust with flour. Brown chops for 3 minutes on each side. Transfer to a flameproof casserole. Remove most of oil from skillet; add onions and cook, stirring often, for 5 minutes. Stir in wine vinegar, bring to a boil and cook it almost away. Spoon the onions and juices over the chops and add the bouquet garni. Cover the casserole and bake for 45 minutes. Remove the chops and keep warm in a 200-degree oven. Pour cream into the casserole and boil, stirring constantly, until it thickens. Add mustard and lemon juice and pour over chops. Garnish with parsley. Serves 6.

Mrs. John Codington (Betsy)

PEACH-GLAZED SPARERIBS

4 pounds boneless spareribs
1 (16-ounce) can yellow cling
    sliced peaches, drained
½ cup brown sugar
¼ cup ketchup
¼ cup vinegar

2 tablespoons soy sauce
½ teaspoon salt
¼ teaspoon pepper
1 teaspoon garlic powder
1 teaspoon ground ginger

Grill spareribs 15 minutes on each side. In a blender purée the peaches, brown sugar, ketchup, vinegar, soy sauce, salt, pepper, garlic powder and ginger. Place ribs on foil, pour peach sauce over ribs, wrap securely, and grill for 30 minutes or place ribs in a shallow casserole, pour sauce over ribs, cover and bake at 350 degrees for 1 hour. Serves 6 to 8.

Mrs. John Krohn (Dorene)

BETTY'S SWEET AND SOUR PORK

2 quarts water
¼ cup vinegar
2 to 4 pounds boneless pork,
   cut into bite-sized pieces
½ cup cornstarch
½ cup soy sauce
¼ cup dark molasses
4 cups oil

¾ cup water
½ cup sugar
¾ cup vinegar
¾ cup pineapple syrup
2 green peppers, cut into 1-inch
   pieces
1 (20-ounce) can pineapple
   slices, cut into 1-inch pieces

Heat 2 quarts of water to boiling and add ¼ cup vinegar. Add meat; cover until water begins boiling again; uncover and simmer 10 to 15 minutes. Drain meat. (This may be done a day ahead.) Mix cornstarch, soy sauce and molasses in a large bowl. Add meat and soak in mixture until most of liquid is absorbed, stirring frequently. Heat oil to 375 degrees and fry meat, a few pieces at a time, until well browned. Set meat aside. Combine ¾ cup water, sugar, ¾ cup vinegar and pineapple syrup in a large pan. Heat to boiling. Add meat to hot syrup, cover and simmer until meat is glazed and tender—about 30 minutes. Add peppers and pineapple and continue cooking until peppers and pineapple are heated through, but peppers are still crisp. Serves 4 to 8.

Mrs. William B. Leach (Betty)

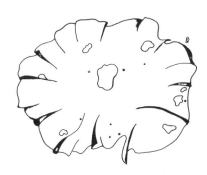

FRUITED PORK CHOPS

6 center-cut loin pork chops,
  1-inch thick
¼ teaspoon salt
¼ teaspoon sage
1 tablespoon oil
3 large tart apples
3 tablespoons molasses

1 (11-ounce) can Mandarin
  orange slices, drained,
  reserving syrup
3 tablespoons flour
1 tablespoon cider vinegar
½ teaspoon salt
⅓ cup golden raisins

Preheat oven to 350 degrees. Sprinkle chops with ¼ teaspoon salt and sage. Heat oil in a skillet, add chops and brown slowly. Reserving meat drippings in skillet, place chops in a large, shallow baking dish. Peel, core and slice apples into ¼-inch pieces and arrange on chops. Pour molasses over chops. Add enough water to reserved Mandarin orange syrup to equal 2 cups. Stir flour into meat drippings reserved in skillet; cook over medium heat until brown, stirring constantly. Gradually stir in water and syrup mixture and cook until boiling. Add vinegar, ½ teaspoon salt and raisins. Pour sauce over chops and apples. Cover and bake for 50 minutes. Remove from oven and arrange orange slices over top and bake an additional 10 minutes. Serves 6.

Mrs. Thomas Mobley (Sue)

SPARERIBS WITH DRIED BLACK BEANS

¾ pound pork spareribs
2 tablespoons dried fermented
  black beans
1 tablespoon oil
1 tablespoon red wine
1 teaspoon sugar
½ teaspoon salt

1 tablespoon soy sauce
2 tablespoons water
1 tablespoon cornstarch
2 tablespoons hot red pepper,
  finely chopped
2 tablespoons garlic,
  finely chopped

Cut spareribs into small pieces. Soak dried beans in cold water for 10 minutes. Rinse to remove salt from beans, drain well and chop finely. Heat oil in frying pan and stir fry black beans. Add wine, sugar, salt and soy sauce; stir fry 10 seconds more. Place spareribs in a bowl and pour bean mixture over meat. Mix water and cornstarch to make a paste, pour over spareribs and mix thoroughly. Place spareribs in shallow bowl and sprinkle with red pepper and garlic. Place bowl in a steamer, cover and steam over high heat for 30 minutes. Serves 2, generously.

Mrs. Alfred Chan (Judy)

CHEESY SAUSAGE QUICHE

¾ pound pork sausage
½ cup onion, chopped
¼ cup green pepper, finely
  chopped
1½ cups sharp Cheddar cheese,
  grated
1 tablespoon flour

2 eggs, beaten
1 cup Pet evaporated milk
1 tablespoon parsley flakes
¾ teaspoon seasoning salt
¼ teaspoon garlic salt
¼ teaspoon pepper
1 deep dish pie crust

Preheat oven to 375 degrees. Crumble and fry sausage until brown; drain, reserving 2 tablespoons fat. Sauté onion and green pepper in reserved fat until golden. In a large bowl combine cheese and flour. Stir in sausage, green pepper and onion. Add eggs, evaporated milk, parsley flakes, seasoning salt, garlic salt and pepper. Mix well. Pour into pie shell and spread evenly. Bake on a cookie sheet for 35 to 40 minutes. Serves 6 to 8.

Mrs. Britton E. Taylor (Harriette)

SAUSAGE CASSEROLE

2 pounds bulk pork sausage
1 (1-pound) can tomatoes
1 (1-pound) can stewed
  tomatoes
½ teaspoon Worcestershire
  sauce

6 bay leaves
8 ounces fine noodles, cooked,
  drained, and set aside
Grated Parmesan cheese

Crumble sausage and cook in skillet over moderate heat until brown. Drain well. Add tomatoes, stewed tomatoes, Worcestershire sauce, bay leaves and noodles. Mix well and turn into 1 large casserole or 2 small casseroles and sprinkle generously with cheese. Bake uncovered at 350 degrees for 45 minutes or until bubbly and the cheese is melted. Serves 6 generously.

Mrs. James W. Markworth (Ruthe)

BONED LEG OF LAMB WITH MUSHROOM DRESSING

Leg of lamb, approximately 6-
  pounds, deboned and rolled
Parsley
Garlic salt
Savory salt

Onion salt
Celery salt
Rosemary
3 strips bacon
½ cup cooking sherry

Dressing (optional):
2 pounds fresh mushrooms
1 bunch green onions, cleaned
  and cut in thirds
3 tablespoons butter
1 tablespoon oil
½ cup Madeira

½ cup beef stock
Salt to taste
Pepper to taste
½ cup Parmesan cheese,
  freshly grated

Remove lamb from refrigerator 1 hour before preparing. Preheat oven to 450 degrees. Make 5 slits in the roll and stuff with parsley. Sprinkle generously with garlic salt, savory salt, onion salt, celery salt and rosemary. Stuff dressing (recipe below) into center of roll, if desired. Lay 3 strips of bacon over top of roast and place on a rack in a roasting pan. Turn oven temperature to 325 degrees and roast uncovered approximately 30 minutes per pound or until internal temperature reaches 175 degrees for a well done roast or 165 degrees for slightly rare roast. 30 minutes before roast is done, pour sherry over lamb and cover.

Dressing (optional): In a food processor fitted with a steel blade, chop mushrooms and onions finely, ½ pound at a time. Sauté mushrooms and onions in hot butter and oil until mushrooms start to separate and brown. Add Madeira and beef stock, boil down until no liquid remains. Season with salt and pepper, sprinkle with Parmesan cheese and stir.

Mrs. David P. Thomas (Ginny)

GLAZED HAM

4 to 5 pound fully cooked ham
Whole cloves
½ cup brown sugar

1 tablespoon prepared mustard
2 tablespoons bourbon

Preheat oven to 325 degrees. Insert cloves into top of ham. Mix sugar, mustard and bourbon together and spoon over ham. Bake for 1 hour.

Mrs. William P. Robison (Maryann)

STUFFED LEG OF LAMB

4 to 5 pound leg of lamb
1 bunch parsley, chopped
1 bunch fresh mint, chopped
1 head of garlic
Salt
Pepper
1 onion

1 carrot
1 stalk of celery
Strong coffee
1 beef bouillon cube
1 cup water
3 ounces mint jelly

Bone the leg of lamb or have butcher remove bone. Mix parsley and mint together and stuff in the lamb in place of the bone. Make small slits in the skin using a sharp knife; insert slivers of garlic in each slit. Rub the roast with salt and pepper. Place in an uncovered roasting pan, fat side up; place onion, carrot and celery in pan. Bake at 350 degrees for about 2 hours or 30 minutes per pound (if using a meat thermometer, bake to an internal temperature of 175 to 180 degrees). Baste with strong coffee 2 or 3 times during roasting. Remove roast from pan; discard vegetables. Drain grease from pan and add bouillon cube and water; simmer for 10 minutes; add mint jelly and simmer 3 minutes more. Serve as a sauce over lamb.

Mrs. Michael Donahue (Teri)

BRATWURST IN SOUR CREAM

2 (16-ounce) packages cooked
  bratwurst (may use
  knockwurst)
2 tablespoons butter or
  margarine
2 medium onions, thinly sliced

3 tablespoons flour
½ teaspoon salt
1½ cups apple juice
1 cup sour cream
Hot buttered noodles

Brown bratwurst well on all sides in butter or margarine in large skillet. Remove sausages from skillet. Sauté onions until soft in same skillet. Stir in flour and salt; blend well. Stir in apple juice; cook until bubbly. Return sausages to skillet; cover and simmer over low heat for 15 minutes. Spoon sour cream into a small bowl; gradually blend in 1 cup of the hot sauce from the skillet; stir sour cream mixture into skillet. Cook, stirring constantly until hot, but do not allow to boil. Serve with hot buttered noodles. Serves 8.

Mrs. Lyndon U. Anthony (Agnes)

VEAL PICCATA

1 pound veal, off the rib
Flour
Salt
Pepper
1½ tablespoons peanut oil
3 tablespoons dry vermouth

2 tablespoons butter
Juice of 1 lemon
Peel from half a lemon,
  cut into fine pieces
Lemon, sliced thinly
Parsley

Cut veal into pieces and pound with a meat hammer until thin. Dust veal with flour, salt and pepper. Sauté each side of meat in hot peanut oil for 1 minute. Remove veal to a warm plate. Drain fat from pan; deglaze pan with vermouth. Add butter and lemon juice; stir and pour mixture over veal. Sprinkle veal with lemon peel and garnish with lemon slices and parsley. Serves 4.

Note: Vermouth, butter and lemon juice may be increased or decreased to personal taste.

Mrs. Thomas H. Maloy (Jane)

SPAGHETTI SAUCE

½ pound ground beef
1 medium (or large) onion,
  chopped fine
2 cups catsup
1 cup water

¼ teaspoon ground oregano
Sprinkle of granulated garlic
3 ounces American cheese,
  crumbled

Sauté ground beef and onion until beef is slightly brown. Add catsup, water, oregano and garlic. Simmer 15 minutes. Add cheese, simmer 5 minutes more. Serve with thin spaghetti. This is enough sauce for a (12 ounce) box of spaghetti. Yields: 4 servings.

Ben Jones
Los Angeles, California
T.V. personality—Native of Wilmington

STANLEY'S SPAGHETTI SAUCE FOR THE SINGLE MAN

2 pounds top sirloin,
  ground
1 (32-ounce) jar plain Ragu
  spaghetti sauce

1 (3-ounce) can B & B chopped
  mushrooms
1 (3-ounce) can B & B
  mushrooms buds

Brown sirloin. Pour off excess drippings. Add spaghetti sauce and mushrooms. Cook over low heat for 10 minutes. Pour over cooked spaghetti. Yield: 4 to 6 servings. Can be frozen in individual portions for later use.

Stanley Rehder
Wilmington, North Carolina
Azalea Festival Host

HASENPFEFFER

2 rabbits, cut into serving
  pieces
2 sticks butter
¼ cup oil
Salt to taste
Pepper to taste
Flour
1 cup onion, chopped
1 clove garlic, finely chopped

2 bay leaves
¼ teaspoon ground rosemary
¼ teaspoon ground thyme
½ teaspoon salt
½ teaspoon black peppercorns,
  ground
1 (12-ounce) jar Robertson's
  Blackcurrant Preserves
1 tablespoon pickling spice

Preheat oven to 325 degrees. Melt butter and oil in frying pan. Salt, pepper and flour rabbit and fry until golden. Place meat in heavy Dutch oven. Add flour to drippings in frying pan to make gravy. To gravy mixture add onion, garlic, bay leaves, rosemary, thyme, salt, pepper and preserves. Cook until smooth, stirring constantly. Pour gravy mixture over rabbit. Add pickling spice in a spice bag or after grinding well. Bake, covered, for 2 hours. Check after one hour and add water, if necessary. To serve, remove rabbit and use gravy over hot egg noodles. Serves 6.

Robert R. Smalley, M.D.

NORTH STATE CHARCOAL BROILED VENISON

Venison ham, tenderloin or
  back strap, cut into ½-inch
  slices

1 stick butter, melted
Salt to taste
Pepper to taste

Prepare intensely hot charcoal fire. Place venison slices in a two-sided wire grilling rack. Brush on melted butter. Cook 2 to 3 inches above charcoal, basting and turning frequently, until venison is rare or medium rare (not well done). Season with salt and pepper after cooking. Serve with hot pepper vinegar or hot pepper jelly.

Note: Some hunters like to pour Grandma's Molasses over their second serving of broiled venison and hot biscuits.

Charles A. Wilkinson, M.D.

BUL-GOGI

1 cup soy sauce
½ cup sugar
1 teaspoon garlic powder
1 tablespoon sesame oil
  (or another vegetable oil)
1 teaspoon Accént

1 teaspoon pepper
1 tablespoon sesame seed
1 pound venison, cut into
  1-inch cubes
10 green peppers, quartered

To prepare marinade, mix soy sauce, sugar, garlic powder, oil, Accént, pepper and sesame seed. Place meat in marinade, cover and let stand, refrigerated, for 3 to 4 days. Alternate pieces of venison and green pepper on skewers. Cook over low heat on a charcoal grill until done—10 minutes or more. Serves 3 to 4.

Mrs. E. Thomas Marshburn, Jr. (Pat)

seafood

For years a familiar landmark, Zora's, has provided Wilmingtonians with fresh seafood brought in by local shrimp boats.

CRABMEAT CASSEROLE

1 (20-ounce) can artichoke
  hearts
1 pound crabmeat
½ pound fresh mushrooms,
  sautéed
4 tablespoons butter
2½ tablespoons flour
1 cup cream

½ teaspoon salt
1 teaspoon Worcestershire
  sauce
¼ cup medium dry sherry
Paprika to taste
Cayenne to taste
Pepper to taste
¼ cup Parmesan cheese, grated

Preheat oven to 375 degrees. Place artichokes in bottom of 2½-quart baking dish; spread a layer of crabmeat. Add a layer of sautéed mushrooms. Melt butter in a saucepan; add flour, cream, salt, Worcestershire sauce, sherry, paprika, cayenne and pepper. Stir well after each addition to form a smooth sauce. Pour sauce over artichoke-crab layer and sprinkle with cheese on top. Bake 20 minutes. Serves 8.

Nancy Reagan
Washington D.C.

Participated in Azalea Festival—1969 (Ronald Reagan)

PEPPERMILL'S CRABMEAT CRÊPES

Crêpes:

1 cup flour	1 cup half and half cream
1 cup water	2 eggs

Combine flour, water, cream and eggs, beat well. Refrigerate batter at least 1 hour. Brush bottom of 6 or 7-inch crepe pan or heavy skillet with salad oil. Place over medium heat until just hot, not smoking.

Pour 2 tablespoons batter in pan. Quickly tilt pan in all directions so batter covers the pan in a thin film. Cook about 1 minute.

Lift edge of crêpe to test for doneness. Flip the crêpe, and cook about 30 seconds on the other side. Use this side on which to place the filling.

Place hot crêpe on a towel to cool. Stack crêpes between layers of waxed paper to prevent sticking. May be frozen. Yield: 16 6-inch crêpes.

Crabmeat Filling:

½ cup green pepper, chopped	1 cup sour cream
2 tablespoons butter	2 tablespoons Romano cheese,
4 tablespoons all-purpose flour	grated
1¼ cups half and half cream	Salt and pepper to taste
1 egg yolk, beaten	Hollandaise sauce
1 pound crabmeat	

Sauté green pepper in butter. Add flour and cream, stirring constantly and cooking until thick. Add a little of the hot mixture to the egg yolk. Stir back into the mixture in the saucepan. When quite thick, add crabmeat, sour cream, and cheese. Season to taste and heat to serving temperature. Spoon over crêpes and roll up. Top rolled crêpes with Hollandaise sauce. Yield: 3½ cups. Serves 4 to 6.

The Peppermill Restaurant
Wrightsville Beach, North Carolina

MENA'S DEVILED CRAB

2½ cups crabmeat, fresh
  or canned
2 tablespoons prepared
  mustard
15 tablespoons grated bread
  crumbs (Dry out 10 slices of
  bread in 200 degree oven for
  3 hours. Do not brown. Grate
  the bread and sift.)

5½ tablespoons melted butter
1 teaspoon lemon juice
2½ teaspoons Worcestershire
  sauce
1 egg, beaten
1 tablespoon Miracle Whip
  salad dressing
7 crab shells

Preheat oven to 350 degrees. Mix crabmeat, mustard, 5 tablespoons bread crumbs, 1½ tablespoons melted butter, lemon juice, Worcestershire sauce, egg and Miracle Whip. Put in crab shells. Pour 4 tablespoons of melted butter over crab in shells and sprinkle remainder of crumbs on top. Bake for 30 minutes. If desired, wrap separately and freeze. If frozen, thaw first. Serves 7.

Mrs. David B. Sloan, Sr. (Christine)

GRAY GABLES' CRAB IMPERIAL

1 cup Bechamel (white sauce)
½ cup heavy mayonnaise
¼ cup sweet green peppers,
  sautéed in butter
¼ cup sweet red peppers,
  sautéed in butter

2 pounds deluxe crabmeat or
  1 pound deluxe and 1 pound
  King crab
1 dash Tabasco
1 teaspoon chicken base

Bechamel:
2 tablespoons butter
2 tablespoons flour

1 cup milk, warmed

Preheat oven to 350 degrees. To prepare Bechamel, melt butter (be sure not to brown). Add flour and stir vigorously with wire whisk. Slowly add warm milk, stirring constantly and then remove from heat. Fold mayonnaise into slightly cooled Bechamel. Add peppers, Tabasco, and chicken base. Fold in crabmeat. Bake in oven or microwave oven until bubbly hot. Serves 10 to 12.

Sarah Hedgpeth
Gray Gables Restaurant
Wrightsville Beach, North Carolina

CRAB IMPERIAL

2 large eggs
½ cup mayonnaise
½ teaspoon Dijon mustard
¼ cup Durkee's Special Sauce
1 pound crabmeat

1 tablespoon green pepper,
   chopped coarsely
1 tablespoon pimiento, chopped
   coarsely
Paprika

Preheat oven to 350 degrees. Beat eggs, add mayonnaise, mustard, Durkee's. Mix. Add crabmeat, green pepper, and pimiento. Bake in a 1½-quart casserole for 40 minutes or until heated through. Sprinkle with paprika. Serves 4 to 6.

Mrs. Robert Creighton, Jr. (Ruth)

CRAB QUICHE

3 eggs
1 cup evaporated milk
2 tablespoons butter or
   margarine
2 teaspoons onion, minced
¼ pound fresh mushrooms or
   1 (2½-ounce) jar mushrooms,
   drained

2 tablespoons dry white wine
1 (6½-ounce) can crabmeat or
   ½ pound fresh crabmeat
¼ cup Swiss cheese, grated
   (Cheddar may be substituted)
1 prepared or purchased pie
   crust

Preheat oven to 375 degrees. Bake pie crust 5 minutes. Beat eggs, then add milk and beat. Cook onions in butter until soft. Add mushrooms, wine, and crabmeat and cook until liquid is evaporated. Pour crab mixture into milk mixture and mix well. Turn into pie crust. Top with Swiss cheese. Bake 25 to 30 minutes or until knife inserted near middle comes out clean. Serves 4 to 6.

Mrs. Robert H. Hutchins (Seldie)

CEBICHE

1 pound white fish cut in strips or small pieces
Boiled water, enough to cover fish
3 lemons
1 sour orange
½ cup dry white wine
1 large onion, thinly sliced
1 cup tap water
1 teaspoon salt
1 hot pepper, cut in thin strips

Place fish in a glass bowl. Pour boiling water over it. Drain well in colander and return to bowl. Cover with lemon and orange juice and wine. Let stand 1 hour at room temperature. Place onions in 1 cup water with 1 teaspoon salt. Soak 20 minutes. Drain, rinsing a little in fresh water. Toss with hot peppers, fresh ground pepper and salt. Add to fish. Let stand 1 hour, then refrigerate for 2 or 3 hours or more. Serves 8 to 10.

Traditionally (in Peru) served with sliced cold yams, lettuce, and short pieces of cob corn.

Thomas H. Maloy, M.D.

FISH FILETS ELEGANTE

1 (1-pound) package frozen or fresh fish filets (Filets of sole, haddock, halibut, flounder, cod or trout may be used)
½ teaspoon pepper
2 tablespoons butter or margarine
1 (10½-ounce) can condensed cream of shrimp soup
¼ cup Parmesan cheese, grated
½ teaspoon paprika
1 lemon, cut into wedges

Preheat oven to 400 degrees. Butter a 9x13-inch baking dish. Separate filets. Place in baking dish. Dash with pepper; dot with butter. Spread soup over filets; sprinkle with Parmesan cheese and paprika. Bake for 25 minutes. Garnish with lemon wedges. Serves 2 to 4.

Mrs. Howard L. Armistead (Linda)

SAVORY BAKED FISH

1 teaspoon instant minced
   onion
½ teaspoon powdered mustard
¼ teaspoon tarragon leaves,
   crushed
1/16 teaspoon ground black
   pepper
2 teaspoons warm water

1½ pounds filet of flounder,
   whitefish, halibut or cod
Salt to taste
1 teaspoon freshly squeezed
   lemon juice
½ cup mayonnaise
Paprika

Preheat oven to 425 degrees. Combine instant onion, mustard, tarragon and pepper with warm water; let stand ten minutes for flavors to blend. Wipe fish and arrange in greased 9x11-inch baking dish. Sprinkle with salt. Add lemon juice and mayonnaise to tarragon mixture. Spread on fish. Bake for 25 to 30 minutes until browned and fish flakes easily. Garnish with paprika. Serves 6.

Mrs. Oliver Raymond Hunt (Eleanor)

FLOUNDER WITH GRAPES AND MUSHROOMS

2½ pounds filet of flounder
2 cups milk
¾ pound mushrooms,
   sliced
7 tablespoons butter

2 cups seedless grapes,
   skinned
6 tablespoons flour
½ cup breadcrumbs, buttered
¼ cup Parmesan cheese

Preheat oven to 400 degrees. Poach the flounder for 5 minutes in milk. Sauté mushrooms for 3 minutes in 4 tablespoons butter. Combine grapes with mushrooms and place in 13½x8¾x¾-inch buttered casserole. Drain fish and place filets over grapes and mushrooms. Save milk for sauce. Melt 3 tablespoons butter, blend in flour, add milk and cook until thickened; season. Pour sauce over fish and sprinkle with buttered breadcrumbs and Parmesan cheese. Bake 25 minutes until browned. Serves 6.

Mrs. David P. Thomas (Ginny)

BROILED FLOUNDER

2 whole medium size flounder　　**Juice from 2 lemons**
1 stick butter, melted　　　　　　**Salt and pepper to taste**

Preheat oven to Broil. Wipe fish clean with damp paper towels. Line broiler pan with aluminum foil. Heat pan in oven for 10 minutes. Remove pan from oven and brush with butter. Lay fish on foil and squeeze ½ lemon on each fish, brush with butter and season with salt and pepper. Return pan to middle rack of oven and broil 5 minutes. Remove from oven, turn fish and repeat lemon, butter, salt and pepper. Return to oven for 5 minutes on this side. Serves 2.

Mrs. William P. Robison (Maryann)

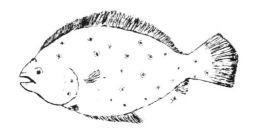

STUFFED WHOLE FLOUNDER

½ cup onion, chopped　　　　　**¼ teaspoon thyme**
½ cup celery, chopped　　　　　**Worcestershire sauce to taste**
1 stick butter　　　　　　　　　　**Tabasco to taste**
1 pound special crabmeat　　　　**18-24 medium shrimp, raw and**
½ cup cracker crumbs　　　　　　**　peeled**
1 cup seasoned breadcrumbs　　**6-8 medium (1½ pound) whole**
4 eggs, beaten　　　　　　　　　　**　flounder**

Preheat oven to 350 degrees. Sauté onion and celery in melted butter. Add crabmeat, cracker crumbs, breadcrumbs, eggs, thyme, Worcestershire sauce and Tabasco. Make a 3-inch slit on dark side of flounder in center of back running from head to tail. Enlarge cavity by slicing directly under skin on both sides of the slit. Fill cavity with stuffing and top with 3 or 4 shrimp. Brush with oil and bake for 20 to 30 minutes. Serves 6 to 8.

B. C. Hedgpeth
The Neptune Restaurant
Wrightsville Beach, North Carolina

GROUPER SALAD

2 pounds grouper filet,
 cut in chunks
Salt and pepper to taste
3 stalks celery (or more),
 finely diced

2 medium onions, finely diced
3 tablespoons pimiento,
 finely diced
Mayonnaise to taste

Bring water to boil with salt and pepper. Cook fish about 8 to 12 minutes until fish is done. Drain water off. Save for fish stock. Cool fish meat in refrigerator. Flake fish, then add to celery, onion and pimiento. Add mayonnaise to make salad consistency. Serve on lettuce with lemon wedges. Serves 4.

Marlene Hieronymus
Hieronymus Market Street Restaurant
Wilmington, North Carolina

STUFFED GROUPER

1 pound shrimp, peeled and
 deveined
4 pounds grouper filet
1½ cups onions, chopped
½ cup celery, chopped
1 stick margarine
½ teaspoon sugar
¼ teaspoon black pepper
1 teaspoon salt

¼ teaspoon gumbo fillé
 (optional)
4 stale hamburger buns
4 eggs
1 heaping tablespoon
 all-purpose flour
¼ cup white wine
½ teaspoon Cayenne pepper

Boil shrimp, drain water and chop shrimp coarsely. Dice 1 pound of grouper filet and set aside. Wilt onions and celery in margarine. Add sugar, black pepper, salt, and gumbo fillé. Add shrimp and diced grouper filet to seasoned onions and celery mixture. Cook for 5 minutes. Crumble hamburger buns (by hand or food processor) and add to lightly beaten eggs; add flour. When well mixed, add shrimp, diced grouper, onion/celery mixture. Add white wine to the stuffing mixture.

To stuff filet: Slash a pocket into the grouper filet. Fill with stuffing. Place in buttered, ovenproof dish and lightly butter the top side of each filet. Broil 10 minutes. Remove from oven, turn filet over very carefully and broil additional 10 minutes. Sprinkle lightly with cayenne pepper, serve with drawn butter. Serves 6.

Wilbur P. Matthews, M.D.

MACKEREL IN WINE SAUCE

2½ pounds mackerel filets
  or steaks
1 tablespoon oil
½ stick butter or margarine
2 large onions, sliced
1 cup dry white wine or
  vermouth
2 beef bouillon cubes

2 cups water
2 tablespoons flour
Salt and pepper to taste
1 can (4 ounces) sliced
  mushrooms, drained
½ cup bread crumbs
½ lemon

Preheat oven to 375 degrees. Clean, wash and dry filets. Cook onions in oil and 2 tablespoons butter or margarine until golden. Add wine or vermouth. Boil to reduce liquid to 3 tablespoons. Add bouillon cubes and water. Mix flour with 2 tablespoons butter or margarine. Add to liquid. Stir continuously while cooking over medium heat until sauce reaches medium thickness. Salt and pepper to taste. Add mushrooms. Pour half the sauce into 2-quart pyrex casserole; lay fish on top and cover with remaining sauce. Sprinkle with bread crumbs; dot with butter. Squeeze lemon on top. Bake 35-40 minutes or until fish is done. Serves 6.

Kenny J. Morris, M.D.

BAKED SHAD

1 shad, cleaned
3 lemons, juiced
Salt and pepper to taste

Milk
Bacon strips to cover shad
1 large onion, chopped

Preheat oven to 250 degrees. Place shad in roasting pan. Cover with lemon juice, salt, and pepper. Let stand for 1 hour. Place bacon strips over shad. Cover almost completely with milk. Sprinkle chopped onion over and around shad. Bake for 8 hours. Remove shad from oven. Dip out most of the milk and bake for 20 minutes at 300 degrees. More salt, pepper, and lemon juice may be needed. Serves 4-6.

Robert R. Smalley, M.D.

OYSTERS AND HAM CAPE FEAR

2 dozen select oysters
2 tablespoons butter
6 eggs
4 medium sized slices country
ham, cooked

4 large buttermilk biscuits
1 cup Hollandaise sauce
Fresh parsley

Sauté oysters in butter. Scramble the eggs in a separate pan. On a warm plate place each opened biscuit, cover with scrambled eggs, one ham slice, then the oysters. Top with a generous portion of Hollandaise sauce. Garnish with fresh parsley. Serve immediately with a tangy Bloody Mary. Serves 4.

Lucien S. Wilkins, M.D.

MAMA OLIVE'S SCALLOPED OYSTERS

½ cup bread crumbs
1 cup saltine cracker crumbs
½ cup melted butter
1 pint oysters

1 tablespoon oyster liquid
2 tablespoons canned milk
  or cream
Salt and pepper

Preheat oven to 400 degrees. Mix the bread and cracker crumbs and stir in the butter. Spread ⅓ of the crumb mixture in the bottom of an 8x8-inch baking dish that has been buttered. Cover crumbs with a layer of half the oysters. Sprinkle with salt and pepper. Add half of the oyster liquid and cream. Repeat the layering process with the remaining ingredients and top with the last ⅓ of crumbs. Bake for 30 minutes. Serves 4.

Mrs. Lucien S. Wilkins (Freda)

WILD RICE AND OYSTER CASSEROLE

2 cups wild rice (or ½ wild and
  ½ brown rice)
1 stick butter, melted
4 dozen raw oysters, shucked
Salt and pepper to taste
Hot pepper sauce to taste
1 can (10½-ounce) cream of
  chicken soup

1 cup light cream
1½ tablespoons onion powder
¾ teaspoon thyme
1½ tablespoons curry powder
¼ cup hot water

Preheat oven to 300 degrees. Cook rice and drain well. Add butter to rice. Place half the rice in shallow baking dish. Drain oysters and place on top of rice. Season oysters with salt, pepper and hot pepper sauce. Spoon remaining rice over oysters. Heat soup with cream, seasoned with onion powder, thyme and curry powder, which has been dissolved in the hot water. Pour mixture over rice and oysters. Bake for 45 minutes. Serves 10 to 12.

Mrs. Fletcher Rieman (Harriet)

OYSTER-SPINACH CASSEROLE

1 (10-ounce) package frozen
  chopped, spinach
1 pint oysters
1 small onion, chopped
2 tablespoons salt-free or corn
  oil margarine

2 heaping tablespoons flour
⅓ cup oyster liquor
⅔ cup milk
¼ teaspoon nutmeg
½ cup bread crumbs

Preheat oven to 400 degrees. Drain oysters, saving liquor. Cook spinach according to package instructions, then *drain thoroughly*. Over medium low heat, sauté onion in melted margarine until tender, then sprinkle with flour. Add oyster liquor and milk, stirring constantly until sauce begins to bubble. Stir in nutmeg, then gently fold in oysters. Allow mixture to simmer until edges of oysters begin to curl. Spray 1½-quart casserole with Pam. Place cooked spinach in bottom of casserole, then pour oyster mixture over this. Top with bread crumbs and dot with margarine. Bake for 15 minutes. Turn oven off and let casserole remain in oven for 10 to 15 minutes for casserole to set. Serves 2 to 3 generously. (Delicious served with cornmeal muffins baked at same time.)

Mrs. J. Calvin MacKay (Shirley)

OYSTERS ROCKEFELLER

24 oysters in shells
2 tablespoons parsley, minced
1 tablespoon onion, chopped
1 tablespoon butter, melted
Paprika, to taste

1 cup cooked spinach,
 chopped, drained
¼ cup fine dry bread crumbs
1 stick butter
Rock salt

Open oysters with knife; cut away from shell. Leave oyster in deep half of shell. Combine parsley, onion, and 1 tablespoon melted butter; spread over oysters. Sprinkle with a small amount of paprika. Top each with 2 teaspoons spinach, then ½ teaspoon bread crumbs and about 1 teaspoon butter. Arrange shells on bed of rock salt in a shallow pan. Bake at 450 degrees until browned, about 10 minutes. Serves 8.

Michael J. Donahue, M.D.

SALMON LOAF WITH SHRIMP SAUCE

2 (1-pound) cans salmon
¼ cup onion, finely minced
¼ cup parsley, chopped, or
 1 teaspoon dried parsley
¼ cup lemon juice
½ teaspoon salt
½ teaspoon pepper

½ to 1 teaspoon ground thyme
2 cups coarse bread crumbs
About ½ cup milk
4 eggs, well beaten
¼ cup butter or margarine,
 melted
Shrimp Sauce

Sauce:
1 (10¾-ounce) can Campbell's
 cream of shrimp soup

½ cup milk
¼ cup Parmesan cheese

Preheat oven to 350 degrees. Drain salmon, saving liquid. Flake salmon into bowl; add onion, parsley, lemon juice, salt, pepper and thyme. Add bread crumbs and mix lightly. Add salmon liquid plus enough milk to make 1 cup; add eggs and melted butter or margarine. Mix lightly. Spoon into greased 2-quart loaf pan or casserole. Bake for 1 hour or until loaf is set in center. This dish may be made in advance and refrigerated or frozen for later use. For the sauce, heat the soup with milk and stir until smooth. Stir in cheese. Spoon onto hot salmon loaf. Serves 8.

Mrs. Howard L. Armistead (Linda)

SALMON AND NOODLE ONE-DISH MEAL

4 tablespoons butter
4 tablespoons flour
¼ teaspoon dry mustard
¼ teaspoon paprika
1 teaspoon salt
3 cups milk
1 teaspoon Worcestershire
  sauce
1 tablespoon lemon juice
½ cup cheese, grated

1 (1-pound) can salmon
½ cup stuffed olives, sliced
2 (4-ounce) cans sliced
  mushrooms
8 ounces noodles, cooked
  and drained
Buttered dry bread crumbs
8 to 10 canned asparagus tips
Parsley, pimiento, and paprika

Preheat oven to 375 degrees. Melt butter, blend flour, mustard, paprika, and salt. Gradually add milk and cook, stirring until thickened. Stir in Worcestershire sauce, lemon juice, and cheese, and stir until cheese is melted. Add salmon, olives and mushrooms. Combine noodles and sauce in lightly greased 2-quart casserole. Sprinkle with buttered bread crumbs and bake for 30 minutes. Garnish with asparagus, parsley, pimiento, and paprika. Serves 4 to 6.

Mrs. Sigmond A. Bear (Kay)

BRIDGE TENDER'S SCALLOPS

1 pound scallops
1 stick butter
¾ cup white wine
½ teaspoon garlic powder
2 teaspoons salt
1 small onion, chopped

1 green pepper, chopped
4 ounces fresh mushrooms,
  sliced
1 tomato, peeled, seeded
  and chopped

Sauté scallops in butter with wine. Add garlic powder and salt. Add onion, green pepper and mushrooms when scallops are half done. Stir in tomato just before serving. Serve over wild rice. Sprinkle with paprika and garnish with lemon. Makes 2 to 3 servings.

The Bridge Tender
Wrightsville Beach, North Carolina

TENDER BROWN SCALLOPS

½ teaspoon salt
¼ teaspoon black pepper
1 dash cayenne pepper
1 cup fine bread crumbs or
  6 Holland Rusks, crushed

1 egg
2 tablespoons water
1½ pounds scallops
4 tablespoons butter, melted

Preheat oven to 450 degrees. Mix the salt, black pepper, cayenne pepper and bread crumbs. Beat the egg and water with a fork. Dip each scallop first in crumb mixture, then in egg mixture and again in crumbs. Put in 8x8-inch buttered baking dish and let stand for 30 minutes for coating to harden and set. Pour melted butter over scallops and bake 25 to 30 minutes or until scallops are brown and crisp. Serve with Tartar Sauce. Serves 2 to 4.

Mrs. R. Bertram Williams, Jr. (Ellen)

SCALLOPS AU GRATIN

1½ pounds fresh scallops
1 cup fine dried bread crumbs
½ cup celery, finely chopped
½ cup fresh or canned
  mushrooms
1 teaspoon salt

2 tablespoons butter or
  margarine
1 cup light cream
2 tablespoons Parmesan
  cheese, grated

Preheat oven to 350 degrees. Rub baking dish with butter or margarine. Rinse scallops and drain. Cover with cold water. Heat slowly to boiling. Drain again. Cover bottom of baking dish with bread crumbs. Add a layer of celery and a layer of mushrooms. Add scallops and season with salt and butter. Add part of cream. Repeat until all ingredients are used. Sprinkle top with cheese. Heat in oven. Serves 4. (Crabmeat may be used in place of scallops.)

Blue Water Point Restaurant
Long Beach, North Carolina

SCALLOPS IN CREAM SAUCE

1 pound scallops
½ cup flour
Salt and pepper to taste
6 tablespoons butter
¼ pound fresh mushrooms,
  sliced

1 lemon, juiced
1½ cups whipping cream,
  unwhipped
1 tablespoon fine dry bread
  crumbs, optional
Mild-flavored cheese, grated

Preheat broiler. Roll scallops in flour; season with salt and pepper. Melt butter in 12-inch skillet, add scallops, and sauté until they are light brown on all sides. Remove scallops from skillet.

To the pan drippings add mushrooms, lemon juice, and unwhipped cream. Season to taste with salt and pepper. Return scallops to skillet, and cook a few minutes longer just until done. If a thicker sauce is desired, blend in bread crumbs and cook and stir gently until they dissolve. Sprinkle cheese on top and place under broiler until cheese melts. May be served as an entree on a bed of parslied rice or as a first course served in individual scallop shells. Serves 4.

Mrs. Wesley W. Hall (Anne)

SHRIMP CREOLE

4 pieces of bacon
½ cup onions, minced
½ cup green pepper, diced
1 cup celery, diced
2 tablespoons flour
2 (16-ounce) cans tomatoes
1 (16-ounce) can stewed
  tomatoes
1 teaspoon salt

1 teaspoon pepper
2 teaspoons sugar
1 tablespoon Lea & Perrins
  sauce
3 bay leaves
2 pounds shrimp, cooked
  and shelled
2 cups rice, cooked

Cook bacon in 12-inch skillet. Remove cooked bacon. Sauté onion, pepper and celery in bacon grease in skillet until tender. Add flour, blend. Add tomatoes, stirring constantly. Chop up whole tomatoes as you stir. Add salt, pepper, sugar, Lea & Perrins sauce and bay leaves. Cook gently thirty minutes. Remove bay leaves. Add shrimp and crumbled bacon. Heat. Serve over rice. Serves 8 to 10.

Mrs. Frank B. Reynolds (Marguerite)

SHRIMP JAMBALAYA

4 large onions, chopped
¾ cup green pepper, chopped
3 cloves garlic, minced
  (optional)
Salad oil
2 pounds fresh shrimp, peeled
  and deveined

3 cups water
2 cups uncooked regular rice
Cayenne pepper to taste
Black pepper and salt to taste

Sauté onion, green pepper, and garlic in enough oil to cover bottom of a heavy Dutch oven. When vegetables are tender, add shrimp and cook about 15 minutes. Add water and bring to a boil. Stir in rice, cayenne pepper, black pepper, and salt. Cook covered for 20 to 25 minutes over low heat or until rice is tender. Lightly stir; cover and set aside for 10 minutes. Serves 8 to 10.

Mrs. David P. Thomas (Ginny)

SHRIMP MOUSSE

1 envelope unflavored gelatin
½ cup hot water
1 (10¾-ounce) can Campbell's
  tomato soup
1 cup mayonnaise
1 (8-ounce) package cream
  cheese

1½ cups celery, chopped
½ cup onions, chopped
½ pound fresh shrimp, cooked
  and cleaned

Dissolve gelatin in hot water. Heat tomato soup. Mix mayonnaise, cream cheese, celery, onions, and shrimp. Pour gelatin mixture into heated soup. Combine all and pour into a 5-cup mold. Chill overnight. Unmold and serve. Serves 8 to 10.

Mrs. E. Tilghman Poole (Jean)

SHRIMP ORLEANS

1 tablespoon butter or
margarine
1 medium onion, sliced
1 clove garlic, crushed
1 (10¾-ounce) can condensed
cream of mushroom soup

1 cup dairy sour cream
¼ cup catsup
1 (3-ounce) can (⅔ cup) broiled
sliced mushrooms, drained
2 cups cleaned cooked or
canned shrimp

Melt butter in chafing dish or skillet; add onion and garlic; cook until tender but not brown. Combine soup, sour cream, and catsup; stir into onions. Add mushroom and shrimp. Cook over low heat until mixture is heated through. Serve over fluffy hot rice. Serves 4.

Mrs. Robert A. Moore, Jr. (Wanda)

REFRESHING SHRIMP SALAD

2 pounds shrimp, cooked and
peeled
1 medium head of cauliflower
1 green pepper
2 cups celery, chopped

1 (10-ounce) package frozen
peas, defrosted
1 regular package Hidden Valley
Ranch salad dressing

Chop cauliflower and green pepper finely. Mix in large bowl the shrimp, cauliflower, green pepper, celery, and peas. Prepare Hidden Valley Ranch salad dressing according to package directions. Combine one-half of salad dressing with shrimp and vegetables. Chill thoroughly. Serve on lettuce leaves. Serves 6 to 8.

Mrs. James E. Wortman (Martha)

SHRIMP SOUFFLÉ

1½ pounds of shrimp, cooked
   and peeled
¼ cup onion, minced
½ cup celery, chopped
¼ cup green pepper, chopped
¼ cup mayonnaise
Salt and pepper to taste

1 stick margarine, melted
12 slices white bread, crusts
   removed
½ cup mild Cheddar cheese,
   shredded
2 cups milk
5 eggs

Preheat oven to 350 degrees. Chop shrimp finely (may use food processor). Combine shrimp, onion, celery, green pepper, mayonnaise, salt and pepper. Mix well. Dip bread into melted margarine, coating each slice on both sides. Make 6 sandwiches of the butter-dipped bread and shrimp mixture. Cut sandwiches into quarters and place in 9x13-inch baking dish. Sprinkle cheese on top. Beat together eggs and milk and pour over sandwiches. Refrigerate at least 4 hours (or overnight). Set dish in pan of water and bake for one hour. Serves 8.

Mrs. Clifford Lewis (Libby)

SHRIMP SZECHUAN

2 tablespoons peanut oil
1 pound large shrimp, shelled
   and deveined
¼ cup green onion, minced
2 tablespoons fresh ginger,
   minced
3 cloves garlic, finely minced

2 tablespoons dry sherry
2 tablespoons soy sauce
1 teaspoon sugar
¼ teaspoon salt
2 to 3 tablespoons catsup
1 tablespoon chili sauce
1 teaspoon red pepper flakes

Heat oil in a wok or large heavy skillet. Add shrimp, green onion, ginger and garlic. Stir-fry until shrimp are pink. Add sherry, soy sauce, sugar and salt. Stir well and blend in catsup, chili sauce and red pepper flakes. Serve with piping hot rice. Serves 6-8.

(Watch out—it's hot and spicy!)

Wesley W. Hall, M.D.

SHRIMP VOL-AU-VENT WITH BÉCHAMEL SAUCE

6 ready-made (or frozen) vols-au-vent (patty shells)
1½ pounds shrimp, freshly peeled
1 tablespoon or a little more butter
4 medium mushrooms, sliced

¼ to ½ teaspoon salt or to taste
¼ to ½ teaspoon white pepper or to taste
2 to 3 teaspoons of fish or chicken stock
Several drops of cognac or dry sherry

In a pan, sauté mushrooms in butter with salt and pepper to taste. When mushrooms are sautéed, add shrimp. Cook a few minutes longer until shrimp are pink, adding a few spoonfuls of fish or chicken stock to keep the bottom of the pan runny. Sprinkle with several drops of cognac. Finally mix in the Béchamel sauce. If too thick add a little fresh cream. Serve into patty shells. Serves 4 to 6.

Béchamel Sauce:
1½ cups milk
2 tablespoons onion or shallots, chopped
2 tablespoons celery, chopped
6 peppercorns

2 sprigs parsley
2 bay leaves
3 tablespoons butter
3 tablespoons flour
1 egg yolk

Combine, in a saucepan, the milk, onion, celery, peppercorns, parsley and bay leaves. Heat, covered, over low heat until steaming hot. Set aside for 15 minutes. In a second heavy saucepan melt butter, blend in flour. Cook 1 minute and remove from heat. Strain milk mixture and stir it into flour mixture. Cook stirring constantly, until sauce thickens and comes to a boil. Boil 2 minutes. In a small bowl, beat egg yolk with a fork. Stir in about half of sauce, then stir all back into remaining sauce. Cook over low heat 1 minute longer (do not boil). Makes 1½ cups.

Mrs. David Bunn (Dana)

SHRIMP TOM JONES

3 small onions, cut in large
  pieces
3 stalks of celery, cut in large
  pieces
Salt to taste
Pepper to taste
3 to 4 bay leaves

1½ teaspoons oregano
2 cloves of fresh garlic
¼ cup parsley
1½ lemons
1 pound medium shrimp,
  unshelled

Dip for Shrimp:
1 stick butter, melted
Juice of ½ lemon

2 tablespoons Worcestershire
  sauce

Fill large pot with 2½ inches of water. Place onions and celery in water. Add salt, pepper, bay leaves, oregano, garlic, parsley and the juice and rind of the lemons and bring to a boil. Reduce heat to simmer until onions are soft. Add unpeeled shrimp and cook 5 to 7 minutes. Strain. Mix butter, lemon juice and Worcestershire sauce for dip. Pour into individual dip cups and dip shrimp as you peel them. Yield: 2 servings.

Francesca James
New York, New York

Azalea Festival Queen—1977

CURRIED SHRIMP RICE

1½ cups Minute rice
1½ cups boiling water
½ teaspoon salt
¼ cup French dressing
¾ cup mayonnaise
1 tablespoon onion, minced
¾ teaspoon curry powder
  (or more, to taste)

½ teaspoon salt
½ teaspoon pepper
½ teaspoon dry mustard
½ cup celery, diced
1 pound shrimp, cooked
  and cleaned

Combine rice, water and salt and cook according to instant rice package directions. When cooked, cool and toss in the French dressing. Blend mayonnaise, onion, curry powder, salt, pepper, mustard and celery. Stir into the rice. Refrigerate. Combine with shrimp when ready to serve. Serve cold. Serves 6 to 8.

Mrs. Albert B. Brown (Margaret)

GULF COAST CRÊPES

¼ cup onion, chopped
  (green onion if possible)
2 teaspoons curry powder
2 tablespoons butter
1 can (10¾-ounce) cream of
  shrimp soup

2 cups sour cream
2 cups shrimp, cooked
16 crêpes (see recipe below)
Green onions, chopped
  (optional)
Lime wedges (optional)

Preheat oven to 350 degrees. Sauté onion and curry powder in butter. Add the soup; stir and cook over medium heat until heated through. Stir in the sour cream and shrimp. Simmer about 5 minutes. Spoon about ¼ cup of the filling on each crêpe. Roll up and spoon remaining sauce over the crêpes and serve at once. Or, arrange the crêpes in greased 13x9-inch baking dish and heat in oven for 10 minutes. Garnish with chopped green onion and lime wedges, if desired. Serves 8 to 10.

Crêpes:
3 eggs
1½ cups milk
3 tablespoons butter, melted

1 cup all-purpose flour
½ teaspoon salt

Combine eggs, milk, butter, flour and salt in a blender and blend until smooth. Let the batter stand about 1 hour before baking. Cook on lightly greased crêpe pan. Makes about 16 crêpes. Recipe can be doubled.

Mrs. Ellis A. Tinsley (Betty)

95

PINEAPPLE SHRIMP

4 tablespoons flour
4 tablespoons cornstarch
½ teaspoon salt
¼ teaspoon monosodium
  glutamate
2 tablespoons water
1 egg, beaten
1 pound raw shrimp, uncooked,
  peeled and deveined
½ cup white vinegar
½ cup brown sugar
½ cup pineapple juice

1 teaspoon salt
¼ teaspoon pepper
4 slices canned pineapple,
  diced
2 green peppers, cut in 1-inch
  squares
2 fresh tomatoes, peeled and
  quartered
2 tablespoons cornstarch mixed
  with ¼ cup cold water
1 tablespoon green onions,
  chopped

Combine flour, cornstarch, salt, monosodium glutamate, water and egg. Dip shrimp in batter. Fry shrimp in cooking oil, turning to brown both sides; drain on paper toweling. Combine vinegar, brown sugar, pineapple juice, salt and pepper in enameled or stainless steel pan; heat. Add pineapple, green peppers and tomatoes. Bring to boil, reduce heat and simmer five minutes. Stir in cornstarch and cook a few minutes, stirring until sauce thickens and is clear. Add shrimp. Simmer about two minutes longer. Sprinkle with green onions. Serves 6 to 8.

Mrs. Wesley W. Hall (Anne)

MASONBORO GUMBO

1½ sticks butter
⅓ cup Wesson oil
½ cup flour
1 green pepper, chopped
4 onions, chopped
6 stalks celery, chopped
½ cup parsley, chopped
2 garlic cloves, minced
1 pound okra, sliced
2 quarts chicken stock
1 quart water
1 quart frozen or ripe tomatoes
½ cup Worcestershire sauce
1 tablespoon salt

½ teaspoon black pepper
3 bay leaves
¼ teaspoon rosemary
¼ teaspoon thyme
3 cups chicken, cooked
  and diced
Tabasco
4 pounds shrimp, boiled
  and cleaned
1 pound crabmeat
1½ teaspoons brown sugar
1 quart oysters or clams,
  drained
2 lemons

Melt butter and oil in heavy pot. Add flour and stir until flour is golden. Add green pepper, onion, celery, parsley and garlic. Cook stirring continuously for 30 minutes. Brown sliced okra and add to pot. Add chicken stock, water, tomatoes, Worcestershire sauce, salt, pepper, bay leaves, rosemary, thyme. Simmer 2 hours. Add chicken; stir and season with Tabasco. After 30 minutes add shrimp, crabmeat and brown sugar. Add oysters five minutes before serving. Serve gumbo on hot rice and squeeze lemon juice on each serving. Freezes well—reheats best in microwave oven. Serves 10.

Mrs. Robert R. Smalley (Mona)

SEAFOOD CRÊPES: CRÊPES FRUIT DE MER

Crêpes:

1 cup flour
¼ teaspoon salt
3 eggs

2 cups milk
Pinch of sugar

In blender, mix all of the ingredients until well-blended. Use a hot well-buttered crêpe pan to fry. Use about 1 ounce batter for each crêpe. Roll around pan till very thin. Makes 24 to 30 (8-inch) crêpes.

Seafood Filling:

1 pound fresh shelled shrimp,
   cooked
1 pound scallops, cooked in
   1 cup water (reserve liquid)
1 tablespoon butter
1 pound mushrooms, sliced
   (fresh)

2 tablespoons butter
2 tablespoons flour
1 cup milk or cream
Salt and pepper to taste
½ cup Swiss cheese,
   finely shredded

Cook shrimp and scallops (reserving liquid from scallops). Melt 1 tablespoon butter in large pan. Heat on medium heat until bubbles form. Add mushrooms and sauté for approximately 5 minutes. Remove mushrooms from pan; add to pan 2 tablespoons of butter; melt; add flour. Stir until smooth; add milk or cream and the reserved scallop liquid; stirring constantly until the sauce has thickened. Add salt and pepper to taste. Add shrimp, scallops, and mushrooms. Heat until thoroughly warmed. Put a generous tablespoon in each crêpe and roll up. Sprinkle top with a small amount of Swiss cheese. Serves 8.

Mrs. Michael Donahue (Teri)

SEAFOOD LOUISIAN IN AVOCADO

Lobster, cooked meat from four
lobster tails or two whole
lobsters
1 pound shrimp, cooked, peeled
and deveined
½ pound deluxe crabmeat
1 cup mayonnaise
2 tablespoons French dressing
(oil and vinegar type)

½ cup chili sauce
1 tablespoon onion, minced
2 tablespoons capers
2 teaspoons lemon juice
2 teaspoons horseradish
½ teaspoon Worcestershire
sauce
1 teaspoon salt
Dash pepper

Mix lobster, shrimp, and crabmeat. In separate bowl mix mayonnaise, french dressing, chili sauce, onion, capers, lemon juice, horseradish, Worcestershire sauce, salt and pepper. Mix seafood and sauce well, cover and put in refrigerator for two to three hours. Brush surface of avocado halves with lemon juice. Fill with seafood mixture. Serve with crescent rolls, small tomatoes and relishes. Serves 12.

Mrs. R. Bertram Williams, Jr. (Ellen)

SHRIMP AND CRABMEAT CASSEROLE

1½ pounds fresh shrimp,
cooked, peeled and deveined
1 pound fresh crabmeat
2 cups celery, diced
1 medium onion, chopped
2 teaspoons seasoned salt
1 teaspoon pepper
2 teaspoons Worcestershire
sauce

8 ounces cream cheese,
softened
2 teaspoons green pepper,
chopped
1 cup mayonnaise
2 slices white bread, grated into
crumbs
1 tablespoon margarine, melted

Preheat oven to 350 degrees. Cut shrimp in pieces. Mix shrimp, crabmeat, celery, onion, salt, pepper, Worcestershire sauce, cream cheese, green pepper, and mayonnaise and put in greased 1½-quart casserole dish. Top with bread crumbs and sprinkle with margarine. Bake for 20 minutes. After baking, serve warm or cold as salad. Serves 8.

Mrs. Donald MacQueen (Lynn)

SHRIMP-CRABMEAT COBBLER
WITH CHEESE BISCUIT TOPPING

1 stick butter
½ cup green pepper, chopped
½ cup onion, chopped
½ cup plain flour
1 teaspoon dry mustard
½ teaspoon Aćcent
1 cup milk
1 cup cheese, shredded

1 pound crabmeat, boned
1 (8-ounce) can tomato paste
2 teaspoons Worcestershire
   sauce
½ teaspoon salt
1 pound shrimp, boiled and
   cleaned

Cheese Biscuit Topping:
1 cup flour
½ teaspoon salt
2 teaspoons baking powder

¼ cup cheese, shredded
2 tablespoons butter
½ cup milk

Preheat oven to 450 degrees. Melt 1 stick butter in double boiler. Add green pepper and onions. Cook over boiling water until tender, about 15 minutes. Blend in ½ cup flour, dry mustard, Aćcent, 1 cup milk, 1 cup cheese. Cook, stirring constantly until cheese is melted and mixture is very thick. Add crabmeat, tomato paste, Worcestershire sauce, ½ teaspoon salt, and shrimp. Blend thoroughly. Pour into an 11 x 9-inch casserole.

To make topping: Sift together 1 cup flour, baking powder, and ½ teaspoon salt. Add ¼ cup cheese. Cut in 2 tablespoons butter. Add ½ cup milk. Drop by spoonfuls on mixture and bake 20 to 25 minutes. Serves 8 to 10.

Mrs. Thad Shearin (Bettie Lou)

CHARCOAL SHRIMP AND SCALLOPS

1 pound raw shrimp, cleaned
1 pound scallops
½ pound fresh mushrooms,
  sliced
1⅓ cups cooked rice

2 tablespoons brandy
1 tablespoon salt
½ teaspoon pepper
1 cup heavy cream
⅓ cup milk

Mix shrimp, scallops, mushrooms, rice, brandy, salt, pepper, cream, and milk. Divide into four tightly sealed foil pouches. Place on grill over hot coals or directly on ashes and cook for 10 minutes—OR—bake in 425 degrees oven for 20 minutes. Serves 4.

William Phillips, M.D.

SPAGHETTI AND SEA SAUCE

1 pound assorted seafood
3 tablespoons olive oil
1 tablespoon garlic, chopped
3 tablespoons parsley, chopped
1 pinch red pepper, chopped
½ pound butter, melted

4 ounces dry Italian white wine
1 teaspoon salt
1 pound spaghetti, cooked
  al dente and drained
2 cups tomato sauce

Note: Clams may be steamed to open shells. Clams and squid may be chopped for extra tenderness. Scallops may be cut into small pieces if desired.

Parboil seafood. Drain. Put in frying pan 3 tablespoons olive oil. Add garlic, parsley, red pepper, frying until garlic and parsley change color. Add all seafood that has been *drained well,* and melted butter. Mix with fork for two minutes. When very hot, add white wine, salt. Add spaghetti. Add tomato sauce and serve. Serves 4.

Carlo Landi
Mediterraneo Restaurant
Wrightsville Beach, North Carolina

TUNA TETRAZZINI

7 tablespoons butter or
  margarine
½ pound mushrooms, sliced
½ package (1-pound size) large
  shell macaroni
¼ cup unsifted all-purpose flour
1 teaspoon salt

½ teaspoon dry mustard
⅛ teaspoon pepper
2 cups milk
½ cup dry sherry
1 (8-ounce) package sharp
  cheddar cheese, grated
3 (7-ounce) cans tuna, drained

Preheat oven to 375 degrees. In 3 tablespoons hot butter in a medium skillet, sauté mushrooms for 5 minutes, stirring occasionally. Cook macaroni as directed on package and drain. Melt remaining butter in medium saucepan. Remove from heat, stir in flour, salt, mustard and pepper. Gradually stir in milk and sherry. Bring to boil while stirring. Remove from heat. Add 1½ cups cheese, stir until melted. In a 2-quart casserole, combine tuna, mushrooms, macaroni and cheese sauce. Sprinkle with remaining cheese. Bake uncovered for 20 to 25 minutes or until golden and bubbly. This may be frozen and then thawed before baking. Serves 6 to 8.

Mrs. James Tidler (Peg)

poultry, cheese, Egg Dishes

The Cameron-Hollman House, circa 1800, offers a grand welcome to all crossing the Cape Fear River while the Corinthian columns of the Market Street Bellamy mansion hint of a luxurious life of Wilmington past.

BAKED SCRAMBLED EGGS

6 eggs, large
½ teaspoon salt
Pepper to taste
6 (1 inch square slice, cooked) bacon

6 (1 inch square slice) Cheddar cheese

Preheat oven to 400 degrees. Grease 6 cups in a muffin pan generously with butter. Place a piece of bacon in bottom of each cup. In mixing bowl beat eggs, salt and pepper with fork or whisk for 30 seconds. Dividing evenly, pour eggs into muffin cups. Place a piece of cheese on top of egg mixture. Bake in a preheated 400 degree oven for 12 minutes or until eggs puff and cheese begins to melt. Serve on heated plates. Serves 3 to 6.

Robert L. Morrison, M.D.

BRUNCH CASSEROLE

½ cup onions, minced
2 tablespoons oil
4½ tablespoons butter
½ cup cooked ham, diced
4 large eggs
½ clove garlic, mashed

2 tablespoons parsley, minced
1 cup Swiss cheese, grated
¼ cup heavy cream
¼ teaspoon salt
Good grind of whole pepper
3 medium potatoes

Preheat oven to 375 degrees. Cook onions until tender in 2 tablespoons oil and 2 tablespoons butter. Raise heat slightly, stir in ham and cook one minute longer. Beat eggs with garlic, parsley, ⅔ cup cheese, cream, salt and pepper. Stir in ham and onions. Peel and grate potatoes, using large holes of grater. Squeeze moisture out of potatoes. Stir the potatoes into the egg mixture. Melt 2 tablespoons butter in a 8½x12-inch oval baking dish, pour in the mixture. Dot with ½ tablespoon butter and sprinkle with remaining ⅓ cup cheese. Bake in preheated 375 degree oven for 35 minutes or until nicely browned. Serves 6.

Mrs. Sigmond A. Bear (Kay)

GERMAN APPLE PANCAKES

Batter:

8 extra large eggs
1 cup all-purpose flour
2 tablespoons sugar
1 teaspoon baking powder
⅛ teaspoon salt

2 cups milk
½ stick butter, melted
2 teaspoons vanilla
¼ teaspoon nutmeg,
   freshly grated

Batter: Combine eggs, flour, sugar, baking powder, salt and milk. Blend until smooth. Add melted butter, vanilla and nutmeg. Blend thoroughly. Let batter stand at room temperature for 30 minutes.

Fruit Mixture:

1 stick butter
1⅓ cups sugar
1 teaspoon cinnamon
¼ teaspoon nutmeg,
   freshly grated

2 large tart apples (Granny
   Smith is best), peeled, cored
   and thinly sliced (2 cups)
2 tablespoons lemon juice

Fruit Mixture: Position rack in center of oven and preheat to 425 degrees. Divide butter evenly and melt in two 10-inch ovenproof skillets, brushing butter up sides of pan. Remove from heat. Combine sugar, cinnamon and nutmeg and blend well. Sprinkle ⅓ cup sugar mixture over butter in each skillet. Divide apple slices and layer evenly on top of sugar mix. Sprinkle with lemon juice and the remaining sugar mixture. Place skillets over medium-high heat on top of stove until mixture bubbles. This layer will form a crusty, tasty bottom layer. Divide batter evenly and gently pour over apples. Transfer skillets to oven and bake 15 minutes. Reduce heat to 375 degrees and bake an additional 10 minutes. Slide onto heated serving platters, cut into wedges and serve immediately. Serve with sausage, juice and coffee for a delicious and satisfying meal. Serves 6-8.

Wilbur P. Matthews, M.D.

LOU'S EGGS AND TOMATOES

6 thick slices of fresh ripe
  tomatoes
6 eggs
Salt to taste
Pepper to taste

6 teaspoons butter
6 rounds of toasts
Parsley
Cheddar cheese, grated

Preheat oven to 350 degrees. Place one thick slice of tomato in 6 well buttered large muffin tins. Season with salt and pepper. Break an egg on top of each tomato. Season again with salt and pepper. Place one teaspoon of butter on top of each egg. Bake until eggs are set. Scoop each egg tomato out and place on round of buttered toast. Garnish with grated cheese and parsley. This can be served with hollandaise sauce and parsley. Serves 6.

Mrs. W. Thad Shearin, Jr. (Bettie)

CHEESY GRITS

1 cup instant grits
½ pound Velveeta cheese
½ pound sharp cheddar cheese
  grated or cut in small chunks

½ stick margarine
3 eggs, beaten
½-¾ cup milk

Preheat oven to 325 degrees. Cook grits according to directions on package. Stir cheeses and margarine into hot grits. Mix beaten eggs with milk and add to grits mixture. Pour into greased 7¾x11½-inch casserole. Bake approximately 45 minutes in preheated oven. Serves 10 to 12.

Mrs. Oliver Raymond Hunt (Eleanor)

MACARONI AND CHEESE PIE

1 cup flour
½ teaspoon salt
⅓ cup shortening
½ cup Cheddar cheese,
  shredded
4 or 5 tablespoons ice water
1½ cups elbow macaroni
¼ cup butter
¼ cup flour

2 cups milk
2 tablespoons parsley, chopped
1 teaspoon salt
⅛ teaspoon cayenne pepper
1 (3-ounce) package cream
  cheese
2 cups Cheddar cheese,
  shredded

Preheat oven to 425 degrees. Mix flour and salt. Cut in shortening. Stir in cheese. Add water gradually and stir with fork. Pat mixture into a ball. Roll out pastry large enough to cover bottom and sides of 9-inch quiche dish. Prick bottom and sides with fork. Bake 15 minutes. Set aside until ready to fill. Reduce oven temperature to 350 degrees. Cook elbow macaroni as directed on package. Drain. In a medium saucepan melt butter. Add flour to butter and gradually add milk. Cook mixture until thick, stirring constantly. Add parsley, salt and cayenne pepper. Remove from heat and add cream cheese and 1¼ cups Cheddar cheese, stirring until melted. Add macaroni and pour into crust. Bake for 20 minutes. Sprinkle ¾ cup Cheddar cheese over macaroni and bake 10 to 15 minutes longer. Serves 8.

Mrs. W. Thad Shearin, Jr. (Bettie)

VERY CHEESY MACARONI AND CHEESE

4 cups macaroni, uncooked
1 stick margarine, sliced
1 pound Velveeta cheese, cubed
1 (10¾-ounce) can Cheddar
  cheese soup

1 cup milk
Salt
Pepper

Preheat oven to 350 degrees. Cook and drain macaroni according to package directions. In a three-quart, greased casserole, layer one half the macaroni and top with half of the margarine and half of the cheese. Repeat the layers. Stir the soup and milk together and pour over the casserole. Bake for 35 to 45 minutes in a 350 degree preheated oven. Serves 8 to 10.

Mrs. Ellis A. Tinsley (Betty)

CHRISTMAS BREAKFAST BAKE

6 eggs—whisked until frothy
2 cups milk
1 teaspoon salt
1 teaspoon dry mustard

2 slices toasted bread, cubed
1 pound bacon—cooked and
  crumbled
1 cup grated Cheddar cheese

Preheat oven to 350 degrees. Beat together eggs, milk, salt and mustard. In a 9x13-inch greased baking dish arrange in layers bread cubes, bacon and cheese. Pour egg mixture over the top. Bake in oven for about 45 minutes. Cut in squares to serve. Sausage may be substituted for the bacon. Serves 4 to 5.

Mrs. Edgar Cardwell (Ethel)

CINDY'S BRUNCH CASSEROLE

16 slices bread, crusts removed
8 thin slices Canadian bacon or
  ham
8 slices sharp Cheddar cheese
6 large eggs, beaten
½ teaspoon salt
Pepper to taste
½ to 1 teaspoon dry mustard

¼ cup onions, minced
Dash of red pepper
¼ cup green pepper, chopped
1 to 2 teaspoons
  Worcestershire sauce
3 cups whole milk
1 stick butter, melted
1 cup potato chips, crushed

This dish is cooked the day after preparation. Lay 8 slices of bread in a shallow 9x13-inch buttered casserole. On each slice of bread place a slice each of bacon and cheese. Place remaining bread slices on top of cheese. Mix eggs, salt, pepper, mustard, onion, red pepper, green pepper, Worcestershire sauce and milk. Pour over bread. Cover and refrigerate overnight. Before cooking pour butter over top and sprinkle top with potato chips. Bake 1 hour in a preheated 350 degree oven. Serves 8.

Mrs. Andrew R. Cracker (Mary)

CHEESE PIE

2 eggs
¾ cup flour
½ teaspoon salt
⅛ teaspoon pepper

1 cup milk
2 cups shredded cheese
(Mozzarella, Cheddar or
Swiss)

Preheat oven to 425 degrees. Combine eggs, flour, salt, pepper and ½ cup milk. Beat until smooth. Add rest of milk and 1½ cups cheese. Pour in well greased 9-inch pie pan. Bake for 30 minutes. Add rest of cheese the last 5 minutes. Serves 6.

Mrs. Andrew R. Cracker (Mary)

MUSHROOM QUICHE

Pastry for 9-inch pie shell
1 small onion, chopped
8 ounces fresh mushrooms,
  sliced
2 tablespoons cooking oil
3 eggs, beaten
½ cup evaporated milk

8 ounces dairy sour cream
½ teaspoon ground nutmeg
1 teaspoon salt
½ teaspoon pepper
½ pound Swiss cheese, diced
1 tablespoon flour

Preheat oven to 425 degrees. Line 9-inch quiche dish with pastry. Prick pastry with fork and bake for 6 minutes at 425 degrees. Remove from oven and cool. Reduce oven temperature to 350 degrees. Saute onion and mushrooms in cooking oil until tender. Combine eggs, milk, sour cream, nutmeg, salt and pepper in a large bowl stirring until blended. Combine cheese and flour and stir into the egg mixture. Add onions and mushrooms to egg mixture, mix well and pour into pastry shell. Bake for 45 minutes at 350 degrees. Serves 6.

Mrs. Donald W. MacQueen (Lynn)

CHEESE ONION PIE

3 tablespoons butter
2½ cups sliced onions
1 cup milk
2 eggs

3 tablespoons flour
1 teaspoon salt
8 ounces Swiss cheese, diced
1 (9-inch) pie shell, unbaked

Preheat oven to 400 degrees. Melt butter in saucepan and steam onions ten minutes. Mix milk, eggs, flour, salt and cheese. Stir until well blended. Add mixture to steamed onions and pour into the pie shell. Bake at 400 degrees for 30 minutes or until golden brown. Cool 10 minutes before serving to allow the cheese to set. Serves 6 to 8.

Mrs. J. Calvin MacKay (Shirley)

CHEESE SOUFFLÉ NEVER FAIL

3½ tablespoons margarine
  or butter
3½ tablespoons flour
1½ cups milk

½ teaspoon salt
1 cup grated sharp cheese
4 eggs, separated

Preheat oven to 325 degrees. Melt butter in top of double boiler and blend in flour. Stir in milk and salt. Cook over boiling water, stirring until mixture thickens. Add the grated cheese and stir until melted. Beat the egg yolks until thick. Slowly stir the hot cheese mixture into the egg yolks. With clean beaters, beat the egg whites until they stand in stiff peaks and are dry. Slowly pour the egg yolk mixture over the whites, folding to blend (*do not stir*). Pour into a greased six-cup baking dish. Using a table knife, trace a circle through the mixture one-inch deep about one-inch from the edge of dish. Place baking dish in shallow pan of hot water in a preheated 325 degree oven and bake approximately 1 hour or until soufflé feels firm when pressed down with a teaspoon. Serves 3 to 4. Delicious served with tomato sauce.

Mrs. David P. Thomas (Ginny)

HERBED CHICKEN CASSEROLE

3 large whole chicken breasts,
   cut in half
Salt
Pepper
¼ cup butter or margarine
1 (10¾-ounce) can cream of
   chicken soup
¾ cup white wine

1 (5-ounce) can water
   chestnuts, drained, sliced
1 (3-ounce) can sliced
   mushrooms, drained
2 tablespoons green pepper,
   chopped (optional)
¼ teaspoon thyme, crushed

Preheat oven to 350 degrees. Season chicken with salt and pepper. Melt butter in skillet and brown chicken. Arrange browned chicken in shallow 11½ x 7½-inch casserole. Add soup and wine to drippings in skillet, stirring until smooth. Add chestnuts, mushrooms, green pepper and thyme to skillet. Heat to boiling and pour over chicken. Cover casserole with foil and bake in preheated 350 degree oven for 25 minutes. Uncover and cook 30 minutes or until chicken is tender. Serve with rice. Serves 6.

Mrs. John Olin Perritt (Carolyn)

CHICKEN IN WINE SAUCE

1 package (6 ounces) long grain
   and wild rice mix
3 large whole chicken breasts,
   boned, halved lengthwise
Salt
Pepper
¼ cup butter or margarine
1 can (10¾-ounce) cream of
   chicken soup

¾ cup sauterne wine
½ cup sliced celery
1 jar (4½-ounce) sliced
   mushrooms, drained
1 jar (4-ounce) diced pimento,
   drained

Preheat oven to 350 degrees. Prepare rice mix according to directions on package. Season chicken with salt and pepper. Melt butter in skillet and slowly brown chicken. Spoon rice into 1½-quart greased casserole, top with chicken, skin side up. Add soup to skillet. Slowly add sauterne, stirring until smooth. Add celery, mushrooms and pimento to skillet, bring to a boil and pour over chicken. Cover and bake for 30 minutes at 350 degrees. Uncover and bake 20 minutes or until tender. Serves 6.

Mrs. William P. Robison (Maryann)

EMPRESS CHICKEN

4 whole chicken breasts,
skinned, halved
½ cup flour
1 teaspoon salt
¼ teaspoon pepper
4 tablespoons butter or
margarine

1 pound fresh mushrooms,
sliced
1 cup sour cream
½ cup dry white wine
1 cup chicken broth
Pinch of rosemary

Preheat oven to 350 degrees. Dry chicken and shake in a mixture of flour, salt and pepper. Melt the butter in a skillet and brown the chicken. Arrange chicken in a baking dish 9x13-inches in one layer. Reduce the butter to two tablespoons and brown the mushrooms lightly. Stir sour cream, wine and chicken broth into the mushrooms. Sprinkle the rosemary over the sauce and pour over the chicken. Cover and bake 1½ hours in a preheated 350 degree oven. Serves 8.

Mrs. Norman J. Robinson (Sonja)

CREAMY BAKED CHICKEN (MICROWAVE)

½ cup dry bread crumbs
2 tablespoons Parmesan
cheese
1 tablespoon parsley flakes
½ teaspoon garlic salt
⅛ teaspoon pepper
2½-3 pound frying chicken, cut
into serving pieces

1 (10¾-ounce) can cream
of mushroom soup
2 tablespoons milk
Grated Parmesan cheese
Paprika

Mix bread crumbs, cheese, parsley, garlic salt and pepper together. Coat chicken with mixture. Place chicken skin side up in a 9x13-inch glass baking dish. Cover with waxed paper. Microwave on high 20 to 22 minutes. Combine soup and milk; spoon over baked chicken, sprinkle with cheese and paprika. Cover again with waxed paper and microwave on high setting 5-6 minutes. Serves 6.

Mrs. Alan Thomas (Bridget)

STUFFED CORNISH HENS

4 Cornish hens
1 small onion, chopped
½ green pepper, chopped
2 tablespoons butter

1 (8-ounce) package Rice-A-
Roni, Chicken Flavor
Salt
Pepper

Preheat oven to 350 degrees. Wash hens and set aside. Sauté the onion and pepper in the butter until soft. Prepare the Rice-A-Roni according to the directions on package. When cooked add the onion and pepper to the rice. Dust the hens on the outside and in the cavity with the salt and pepper. Stuff the hens' cavities with the rice mixture. Cover and cook for 1 to 1½ hours, uncovering the last ½ hour. Cook till golden brown, basting in its own juices several times during baking. Serves 4 to 8.

Mrs. Lucien S. Wilkins (Freda)

DOVE BREASTS OR QUAIL BAKED IN WINE

12 dove breasts or quail, drawn
and plucked
1 envelope Lipton onion soup
mix

3 cups dry red or white wine
1 can (10¾-ounce) mushroom
soup
1 soup can water

Preheat oven to 350 degrees. Place dove breasts or quail in a 9x13-inch baking dish. Sprinkle with soup mix. Pour in one cup of wine. Mix can of soup with can of water and pour over breasts or quail. Cook uncovered in preheated 350 degree oven for 2 hours or until breasts or quail are tender. Add wine as needed during cooking. Serve over wild rice. Serves 8 to 12.

Mrs. James H. Robinson (Toppy)

WILD DUCK

2 or 3 wild ducks, cleaned   **Salt and pepper**
Bacon grease   **Water**

Preheat oven to 500 degrees. Use 12 inch cast iron skillet with cast iron top. Take fresh or thawed ducks. Rub inside and out with bacon grease. Shake salt and pepper generously inside the cavity and outside the duck. Put ducks in pan and add ½ inch of water. Put top on tightly. Cook in 500 degree preheated oven for 35 minutes. Remove top. Cook 10 more minutes. This works on any size wild duck. Serves 4-6.

Note: This is a hunter's dish. Cooked juices will be red to deep pink.

Frank R. Reynolds, M.D.

BAKED WILD GOOSE

1 young wild goose   **4 strips bacon**
1 large onion, minced   **3 cups orange juice**
3 large ribs of celery, minced   **1 cup sherry**
3 apples, chopped   **1 orange, sliced**
½ pound raisins   **Parsley**
Salt and pepper, to taste

Preheat oven to 350 degrees. Stuff inside of goose with onion, celery, apples, and raisins. Slightly salt and pepper goose. Cover breast with strips of bacon. Bake in covered pan. Baste with orange juice and sherry every 15 minutes. Cook about 30 minutes to pound or until brown and very tender. When done, remove stuffing and bacon strips. Garnish with orange slices and parsley. Serve with apple jelly. (Allow one pound uncooked goose per serving).

Mrs. Duncan Roland McEachern (Sis)

SMOTHERED QUAIL OR SMALL WILD DUCK

8 quail or 4 small young wild
ducks
Salt and pepper, to taste
½ cup flour

1 stick margarine
Warm water
½ teaspoon salt
⅛ teaspoon pepper

Dust quail with salt and pepper. Roll in flour until well coated. Melt 1 stick margarine in 10 inch skillet. Brown quail. After browning fill to top of pan with warm water. Add salt and pepper. Cover pan with lid. Simmer 1 hour adding warm water as needed. Serve with wild rice. Serves 4 to 6.

Mrs. Duncan Roland McEachern (Sis)

CELEBRATION CHICKEN SALAD

2 cups celery, sliced ¼-inch
thick diagonally
½ cup water
5 cups cooked chicken breast,
diced
¾ cup mayonnaise

½ cup sour cream
½ teaspoon onion powder
1 teaspoon salt
1 teaspoon dill
½ cup almonds, slivered

Cook celery until tender-crisp in ½ cup water in a covered saucepan. (May be cooked in microwave oven.) Combine chicken with celery, mayonnaise, sour cream, onion powder and salt. Serve on bed of lettuce. Garnish with dill and almonds. Serves 6 to 8.

Mrs. Wilbur P. Matthews (Katherine)

CHINESE CHICKEN SALAD (SAI SOO GAI)

1 small head of lettuce, shredded
1 pound white chicken meat, cooked, shredded
8 ounces bean sprouts, deep fried, drained
4 green onions, chopped
2 tablespoons sesame seeds, toasted
1 teaspoon salt
½ teaspoon pepper
3 tablespoons white vinegar
2 tablespoons sugar
1 teaspoon Accent (optional)
¼ cup salad oil
2 tablespoons toasted almonds, peanuts or cashews, chopped

Combine lettuce, chicken, bean sprouts and onions. Mix in sesame seeds, salt, pepper, vinegar, sugar, Accent and salad oil. Sprinkle nuts over top. Combine all these ingredients just before serving. Makes 4 large or 6 average servings.

Mrs. Henry D. Jordan (Jean)

HOT CHICKEN SALAD CASSEROLE

4 cups chicken, cooked, diced
2 cups celery, chopped
1 small onion, chopped
½ cup slivered almonds
1½ cups Pepperidge Farm dressing mix
1½ cups mayonnaise
1½ teaspoons lemon juice
1½ cups grated Cheddar cheese

Mix chicken, celery, onion, almonds, dressing mix, mayonnaise and lemon juice together and refrigerate overnight. Preheat oven to 350 degrees. Pour mixture into a 9x13-inch shallow baking dish. Sprinkle cheese over the top and bake in a 350 degree preheated oven for 40 to 50 minutes. Serves 6 to 8.

Mrs. R. Durwood Almkuist, III (Gloria)

CHICKEN TETRAZZINI

2 chickens, each 3 pounds
1 teaspoon salt
Water
1 package (12 ounces) egg
  noodles
1½ quarts chicken broth
¼ pound butter or margarine
1 medium green pepper,
  chopped
1 medium onion, minced
1 can (4 ounces) sliced
  mushrooms, drained

⅔ cup flour
2 cups milk
2 cups chicken broth
½ pound Velveeta cheese,
  cut in chunks
¼ pound sharp Cheddar
  cheese, shredded
Salt
Pepper

Preheat oven to 350 degrees. Place chickens in a soup kettle and add 1 teaspoon salt and enough water to cover chickens. Cook until chickens are tender. Remove chickens, cool, bone and cut into pieces. Strain broth, cool and remove fat. If less than two quarts, add water. Bring 1½ quarts of broth to a boil and add noodles, cooking according to package directions. Drain. Melt butter in a large saucepan. Add green pepper and onion, cooking until tender. Add mushrooms and flour, stirring to remove lumps. Gradually stir in milk and 2 cups of broth. Cook, stirring constantly, over medium heat until sauce begins to thicken. Add cheeses, stirring and cooking until they melt. Combine chicken, noodles and cheese sauce, adding salt and pepper to taste. Pour into a 2½-quart greased casserole. Bake in a preheated 350 degree oven for 30 to 40 minutes or until heated through. Serves 12. (Can be frozen)

Mrs. Kenny J. Morris (Carolyn)

CHICKEN BROCCOLI CASSEROLE FOR A CROWD

8 ounces egg noodles
1 package (10 ounces) frozen
chopped broccoli
16 ounces creamed cottage
cheese
1 egg, large, slightly beaten
2 2½-pound chickens,
disjointed
1 teaspoon salt
1 carrot, chopped

1 medium onion, chopped
1 celery stalk, chopped
6 cups water
1 stick margarine
½ cup flour
1½ teaspoons salt
1 teaspoon dried basil
½ teaspoon pepper
½ cup Parmesan cheese, grated

Preheat oven to 350 degrees. Cook noodles for eight minutes. Cook broccoli according to directions on package. Drain noodles and broccoli and mix them with the cottage cheese and egg. In a soup kettle place chickens, salt, carrot, onion, celery and water. Bring to a boil and simmer one hour. Remove chicken from pot and reserve broth. Bone and dice chicken. Melt margarine in a saucepan. Add flour, 1½ teaspoons salt, basil and pepper. Blend and slowly add 3 cups of the reserved broth. Cook, stirring until mixture thickens and comes to a boil. Remove from heat. Combine the noodle mixture with the chicken and thickened broth. Pour into a greased 4 quart casserole or two 2 quart casseroles. Sprinkle with cheese and bake in a 350 degree oven for 45 minutes. (Casserole may be frozen prior to baking. Frozen casserole should be baked 1½ hours at 350 degrees.) Serves 16 to 32.

Mrs. Ralph B. Moore (Victoria)

CHICKEN TETRAZZINI

1 cup almonds, slivered
2 tablespoons butter
8 ounces thin spaghetti,
  uncooked
5 cups cooked chicken or
  turkey, diced
2 (10¾-ounce) cans cream of
  mushroom soup, undiluted
2 teaspoons Worcestershire
  sauce
¼ teaspoon nutmeg
1 cup mayonnaise
½ cup sherry
½ cup whipping cream,
  whipped (or half and half,
  unwhipped)
½ cup Parmesan cheese, grated

Preheat oven to 350 degrees. Toast almonds in butter and reserve. Cook spaghetti by package directions. Drain and place in greased shallow 9x13-inch casserole. Spread chicken over spaghetti. Sprinkle almonds over chicken. Combine soup, Worcestershire sauce, nutmeg, mayonnaise, sherry, cream and pour over almonds. Sprinkle cheese over sauce and bake in a 350 degree preheated oven for about 30 minutes. Serves 10 to 12. (Casserole can be made a day ahead)

Mrs. Robert M. Fales (Sarah)

LOU'S QUICK CHICKEN PIE

2 cups cooked chicken, diced
1 cup celery, diced
½ teaspoon salt
½ teaspoon pepper
1 stick butter, melted
1 cup flour
3 teaspoons baking powder
1 cup milk
1 (10¾-ounce) can chicken
  broth

Preheat oven to 425 degrees. In a 9-inch quiche dish mix chicken, celery, salt and pepper. Stir in melted butter. Sift flour and baking powder together into a small bowl. Slowly add milk to flour, stirring until smooth. Spread the batter over the chicken. Heat the broth to boiling and pour over batter. Bake in a 425 degree preheated oven for 45 minutes to 1 hour or until brown on top. Serves 6.

Mrs. W. Thad Shearin, Jr. (Bettie)

CHICKEN FOR ALICE

This is a quick tasty version of a la Kiev.

8 half breasts of chicken, boned
1 stick butter
2 tablespoons dry or fresh
  chives, chopped
1 teaspoon garlic, pressed
Salt to taste
White pepper to taste

½ cup flour
2 eggs, beaten
2 cups dry bread crumbs or
  Progresso "Italian style"
  bread crumbs
Crisco oil sufficient to half
  cover chicken

Skin chicken and remove the long tendon running through the breast meat. Flatten boned chicken pieces on waxed paper on a cutting board. Cover with a piece of waxed paper and pound with a rolling pin or wooden mallet until less than half original thickness.

Four pieces will form the bottoms and four the tops. Put 2 tablespoons of soft butter in the middle of each bottom piece. Top with ½ tablespoon chives and ¼ teaspoon pressed garlic. Add a pinch of salt and pepper. Place top pieces on and press edges together with fork. Dust each of the four double pieces with flour and gently, but generously, brush with beaten eggs. Gently roll in bread crumbs. Place in hot oil and fry until lightly browned. If using Italian style bread crumbs, keep oil temperature a little lower as the cheese in the crumbs will brown faster than the chicken will cook. Turn gently once. Remove, drain, and serve immediately. Total time in oil should not exceed 10 minutes. Chicken will be firm to touch. Serves 4.

William D. Kassens, Jr., M.D.

PAPER BAG BARBECUE CHICKEN

3 tablespoons catsup
2 tablespoons vinegar
1 tablespoon lemon juice
2 tablespoons Worcestershire
  sauce
4 tablespoons water
2 tablespoons butter
3 tablespoons brown sugar

1 teaspoon salt
1 teaspoon dry mustard
1 teaspoon chili powder
1 teaspoon paprika
½ teaspoon red pepper
1 (3-pound) fryer, disjointed
1 medium size heavy paper bag,
  greased inside

Mix catsup, vinegar, lemon juice, Worcestershire sauce, water, butter, brown sugar, salt, mustard, chili powder, paprika and red pepper in a saucepan and bring to a boil. Remove from heat. Preheat oven to 500 degrees. Dip each piece of chicken in sauce and place in paper bag. Pour remaining sauce over chicken in bag. Fold top of bag twice and secure with skewer. Place bag in roasting pan and bake one hour and fifteen minutes. Do not open bag during cooking time. Serves 4.

Mrs. W. Thad Shearin, Jr. (Bettie)

CHICKEN PAPRIKA

¼ cup shortening
1 large onion, minced
2 teaspoons paprika
1 large broiler/fryer, disjointed
1 tablespoon flour
1 teaspoon salt
¼ teaspoon pepper

1 chicken bouillon cube
1 cup hot water
4 medium potatoes, peeled,
  quartered
½ cup commercial sour cream
Parsley, chopped for garnish

Heat shortening until quite hot in Dutch oven or electric fry pan. Add minced onion and sauté until glossy. Stir in paprika. Add chicken and cook over medium heat, stirring with a fork, until chicken is a reddish-golden color. Sprinkle chicken with a mixture of flour, salt and pepper. Dissolve bouillon cube in hot water and pour over chicken. Cover and cook slowly, about 25 minutes, until chicken is almost tender. Add potatoes and cook 20 minutes or until chicken is tender. Remove chicken and potatoes to a warm serving dish. Stir sour cream into pan juices and heat almost to boiling. Pour over chicken and sprinkle with parsley. Serves 4 to 6.

Mrs. Oliver Raymond Hunt, Jr. (Eleanor)

CHICKEN BREASTS ROMANO

3 whole chicken breasts,
skinned, cut in half
⅓ cup flour
½ teaspoon salt
¼ teaspoon pepper
2 tablespoons oil
¼ cup onion, chopped
2 cups tomato juice
2 tablespoons Romano or
Parmesan cheese

1 tablespoon sugar
½ teaspoon garlic powder
½ teaspoon oregano
¼ teaspoon basil
1 teaspoon vinegar
1 (4-ounce) can mushrooms,
drained
1 tablespoon chopped parsley

Combine flour, ½ teaspoon salt, and pepper. Dredge chicken in flour mixture and brown in hot oil. Drain chicken on paper towels. Sauté onion in pan drippings (add 1 tablespoon more oil if necessary) until tender. Add tomato juice, cheese, sugar, garlic powder, oregano, basil, vinegar and mushrooms, stirring well. Return chicken to skillet, cover and simmer 45 minutes or until tender. (Sprinkle chicken with additional Parmesan cheese if desired prior to serving.) Garnish with parsley. Serves 4 to 6.

Note: Recipe may be doubled if cooked in large skillet or electric frying pan. Good served with buttered noodles and steamed broccoli.

Mrs. Robert H. Hutchins (Seldon)

CHICKEN CASSEROLE SUPREME

1 (4-ounce) package dried beef
3 whole chicken breasts
6 slices bacon
Black pepper

1 (4-ounce) can mushrooms
1 can (10¾-ounce) cream of
mushroom soup
1 cup thick dairy sour cream

Preheat oven to 275 degrees. Shred dried beef into the bottom of a 9x13-inch greased casserole. Halve each chicken breast lengthwise and bone. Wrap a slice of bacon around each half of the breasts and place on top of the dried beef. Sprinkle with pepper. Top with mushrooms. Blend un-diluted soup with sour cream and pour over the chicken. Cover and bake for 3 hours in a 275 degree oven. Serves six.

Mrs. R. Bertram Williams, Jr. (Ellen)

CHINESE SMOKED CHICKEN

1 chopped green onion
6 tablespoons soy sauce
3 tablespoons Hoisin sauce
2 tablespoons dry white wine
1 teaspoon brown sugar
1 teaspoon fresh ginger, minced
1 teaspoon salt

1 teaspoon Liquid Smoke
1 plastic cooking bag
1 4 pound fryer, washed
  and dried
Slivered green onion for
  garnish

Mix chopped green onion, soy sauce, Hoisin sauce, wine, sugar, ginger, salt and Liquid Smoke in a bowl and pour into the cooking bag. Tie wings closely to the chicken and place chicken in cooking bag. Tie mouth of bag securely and rotate bag to coat chicken with marinade. Refrigerate overnight. Preheat oven to 350 degrees. Slit steam vents in cooking bag. Bake chicken about 1½ hours or until well browned. Allow chicken to cool slightly, slice and arrange on platter. Pour liquid in cooking bag over chicken and garnish with green onion. Serve with steamed rice. Serves 4.

(Chicken may be marinated and frozen, uncooked.)

Mrs. Thomas B. Mobley, III (Sue)

CHICKEN CEYLON STYLE

1 cup buttermilk or yogurt
1 clove garlic, mashed
2 fryers, disjointed
2 tablespoons butter
2 onions, chopped fine

1½ teaspoons salt
½ teaspoon powdered ginger
1¼ tablespoons curry powder
1 teaspoon cornstarch

Mix buttermilk or yogurt and garlic powder in a bowl and add the chicken. Marinate 2 hours, turning and basting frequently. Melt butter in a deep skillet and add onions. Sauté 10 minutes, stirring frequently. Add salt, ginger, curry and cornstarch to the onions, stirring until well blended. Drain the chicken, reserving the marinade. Add chicken to the skillet and cook until chicken is lightly browned. Stir in marinade, cover and cook over low heat for 1½ hours, or until chicken is tender. Serves 6 to 8.

Mrs. James F. McMillan (Cookie)

HONEY CHICKEN

1 cup dry white wine
4 tablespoons soy sauce
¼ teaspoon garlic powder
4 whole chicken breasts, boned,
    skinned, cut in chunks

1 cup flour
1 teaspoon salt
¼ teaspoon pepper
4 tablespoons cooking oil
½ cup honey

In a large bowl mix wine, soy sauce and garlic powder. Add chicken to this mixture, stir to coat and marinate 1 hour. Drain chicken and reserve marinade. In a shallow dish mix flour, salt and pepper. Dredge each piece of chicken in the flour mixture, coating completely. Heat oil in a skillet over moderate heat. Add chicken and cook about 10 minutes or until chicken is brown on all sides. Drain chicken and place in a saucepan. Stir honey into the reserved marinade and pour over chicken. Cover and simmer about 20 minutes or until chicken is fork tender. Spoon sauce over chicken when serving. Serves 4.

Mrs. David P. Mason (Phyllis)

PINEAPPLE CHICKEN

2 whole chicken breasts, boned
    and cut into 1-inch chunks
1 tablespoon dry sherry
2 teaspoons oyster sauce
    (Oriental food store)
3 tablespoons peanut oil
3 slices ginger root (according
    to taste, 2 could be sufficient)
1 (11-ounce) can pineapple
    chunks, drained, reserve juice

1 tablespoon cornstarch
2 tablespoons water
1 small onion, cut into 1-inch
    chunks
1 bell pepper, cut into 1-inch
    chunks
1 tablespoon sugar

Combine chicken, sherry and oyster sauce. Set aside for 10 minutes. Heat oil and add ginger root. Stir fry for 30 seconds. Add chicken mixture and stir fry over high heat for 2 minutes. Measure enough pineapple juice to make 1 cup, add water if needed. Blend 1 tablespoon cornstarch in 2 tablespoons water, add to mixture in wok. Cover and cook for 2 minutes over medium heat. Add pineapple chunks, onion, bell pepper and sugar. Blend well and cook for 3 minutes. Serve over steamed rice. Serves 6.

Egg Roll Factory
Wrightsville Beach, North Carolina

RIGATONI AU GRATIN

1 pound rigatoni
1 quart heavy white sauce
   (recipe below*)
½ pound fontina or Swiss
   cheese, grated

¼ pound Parmesan cheese,
   grated
3 tablespoons consommé
1 stick butter
Parsley, chopped

*White Sauce (1 quart):
Melt over low heat, 1 stick butter. Add ½ cup all-purpose flour. Continue over low heat, stir continuously for five minutes or until well blended. Stir in slowly 4 cups milk. Add salt to taste. Simmer and stir with a wire whisk until it has thickened and is smooth.

Cook rigatoni al dente according to package directions. Drain well. Toss with mixture of white sauce, cheeses, consommé and butter. Pour into a 2-quart flat baking dish. Sprinkle with chopped parsley. Bake at 400 degrees for 10 minutes. Serves 8.

Note: Chopped ham and sliced fresh mushrooms may also be added to the top of casserole before baking.

Carlo Landi
Mediterraneo Restaurant
Wrightsville Beach, North Carolina

TURKEY ANDALUSIAN

3 medium onions, finely
   chopped
6 tablespoons butter
2½ cups canned condensed
   tomato soup
1 cup Half and Half
½ cup drained canned pimiento,
   ¼" x 2" strips

1 cup stuffed olives, thinly
   sliced
½ cup chutney, any flavor
1 teaspoon salt
½ teaspoon pepper
4 cups turkey, large chunks
½ cup sherry

Cook onions in butter. Mix soup with cream and add to onions. Add pimientoes, olives, chutney, salt, pepper, and turkey. Heat, but do not boil. Stir in sherry and serve over rice. Serves 6 to 8.

Mrs. Albert B. Brown (Margaret)

CHICKEN HAWAIIAN

1 3½-4-pound chicken
1 cup Kikkoman soy sauce
1 cup unsweetened pineapple
  juice
2 cloves garlic, minced
1 tablespoon grated ginger root
½ cup cooking oil
1 cup unsweetened pineapple,
  diced

1 can (10¾-ounce) chicken
  broth
2 tablespoons cornstarch
¼ cup water
Salt
Pepper

Disjoint chicken. Mix soy sauce, pineapple juice, garlic and ginger in a glass or stainless steel container. Add chicken to mixture and allow to marinate several hours, turning chicken occasionally. Remove chicken from marinade and sauté in hot cooking oil until browned. Remove chicken from oil and drain. Pour marinade into a saucepan, add pineapple and bring to a boil. Place chicken in a baking dish and pour boiling marinade over chicken. Bake uncovered in a preheated 350 degree oven for 1 hour. In a small saucepan dissolve cornstarch in the chicken broth and water. Stirring constantly, cook until broth thickens. Season with salt and pepper to taste. Serve over rice. Serves 6.

Mrs. John Cashman (Diane)

SHERRY CREAMED CHICKEN

1 cup mushrooms, sliced
2 tablespoons green or sweet
  red pepper, chopped
½ cup butter
4 tablespoons flour
Dash cayenne pepper
1½ cups chicken stock

1 cup yogurt
2½ cups cooked chicken,
  chopped
1 cup green peas, cooked
Salt
¼ cup sherry

Sauté mushrooms and peppers in 4 tablespoons of butter until lightly browned. Set aside. In another pan, blend flour, 4 tablespoons of butter and pepper. Cook over low heat until bubbling. Remove from heat, add stock and stir well. Beat yogurt and blend into stock mixture gradually. Bring to boiling point, stirring constantly. Cook 1 minute. Add chicken, peas, mushrooms, and peppers. Salt to taste. Just before serving, reheat and add sherry. Serve over toast or rice. Serves 4.

Mrs. H. Mack Pickard (Doris)

TURKEY STUFFING

1½ cups onion, chopped
2 cups celery, diced
3 sticks butter
3 teaspoons poultry seasoning
3 teaspoons salt
½ teaspoon pepper

1 quart oysters, chopped
15 cups day-old bread crumbs
1 cup parsley, chopped
1 can (6½-ounces) water
  chestnuts, chopped
1 cup mushrooms, chopped

Cook chopped onion and diced celery in butter until onion is tender. Blend in poultry seasoning, salt, and pepper. Drain the oysters and chop. Toss onion mixture with bread crumbs, oysters, parsley, mushrooms, and chestnuts. Stuff turkey cavities and bake according to turkey directions. Enough stuffing for 16-18 pound turkey.

Robert R. Smalley, M.D.

vegetables

The pelican, prolific on the Azalea Coast, makes the Bald Head Island lighthouse area home for a nesting site.

APPLE CRANBERRY CASSEROLE

3 cups apples, unpeeled and
  cut into bite-size pieces
2 cups whole raw cranberries
1½ cups sugar
1 cup oatmeal (uncooked)

½ cup brown sugar
⅓ cup flour (all-purpose)
½ cup pecans, chopped
1 stick margarine or butter

Preheat oven to 350 degrees. Mix apple, cranberries, and sugar and put into a greased 3-quart casserole dish. Then mix the oatmeal, brown sugar, flour and pecans and pour over the above. Cut the margarine or butter into pieces and place on top of the casserole. Bake covered for 50 minutes, then remove cover and bake for 10 more minutes. Serves 6-8.

Note: This is delicious served with pork or poultry.

Mrs. Howard L. Armistead (Linda)

ASPARAGUS WITH BLUE CHEESE

1 (10-ounce) package pie crust
  mix
1 (4-ounce) can button
  mushrooms, drained, or
  ½ pound small fresh
  mushrooms
2 tablespoons onion, minced
¼ cup butter

1 (10¾-ounce) can cream of
  asparagus soup
2 tablespoons sherry
1 (6-ounce) package blue
  cheese, crumbled
2 (14½-ounce) cans Mary
  Washington asparagus

Preheat oven to 400 degrees. Prepare pie crust mix according to directions. Roll out on cookie sheet to ¼ inch thickness. Bake pastry until done, about 20 minutes. Cut into 8 pieces and place on a large bake-and-serve platter or a large casserole dish. Sauté mushrooms and onion in butter, just slightly. Blend in soup and sherry. Simmer until heated. Add cheese and stir until melted. Heat asparagus in separate pan; drain. Place asparagus on pastry and cover with sauce. Broil 3-5 minutes at least 4 inches below heat. Garnish with extra mushrooms, if desired. Serves 8.

Mrs. Frank R. Reynolds (Marguerite)

BARLEY CASSEROLE

1 cup barley (medium or small)
½ stick butter
½ cup onion, chopped
½ cup parsley, chopped
3 cups bouillon or chicken broth (have 1 cup extra on hand in case casserole becomes too dry while baking)

Salt and pepper to taste
½ cup sautéed nuts, optional

Preheat oven to 350 degrees. Sauté onion in butter. Add barley and brown lightly. Add parsley and 1½ cups broth. Salt and pepper to taste. Place in 2 quart casserole and bake covered for 1½ hours. After first 30 minutes, add ¾ cup broth and stir. Repeat after 30 more minutes of baking. Add nuts, if desired, during last 15 minutes of baking. Serves 6.

Note: If casserole becomes too dry during baking, add broth which has been kept in reserve.

Mrs. Samuel Warshauer (Miriam)

BROCCOLI DELUXE CASSEROLE

1½ pounds fresh broccoli or one (10-ounce) package frozen chopped broccoli
1 (10¾-ounce) can cream of chicken soup
1 tablespoon all-purpose flour
½ cup dairy sour cream
¼ cup carrot, grated

1 tablespoon onion, grated
¼ teaspoon salt
⅛ teaspoon pepper
¾ cup herb-seasoned stuffing mix
2 tablespoons butter or margarine, melted

Preheat oven to 350 degrees. Cook broccoli and drain. Chop into small pieces. Blend soup and flour. Add sour cream, carrot, onion, salt, and pepper. Add this to broccoli and stir gently until mixed well. Place in 2 quart casserole. Combine stuffing mix and butter or margarine. Sprinkle around top edge of baking dish. Bake for 30-35 minutes or until heated through. Serves 4-6.

Mrs. R. Durwood Almkuist (Gloria)

SAUCY VEGETABLES

2 pints fresh broccoli or brussel
  sprouts or 2 (10-ounce)
  frozen packages
½ cup onion, chopped
2 tablespoons butter
1 tablespoon all-purpose flour

1 tablespoon brown sugar
1 teaspoon salt
½ teaspoon dry mustard
½ cup milk
1 cup sour cream
1 tablespoon snipped parsley

Cook vegetables in lightly salted boiling water until just tender. Drain and set aside. Sauté onion in butter. Add flour, sugar, salt, and mustard. Add milk and blend. Place over medium heat and stir constantly. Allow to bubble and thicken. Slowly blend in sour cream. Add vegetables and place in serving dish. Sprinkle with parsley. Serves 6-8.

Note: Sauce is excellent with any cole vegetable such as cauliflower or cabbage.

Mrs. Neill H. Musselwhite (Nancy)

LOTTIE MAE'S MARINATED CARROTS

2 pounds carrots, medium
  slices
1 cup sugar
½ cup oil
½ cup vinegar
1 teaspoon prepared mustard
1 teaspoon Worcestershire
  sauce

1 (10¾-ounce) can cream of
  tomato soup
1 medium size onion, chopped
1 medium size green pepper,
  sliced in thin strips

Cook carrots until tender. Mix together sugar, oil, vinegar, prepared mustard, Worcestershire sauce, and cream of tomato soup. Pour mixture over cooked carrots, chopped onions, and green pepper strips. Store in refrigerator one day prior to serving. Serves 6-8.

Mrs. J. J. Pence, Jr. (Joan)

EGGPLANT PARMIGIANA

1 large eggplant, about 1½ pounds
¼ cup mayonnaise
1 cup fine bread crumbs
½ cup grated Parmesan cheese

3 to 4 cups spaghetti sauce (homemade or your favorite brand)
8 ounces Mozzarella cheese
½ cup grated Parmesan cheese

Preheat oven to 375 degrees. Do not peel eggplant. Wash and cut off stem and blossom ends. Cut eggplant crosswise into uniform slices approximately ¼ to ½ inch thick. Spread mayonnaise very thin on both sides of each slice. On a sheet of wax paper, combine bread crumbs and ½ cup of Parmesan cheese. Dip slices of eggplant in this mixture. Place the breaded slices on an ungreased cookie sheet. Bake for 15 minutes or until golden brown. Place a layer of the cooked eggplant in a lightly greased 9x13x2-inch baking dish. Place a slice of Mozzarella cheese on each slice of eggplant; spoon spaghetti sauce over all. Continue the layers until all the eggplant is used, ending with spaghetti sauce. Sprinkle ½ cup of Parmesan cheese over top and bake uncovered in a preheated 350 degree oven for 25 minutes or until cheese melts and top is browned. Serves 6-8.

Note: Any remaining bread crumb and cheese mixture may be refrigerated or frozen for future use. The cooked eggplant without the spaghetti sauce and Mozzarella cheese is a delicious vegetable dish.

Mrs. Robert L. Morrison (Marion)

CURRIED FRUIT

1 (16-ounce) can pear halves
1 (16-ounce) can pineapple chunks
1 (16-ounce) can apricot halves
12 maraschino cherries

¾ cup brown sugar
3 teaspoons curry powder
⅓ cup margarine, melted
⅔ cup blanched, slivered almonds

Preheat oven to 325 degrees. Drain fruit. Add sugar and curry powder to melted margarine. Arrange fruit and nuts in layers in a 9x13-inch pyrex dish. Pour margarine mixture over fruit. Bake for 1 hour. Serves 8-10.

Mrs. Clifford Lewis (Libby)

HOT FRUIT CASSEROLE

1 (29-ounce) can peach halves
1 (29-ounce) can pear halves
1 (20-ounce) can pineapple
  slices
1 (15-ounce) jar red apple rings
¼ cup sugar

1 cup sherry
2 tablespoons flour
1 stick butter
1 (10-ounce) jar maraschino
  cherries with stems

Drain all fruit well. In a saucepan mix sugar, sherry, flour, and butter. Cook until thick as heavy cream, stirring constantly. Arrange fruit in layers in a 9x13x1-inch casserole, placing a layer of peaches, then a layer of pears, then pineapple. Scatter the apple rings in each layer for color. In center of each pineapple slice, place a cherry. Pour the sauce over fruit. Refrigerate overnight. Before serving, take out of refrigerator 30 minutes, then bake in 350 degree oven for about 20 minutes, or until bubbly and heated thoroughly. Serve hot. Serves 12.

Mrs. James H. Robinson (Toppy)

MOM'S LIMA BEAN CASSEROLE

2½ cups small lima beans,
  cooked (reserve liquid)
1 tablespoon butter
1 tablespoon flour
½ cup liquid from the beans
1 tablespoon brown sugar
½ teaspoon salt

⅛ teaspoon pepper
2 teaspoons dry mustard
2 teaspoons lemon juice
½ cup buttered bread crumbs
½ cup grated Cheddar cheese
4-6 strips of bacon, uncooked

Preheat oven to 350 degrees. Drain beans and reserve the liquid. Place beans in a greased 8x8-inch casserole. Heat butter over low heat. Add flour and stir until well blended. Slowly add ½ cup of bean liquid, stirring until smooth and thickened. Add brown sugar, salt, pepper, mustard, and lemon juice. Pour sauce over the beans. Sprinkle with bread crumbs and grated cheese. Arrange bacon strips over the top. Bake for 25-35 minutes until bacon becomes crisp and brown. Serves 6.

Mrs. Lucien S. Wilkins (Freda)

NOODLE PUDDING

1 pound broad egg noodles
1 pint sour cream
1 pound cottage cheese
1 cup milk
2½ teaspoons salt

4 tablespoons sugar
6 tablespoons butter, melted
1 cup cornflakes, crushed
2 tablespoons butter

Preheat oven to 375 degrees. Cook noodles according to package directions. Rinse with cold water and drain. Mix noodles with sour cream, cottage cheese, milk, salt, sugar, and 6 tablespoons butter. Place in greased deep 3-quart casserole. Top with crushed cornflakes. Dot with 2 tablespoons butter. Bake uncovered for 1½ hours. Serves 10-12.

Note: Can be frozen or made a day in advance and refrigerated.

Mrs. William Parker (Connie)

MUSHROOM CASSEROLE

6 slices white bread
¼ pound butter
1 pound mushrooms, sliced
½ cup celery, chopped
½ cup onion, chopped
½ cup mayonnaise

2 eggs
½ cup milk
1 (10¾-ounce) can cream of
   mushroom soup, undiluted
1 cup cracker crumbs

Break up 3 slices of white bread and place in bottom of 2-quart casserole. Sauté mushrooms in butter 5 minutes. Add celery, onions, and mayonnaise, and pour over bread. Break up the additional three slices of white bread and place on top of mushroom mixture. Beat eggs with milk and pour over top of casserole. Refrigerate 1 hour. Spread mushroom soup on top and sprinkle with cracker crumbs. Bake in preheated 350 degree oven 1 hour. Serves 6.

Mrs. David P. Thomas (Ginny)

STIR-FRIED OKRA

2 cups okra, sliced ½-inch thick
1 small onion, diced
1 medium green pepper, diced
½ cup celery, diced
½ teaspoon salt
⅛ teaspoon pepper
¼ teaspoon dried thyme
3 tablespoons hot salad oil
1 medium tomato, cut into
  8 wedges
Soy sauce to taste

Stir-fry okra, onion, green pepper, celery, salt, pepper, and thyme in hot oil over high heat for 6-8 minutes. Add tomato. Stir-fry for 2 more minutes. Sprinkle with soy sauce to taste. Serves 4-6.

Note: This dish should be prepared when the vegetables are fresh and plentiful.

Mrs. John Codington (Betsy)

PURÉE OF GREEN PEAS AND BROCCOLI
Excellent with roast of beef, pork, veal, or lamb

4 cups fresh or frozen
  green peas
3 broccoli stalks
2 cups water
3 tablespoons butter
3 tablespoons flour
1-2 tablespoons sour cream
1 teaspoon sugar
Salt, to taste
White pepper, to taste
1 teaspoon lemon juice

Cook peas and broccoli in water, sugar, and salt. Boil slowly for 8-10 minutes. A short cooking time retains the color. Drain. Put vegetables through a food mill with a fine pore size. A food processor or blender will not work, as the pea hulls will be chopped up rather than eliminated. Make a roux by melting butter in saucepan. Remove from heat and blend in flour. Whisk over low heat with mixture bubbling for 2 minutes. Add the purée of peas and broccoli. Blend in sour cream. Taste for salt. Add white pepper and lemon juice. Serve immediately. Serves 4.

William D. Kassens, Jr., M.D.

PEAS IN SOUR CREAM SAUCE

¼ teaspoon tarragon
2 tablespoons warm water
1 (10-ounce) package frozen
  tiny green peas
1 large cucumber, peeled
  and sliced

1 teaspoon salt
½ cup sour cream
½ cup mayonnaise
1 tablespoon lemon juice

Soak tarragon in warm water for 10 minutes. In a large saucepan combine peas, cucumber, salt, and tarragon mixture. Bring to boil. Cover and simmer for five minutes. Drain well. In a small saucepan, blend sour cream, mayonnaise, and lemon juice. Heat thoroughly. Pour hot vegetables into serving bowl, and serve sauce over them. Serves 4.

Mrs. Thomas Mobley (Sue)

ENGLISH PEA CASSEROLE

1 (17-ounce) can tiny English
  peas, drained (reserve liquid)
1 cup celery, chopped
1 cup onion, chopped
½ cup bell pepper, chopped
½ stick butter
½ cup pea juice
1 (10¾-ounce) can cream of
  mushroom soup

3 tablespoons Worcestershire
  sauce
¼ teaspoon Tabasco sauce
Salt and pepper to taste
¾ cup cheese, grated
¾ cup bread crumbs, grated

Preheat oven to 300 degrees. Cook celery, onions, bell pepper, butter, and pea juice for 20 minutes. Add drained peas, mushroom soup, Worcestershire sauce, Tabasco sauce, salt, and pepper and place in 2-quart casserole. Sprinkle with cheese and bread crumbs. Bake uncovered approximately 30 minutes. Serves 5.

Mrs. James L. Cathell (Drukie)

JUDY'S SPECIAL PEAS

2 tablespoons butter
1 (10-ounce) package frozen
  green peas
2 cups lettuce, shredded in
  ¼-inch slices

¼ cup onion, chopped
1 teaspoon salt
¼ teaspoon pepper
1 pinch basil or tarragon

Heat butter in Dutch oven. Add peas. Cover and cook until peas are defrosted. Add lettuce, onions, salt, pepper, and basil or tarragon. Mix lightly. *DO NOT ADD WATER!* Cover tightly and steam 5 minutes, no more. Serves 5.

Mrs. Thomas H. Maloy (Jane)

CHEESY POTATOES

2 tablespoons margarine
½ teaspoon onion salt
3 ounces cream cheese
1 (10¾-ounce) can cream of
  celery soup

12 ounces frozen shredded
  hash brown potatoes, thawed
Salt and pepper to taste

Preheat oven to 375 degrees. With the stove on medium heat, melt margarine in a medium-sized saucepan. Add onion salt, cream cheese, and soup. Stir until smooth. Salt and pepper to taste. Blend in the potatoes. Pour into greased one-quart casserole. Cover and bake for 40 minutes. Serves 3-4.

Note: This is very good with slices of ham layered on top before baking.

Mrs. James W. Markworth (Ruthe)

HOT POTATO SALAD

½ cup onions, chopped
1 tablespoon margarine
½ cup mayonnaise
⅓ cup cider vinegar
1 tablespoon sugar
1¾ teaspoons salt
¼ teaspoon pepper

4 medium potatoes, cooked,
    peeled, and sliced (about
    4 cups)
1 tablespoon parsley, chopped
1 tablespoon bacon, cooked
    and crumbled

Use large skillet over medium heat. Sauté onions in margarine for 2 to 3 minutes. Stir in mayonnaise, vinegar, sugar, salt, and pepper. Add potatoes and continue cooking and stirring constantly for about 2 minutes or until heated through. Do not boil. Garnish with parsley and bacon. Serves 6.

Mrs. Oliver Raymond Hunt (Eleanor)

POMMES DE TERRE CHATEAU
(POTATOES SAUTÉED IN BUTTER)

2 pounds potatoes
2 tablespoons butter
1 tablespoon olive oil
¼ teaspoon salt
2 tablespoons softened
    butter

3 tablespoons minced
    fresh parsley, chives, or
    tarragon, or a mixture of
    fresh green herbs
Salt to taste
Pinch of pepper

Peel potatoes. Scoop out potato balls with melon cutter. Do not wash potatoes. Dry well with paper towels. Melt 2 tablespoons butter and olive oil in skillet and heat until foam begins to subside. Add potatoes and cook about five minutes, shaking skillet back and forth to roll potatoes. When potatoes are a pale golden color all over, sprinkle with salt. Lower heat to simmer and cover with a close-fitting lid. Cook for about 15-20 minutes, shaking skillet occasionally. Drain sautéing fat from skillet. Add remaining butter and seasonings. Arrange potatoes in hot vegetable dish or around meat platter. Serves 4.

Mrs. James M. McMillan (Cookie).

PATRICIAN POTATOES

4 cups freshly cooked mashed
  potatoes
3 cups creamed cottage cheese
¾ cup sour cream
1½ tablespoons onion, grated

2½ tablespoons salt
⅛ teaspoon white pepper
2 tablespoons butter, melted
½ cup chopped toasted
  almonds

Preheat oven to 350 degrees. Cook potatoes and drain. Mash, using no milk or butter. Press cheese through sieve or blend in blender or food processor until consistency is smooth. Mix potatoes and cheese. Add sour cream, onion, salt, and pepper. Mix well. Pour into buttered 2-quart casserole. Brush surface with melted butter. Bake for 30 minutes. Brown surface under broiler and sprinkle with almonds. Serves 8-10.

Mrs. Joseph M. James (Eleanor)

MEXICAN RICE

1 clove garlic, finely minced
1 teaspoon cumin seeds
1 small onion, chopped
2 tablespoons vegetable oil
1½ cups uncooked rice

2¼ cups chicken broth
1 medium tomato, peeled and
  cut into small pieces
¼ cup peas, cooked
½ cup carrots, thinly sliced

Sauté garlic, cumin, and onion in vegetable oil in large saucepan until onion is wilted. Add the rice and stir. Add chicken broth, tomato, peas, and carrots. Bring to boil. Cover tightly and simmer 17 minutes. Serves 6.

Mrs. Clifford Lewis (Libby)

BROCCOLI CASSEROLE

3 (10-ounce) boxes frozen
  chopped broccoli, thawed
1 (10¾-ounce) can cream of
  mushroom soup
1 (10¾-ounce) can cream of
  celery soup

⅓ stick margarine or butter,
  melted
2 cups cooked rice
1 (8-ounce) jar Cheez Whiz

Preheat oven to 350 degrees. Mix all ingredients. Place into two-quart casserole. Bake uncovered for 30 minutes. Serves 8.

Mrs. William A. Phillips (Phoebe)

SPINACH STRATA

10 slices white bread, cut
  in one inch cubes
  (about 7 cups)
1 (10-ounce) package frozen
  chopped spinach
2 cups Cheddar cheese,
  shredded

1 (10¾-ounce) can condensed
  cream of chicken soup
1 cup water
4 eggs, slightly beaten
⅛ teaspoon ground nutmeg
⅛ teaspoon ground black
  pepper

Cook spinach according to directions and drain well. In buttered 2-quart shallow baking dish (12x8x2), arrange half of bread cubes. Spread spinach on bread evenly. Sprinkle with 1 cup Cheddar cheese. Top with remainder of bread and cheese. Combine chicken soup, water, eggs, nutmeg, and pepper. Pour over bread mixture. Cover and refrigerate 4 hours or more. Preheat oven to 350 degrees. Uncover and bake for 45 minutes or until set. Serves 6.

Mrs. Ellis A. Tinsley (Betty)

SPINACH PIE

2 (10-ounce) packages frozen
chopped spinach
2 tablespoons butter
2 tablespoons onion, minced
2 tablespoons flour
¼ teaspoon salt
⅛ teaspoon white pepper

Pinch nutmeg
1 cup whole milk
2 teaspoons fresh lemon juice
4 ounces sharp Cheddar
cheese, grated
Paprika

Preheat oven to 375 degrees. Cook spinach according to package directions. Drain dry in a colander. Melt butter over moderate heat. Add onion and cook 2 minutes, stirring constantly. Mix flour with salt, pepper, and nutmeg and add to onions. Stir with wooden spoon until blended. Add milk. Bring to a boil, stirring constantly. Reduce heat and simmer 3 minutes. Add spinach and lemon juice. Blend well. Place in buttered, shallow, one-quart casserole. Cover with cheese and sprinkle with paprika. Bake for 20 minutes. Serves 6.

Note: Spinach must be very dry. Press with back of spoon into colander.

Mrs. John Codington (Betsy)

MUSHROOM SPINACH

3 (10-ounce) packages frozen
chopped spinach
2 tablespoons butter
2 tablespoons olive oil
1 small onion, grated
2 (4-ounce) cans sliced
mushrooms, drained
(reserve liquid)
1 clove garlic, crushed

½ teaspoon seasoned salt
½ teaspoon salt
Pepper to taste
2 tablespoons soy sauce
⅛ teaspoon ground nutmeg
1 tablespoon all-purpose flour
1 cup commercial sour cream
1-2 teaspoons lemon rind

Preheat oven to 375 degrees. Cook spinach according to package directions, drain thoroughly, and set aside. Heat butter and oil in heavy skillet. Add onion and cook for one minute. Stir in drained mushrooms and garlic. Sauté for 5 minutes, stirring constantly. Add spinach, seasoned salt, salt, pepper, soy sauce, and ground nutmeg. Make a paste of flour and mushroom liquid. Blend in sour cream. Combine with spinach mixture. Stir in lemon rind. Heat thoroughly, but do not boil. Place in 9x13x2-inch casserole and heat in oven for about 30 minutes. Serves 8-10.

Mrs. Albert Brown (Margaret)

SPINACH CASSEROLE

1 (10-ounce) package frozen
  chopped spinach
1 (10¾-ounce) can cream of
  mushroom soup
1 cup onion, finely chopped

1 cup sharp cheese, grated
1 cup Pepperidge Farm
  dressing mix
½ cup margarine, melted

Preheat oven to 350 degrees. Thaw spinach and combine with soup, onion, and cheese. Put in a greased one-quart casserole. Combine dressing and margarine and spread over spinach mixture. Bake for 45 minutes. Serves 4 to 6.

Mrs. Lucien S. Wilkins (Freda)

BONNIE'S SPINACH STUFFED TOMATOES

4 medium tomatoes
¼ teaspoon salt
1 (10-ounce) package frozen
  chopped spinach
½ cup bread crumbs
½ cup grated Parmesan cheese
1½ green onions, chopped

1 egg, slightly beaten
1½ tablespoons butter, melted
¼ teaspoon thyme
¼ teaspoon Accent
⅛ teaspoon garlic salt
Dash Tabasco sauce
Salt and pepper to taste

Preheat oven to 325 degrees. Cut tops from tomatoes and remove pulp. Sprinkle insides with salt and invert to drain. Cook spinach according to directions and drain well. Combine spinach with bread crumbs, cheese, onions, egg, butter, thyme, Accent, garlic salt, Tabasco sauce, salt, and pepper. Stuff tomatoes with mixture. Bake 30 minutes. Serves 4.

Note: Can be made a day ahead and refrigerated. Bring to room temperature before baking.

Mrs. Kenny J. Morris (Carolyn)

SQUASH CASSEROLE

1 (8-ounce) package Pepperidge Farm Seasoned Stuffing Mix
1 stick margarine, melted
1 (10¾-ounce) can cream of mushroom soup
1 cup sour cream
1 carrot, grated
1 onion, grated
2 tablespoons pimento, chopped
Pinch of sugar
2 pounds squash, sliced, cooked, and drained

Preheat oven to 350 degrees. Combine stuffing mix with melted margarine. Put half the mix in a 12x7x2-inch baking dish. Combine cream of mushroom soup and sour cream. Stir in carrot, onion, pimento, and sugar. Fold in drained squash. Spoon vegetable mixture on top of stuffing mix. Top with remaining stuffing mix. Bake uncovered 30-35 minutes. Serves 6-8.

Mrs. Robert Moore (Wanda)

SQUASH SOUFFLÉ

2 pounds summer squash, sliced
1 medium onion, chopped
3 eggs
¼ cup butter or margarine
3 tablespoons flour
1½ cups milk
½ cup medium Cheddar cheese, grated
1 cup bread crumbs
2 tablespoons butter or margarine

Preheat oven to 350 degrees. Boil squash and onions until tender. Drain and mash. Place in an approximately 10-inch casserole dish. Beat eggs and mix with squash. In a saucepan, melt ¼ cup butter. Add flour and stir. Add milk and cook until thickened, stirring constantly. Add cheese and stir until melted. Pour sauce over squash. Top with bread crumbs and dot with 2 tablespoons butter. Bake for 30 minutes. Serves 6.

Mrs. Clifford Lewis (Libby)

SAUSAGE SQUASH SPECIAL

1 pound bulk pork sausage,
   medium hot
1 clove garlic, crushed
4 cups summer squash, sliced
½ cup fine dry bread crumbs
½ cup grated Parmesan cheese

½ cup milk
1 tablespoon snipped parsley
½ teaspoon oregano, dried
½ teaspoon salt
2 eggs, beaten

Preheat oven to 325 degrees. Brown sausage and garlic. Drain fat. Cook squash, covered, in a small amount of water until tender. Drain thoroughly. Stir squash, bread crumbs, Parmesan cheese, milk, parsley, oregano, and salt into meat. Carefully fold in eggs. Turn into 10x6x1½-inch baking dish. Bake 25-30 minutes. Serves 4-6.

Mrs. William Eakins (Shelby)

RUM-SPICED SWEET POTATOES

3 pounds sweet potatoes
½ cup sugar
3 tablespoons butter
½ teaspoon cinnamon
¼ teaspoon nutmeg
¼ teaspoon cloves
¼ teaspoon salt

½ cup milk
¼ cup rum
¼ cup brandy
½ cup brown sugar
¼ cup pecans or walnuts,
   chopped

Preheat oven to 350 degrees. Boil sweet potatoes until tender. Peel and mash them. Add sugar, butter, cinnamon, nutmeg, cloves, salt, milk, rum and brandy. Place into two-quart casserole dish. Mix together brown sugar and nuts and sprinkle over top of sweet potato mixture. Bake at 350 degrees for 30 minutes. Serves 8.

Mrs. Britton E. Taylor (Harriette)

GLAZED SWEET POTATOES

6 medium size sweet potatoes
2 tablespoons butter, melted
½ teaspoon salt
Dash of paprika

¼ cup brown sugar
¼ cup butter
¼ cup pecans, chopped

Preheat oven to 350 degrees. Wash and bake potatoes until tender. Cut in halves, and scoop out the pulp. Add the two tablespoons of butter, salt, and paprika, and beat until light and fluffy. Return this mixture to the shells and glaze with the following sauce. Place the brown sugar, ¼ cup butter, and pecans in saucepan. Cook for 3 minutes, then spread on potato halves. Return them to oven for 20 minutes. Serves 6.

Mrs. William P. Robison (Maryann)

SWEET POTATO-COCONUT BALLS

4 cups sweet potatoes, cooked
  and mashed
1 cup sugar
1 stick butter or margarine
1 egg

¼-½ cup milk
1 cup flaked coconut
1 cup pecans, chopped
Whole large marshmallows
Crushed cornflakes

Preheat oven to 350 degrees. Combine potatoes with sugar, butter, and egg. Add enough milk to soften, mashing constantly. Fold in coconut and pecans. Form into balls around a marshmallow. Roll in crushed cornflakes. Bake on a cookie sheet for 5 minutes or until lightly browned. Serves 8 to 10.

Mrs. Ellis A. Tinsley (Betty)

TURNIPS AND POTATOES

**Equal amounts of large turnips
  and white potatoes
Butter to make smooth
  consistency**

**Salt and pepper to taste
Chopped parsley to taste**

Peel equal amounts of turnips and white potatoes. Cut in chunks. Boil each vegetable in water in separate pots until tender. Drain each and mash together with enough butter to make smooth consistency (this can be done in a food processor). Salt and pepper to taste. Add a generous amount of chopped parsley to taste. Keep warm until ready to serve.

Note: Delicious served with roast turkey.

Mrs. David P. Thomas (Ginny)

COLD PARTY VEGETABLE OR SALAD

**2 cans (16-ounce) French cut
  green beans
1 can (16-ounce) very small
  party peas
1 sweet onion, finely chopped
1 green pepper, finely chopped**

**1 cup celery, finely chopped
¼ cup pimento, finely chopped
1 cup vinegar
¼ cup sugar
⅔ cup light salad oil
¼ teaspoon salt**

Drain beans and peas. Place in large nonmetal bowl. Add onion, green pepper, celery and pimento and mix. Mix vinegar, sugar, oil, and salt. Pour over vegetable mixture. Lift vegetables with slotted spoon so they are well coated. Cover and refrigerate at least overnight. Stir occasionally to coat well with oil and vinegar mixture. Serves 10-12.

Note: Can be used two or three days after making if kept refrigerated.

Mrs. O. Raymond Hunt (Eleanor)

GREEN VEGETABLE CASSEROLE

1 medium green pepper
1 (10-ounce) package frozen
  baby lima beans
1 (10-ounce) package frozen
  green peas
1 (10-ounce) package frozen
  French style green beans

Salt and pepper to taste
½ pint whipping cream
1 cup mayonnaise
1 (3-ounce) can grated
  Parmesan cheese
Paprika

Preheat oven to 350 degrees. Slice pepper into strips and boil with lima beans. Drain. Boil green peas and drain. Boil green beans and drain. Mix all drained vegetables together and toss with salt and pepper. Place in a shallow 7x12-inch baking dish. Whip cream until stiff. Fold in mayonnaise and cheese. Spread this mixture over vegetables and sprinkle with paprika. Bake for approximately 20-30 minutes. Serves 6-8.

Note: Do not boil vegetables quite as long as package directions, as they will be baked later.

Mrs. Fletcher Rieman (Harriet)

VEGETABLE CASSEROLE IN WHITE WINE SAUCE

1 pound small white boiling
  onions
3 cups carrots, cut in one-inch
  chunks
2¼ teaspoons salt (total amount
  used)
4 cups celery, cut in one-inch
  chunks

¼ cup butter
½ cup flour, sifted
½ teaspoon dry mustard
⅛ teaspoon pepper
2 cups half and half
⅔ cup sauterne wine
¼ cup Parmesan cheese

Preheat oven to 350 degrees. Peel onions. Cover with water and boil ten minutes. Drain. Return to pot and add carrots and 1½ teaspoons salt. Cover with water. Boil five minutes. Add celery and boil ten more minutes. Drain well. In another pan, melt butter and blend in flour, mustard, pepper, and remaining ¾ teaspoon salt. Gradually stir in half and half and cook, stirring constantly with a wire whisk, until sauce boils and is very thick. Slowly stir in wine. Remove from heat. Combine sauce with drained vegetables and turn into lightly buttered 2-quart baking dish. Sprinkle cheese on top. Bake 35 minutes. Serves 8-10.

Mrs. Fletcher Rieman (Harriet)

VEGETABLE QUICHE

9-inch pastry shell, partially
  baked, or unbaked and
  brushed with egg white,
  then dried
2 small zucchini, thinly sliced
  (½ pound)
1 scallion, sliced
1 medium clove garlic, minced
¼ cup butter or margarine
1 medium tomato, peeled and
  chopped (about 1 cup)
½ cup green pepper, chopped
¾ teaspoon salt, or to taste
¼ teaspoon pepper
¼ teaspoon basil
¼ teaspoon thyme
1 (16-ounce) can Chun King
  beansprouts, drained and
  coarsely chopped
3 eggs
½ cup half and half
½ cup Parmesan cheese

Preheat oven to 375 degrees. Sauté zucchini, scallion, and garlic in butter, about 5 minutes, stirring occasionally. Stir in tomato, green pepper, salt, pepper, basil, and thyme. Cook over low heat 10 to 15 minutes or until vegetables are tender and liquid has evaporated. Mix beansprouts into cooked vegetables and spread evenly in pastry shell. Beat eggs and half and half until mixed but not frothy; pour over vegetables. Sprinkle with Parmesan cheese. Bake 30-35 minutes or until knife inserted near center comes out clean. Serves 6-8.

Mrs. Robert Moore (Wanda)

ZUCCHINI DELUXE

6 large zucchini
1 cup bread crumbs
¼ cup onion, chopped
1 medium tomato, chopped
½ teaspoon salt
¼ teaspoon pepper
2 tablespoons margarine,
  melted
¼ pound Cheez Whiz
¼ cup milk
6 slices crisp fried bacon,
  crumbled

Preheat oven to 350 degrees. Cook zucchini in boiling salted water for 5-8 minutes. Drain and cut in half lengthwise. Scoop out center of each. Chop. Combine chopped zucchini, bread crumbs, onion, tomato, salt, pepper, and margarine. Fill each shell with mixture. Place in baking dish; bake at 350 degrees for 25-30 minutes. Heat cheese and milk in saucepan; add bacon and serve over zucchini. Serves 12.

Note: May also be done as a casserole.

Mrs. Lockert B. Mason (Mary)

SAUTÉ OF ZUCCHINI

An excellent quick recipe to use a relatively
large amount of zucchini per serving.

**4 large or 8 small to medium
zucchini
1 teaspoon salt**

**½ stick butter
Freshly ground pepper, to taste**

Wash and grate zucchini, cutting off stem and flower ends. Sprinkle salt
over grated zucchini and toss in colander. Set aside for ½ hour. If time is
critical, omit the salt and setting aside. Squeeze vigorously a handful at
a time to remove juice. Discard juice. Place squeezed zucchini in skillet
containing butter. Add salt, if omitted above, and pepper. Sauté over moderately high heat for 5-10 minutes according to personal preference. The
high heat and constant stirring will evaporate the remaining juice. Do not
brown. Taste for salt. Serve immediately.

With a light meal, two variations are possible:

1. Add 2 tablespoons whipping cream to sauté just before serving.
2. Add 3 tablespoons Parmesan cheese to sauté just before serving.

Serves 4.

William D. Kassens, Jr., M.D.

CHEESE-STUFFED ZUCCHINI

6 zucchini squash, 6 to 7
  inches long
2 eggs, well beaten
1½ cups sharp Cheddar cheese,
  grated
½ cup small curd creamed
  cottage cheese

2 tablespoons parsley, chopped
2 tablespoons onion, chopped
½ teaspoon salt
⅛ teaspoon pepper
½ cup cracker crumbs
2 tablespoons butter, melted

Preheat oven to 350 degrees. Scrub zucchini well. Cut off ends. Cook whole, covered in boiling salted water about 12 minutes or until barely tender. Remove from water, drain, and cut in halves lengthwise. Scoop out center pulp. Invert shells on paper toweling to drain. Combine eggs, Cheddar cheese, cottage cheese, parsley, onion, salt, and pepper. Fill zucchini shells with this mixture. Toss crumbs with butter. Sprinkle crumbs over zucchini and arrange in greased, shallow pan in single layer. At this point the zucchini pan may be covered with plastic wrap and refrigerated for baking later in the day. When ready to cook, bake for 30 minutes. If desired, run under broiler a few minutes to brown topping. Serves 12.

Mrs. Wesley W. Hall (Anne)

Breads

The porch of the Henry Rehder home and the azaleas of lovely Airlie Gardens—typical Garden Tour sights of Azalea Festival every April.

QUICK SALLY LUNN

2 eggs
¾ cup sugar
2 cups sifted all-purpose flour
4 teaspoons baking powder

½ teaspoon salt
½ stick butter, melted
1 cup milk

Preheat oven to 375 degrees. In medium sized bowl beat eggs, add sugar and beat again. In another bowl, mix together the flour, baking powder, salt, butter and milk. Add flour mixture to the eggs and sugar and beat again thoroughly. Pour batter into a greased tube pan which measures 6 inches across the bottom. Bake for 45-55 minutes or until a straw comes out clean. This may be made in muffin pans and baked 25-30 minutes. (This is a sweetish bread which is nice with cold left over meats and jellied salads. If served at the table, it is dumped out upside down (like a cake) and sliced, then buttered like a muffin or roll.)

Mrs. Fletcher Rieman (Harriet)

GERMAN DARK RYE BREAD

3 cups unbleached flour
  (Pillsbury)
¼ cup unsweetened cocoa
  powder
2 packages active dry yeast
1 tablespoon caraway seeds
3-3½ cups medium rye flour
  (Pillsbury)

2 cups water
⅓ cup unsulphured molasses
2 tablespoons butter
1 tablespoon sugar
1 tablespoon salt

Preheat oven to 400 degrees. Combine unbleached flour, cocoa, yeast and caraway seeds in a large mixer bowl. Heat water, molasses, butter, salt and sugar until warm (115 degrees to 120 degrees), stirring constantly to melt butter. Add to dry ingredients. Beat at high speed with electric mixer for three minutes. By hand, stir in 3-3½ cups of rye flour to make a soft dough. Turn out on lightly floured surface and knead until smooth (about 5 minutes). Cover and let rest for 20 minutes. Punch down and divide and shape into 3 loaves. Brush tops with cooking oil and slash diagonally across top of loaf. Place on greased cookie sheet. Cover and let rise in warm place until double (about 45-60 minutes). Bake for 20 minutes. Remove from oven, brush surface again with cooking oil and return to oven for five more minutes. Remove from cookie sheet and cool on wire rack. Makes 3 round loaves.

Mrs. Lyndon Anthony (Agnes)

DILLY BREAD

1 package active dry yeast
¼ cup lukewarm water
1 cup creamed cottage cheese
⅓ stick butter
2 tablespoons sugar
1 tablespoon minced onion

2 teaspoons dill seed
1 teaspoon salt
¼ teaspoon soda
1 egg, unbeaten
2-2½ cups all purpose flour

Dissolve yeast in ¼ cup lukewarm water. Preheat oven to 350 degrees. Heat cottage cheese and butter to lukewarm. Combine sugar, minced onion, dill seed, salt, soda and egg in a large bowl. Mix thoroughly and then gradually add the flour to form a stiff dough. Cover and let rise for 50-60 minutes in a warm place. Stir down dough and turn into a well greased 8 inch round casserole (1½ to 2 quart size). Let rise for 30-40 minutes until again doubled in size. Bake at 350 degrees for 40-50 minutes until golden brown.

Mrs. Nelson O'Quinn (Libby)

PITA BREAD OR POCKET BREAD

1 package active yeast (dry)
1⅓ cup warm water
   (105-115 degrees)
1 teaspoon salt
¼ teaspoon sugar

1 tablespoon salad oil or olive
   oil
3-3½ cups unbleached flour
   (corn meal)

Preheat oven to 500 degrees. Dissolve yeast in warm water in a large bowl. Stir in salt and sugar, oil and 1½ cups of flour. Beat until smooth. Stir in enough remaining flour to make dough easy to handle. Turn dough onto lightly floured board. Knead until smooth and elastic, about 10 minutes. Place in greased bowl; turn greased side up. Cover. Let rise in warm place until doubles, about 1 hour. (Dough is ready if an indentation remains when touched.) Punch dough down. Divide into 6 equal parts. Shape each part into a ball. Let rise 30 minutes. Sprinkle 3 ungreased baking sheets with corn meal. Roll each ball into a circle ⅛ inch thick. Place 2 circles in opposite corners of each baking sheet. Let rise 30 minutes. Bake until loaves are puffed and light brown, about 10 minutes.

Note: to freeze, wrap cooled bread in aluminum foil and freeze. Reheat foil-wrapped bread in 375 degree oven until hot, 10-15 minutes.

Mrs. Jack Campbell (Toni)

PITA TOAST

1 package of Pita bread (also
called Damascus bread or
Pocket bread)

Butter
Garlic salt
Parsley flakes

Cut each piece of Pita bread in quarters. Then slice each quarter horizontally making 8 small pieces from each original piece. Spread rough side of bread with butter, then dust lightly with garlic salt and parsley flakes. Toast under broiler until bubbly. Serve hot. For breakfast substitute homemade jelly or cinnamon sugar for the garlic salt and parsley.

Lucien S. Wilkins, M.D.

WHOLE WHEAT OAT BREAD

½ cup warm water
2 packages active dry yeast
2¼ cups milk, scalded
⅓ cup honey
2 tablespoons unsulphured
molasses
¼ cup plus 2 tablespoons
butter or margarine

2½ teaspoons salt
4 cups bread flour
2 cups whole wheat flour
2 cups old fashioned oats,
uncooked

Preheat oven to 350 degrees. Dissolve yeast in warm water in a small warm bowl. Into large mixing bowl pour scalded milk over honey, molasses, butter and salt. Mix and cool to lukewarm. Add bread flour and partially mix before adding yeast mixture. Stir in whole wheat flour and oats to form a soft dough. Turn dough out on a lightly floured surface and knead for 8 to 10 minutes by the clock. (Do not skimp on the kneading.) Place dough in a greased bowl and turn dough over so it will have a greased surface up. Cover and put in a warm place free from drafts. Allow to rise until double in volume, approximately 1½ hours. Punch dough down, and divide dough into three equal parts with a sharp knife. Shape each third into a round ball, cover with a towel and allow to rest 20 minutes. Grease three 8 by 4 by 2½ inch bread pans. Shape each ball of dough into a loaf and place in bread pan. Cover and allow to rise until almost double in volume, approximately 45 minutes. Bake in preheated oven at 350 degrees for 40 minutes or until the loaves sound hollow when rapped with knuckles. Remove from pans to wire rack to cool.

Mrs. Robert L. Morrison (Marion)

ITALIAN BREAD

1 package of dry yeast	1 tablespoon salt
5 pounds flour	1 egg
2 tablespoons sugar	shortening (Crisco)

Preheat oven to 450 degrees. In large bowl combine 2 tablespoons sugar, 1 tablespoon salt, 2½ cups warm water (100-120 degrees) and 1 package of dry yeast. Stir until all is dissolved. Add and stir 5 cups flour and stir until it is more or less mixed. (Do not sift. No need to measure each cup). Add another cup of flour and stir. At this time you have a total of 6 cups in a big sticky, gooey blob and only about 80-90 percent mixed. (Great! that is just right!) On the drainboard or any formica top and with the remainder of the sack nearby, reach into your flour sack and grab a small handful. Scatter it on your board and pour your poorly mixed blob out on it. Scatter a dusting of flour over top of blob and knead. With your fingers outstreached and with the heel of your hand, push the dough into the board and away from you. Now slip your right hand under the far right edge of the dough and fold it back on itself and as you are folding, turn the dough a quarter turn to the left. Knead again. As you work you will work in some of the unmixed flour with each knead. Sticky? Dust your hands and the top of the dough. Sticks to the board? Dust the board. Little gobs stick on your fingers? Rub them off your hands, let them fall into the dough, they add character. Dust your fingers. Keep adding flour, enough to prevent stickiness by scattering a little at a time on the board as you knead. In kneading you will add ¾ to 1 cup of flour, bringing the total to 7 cups. Knead about 10 minutes. Take a large bowl, grease the inside with shortening. Dump dough in the bowl and flop it around 2-3 times. Wet and squeeze out a dish towel and place over dough. Set the dough in a warm place to rise, 85-95 degrees for about 1½ hours. After it rises, punch it down (make fist and punch it about 5 or 6 times to push air out). Grease bread pans (4 long ones). Place dough back on drainboard. Punch the dough down and turn it out on clean dry board (no flour is used). Divide dough into 4 equal parts. Working with one piece, squeeze it until it is shaped like a piece of rope. Lay out the rope and roll it back and forth between your two palms on board, rolling the rope dough back and forth until it is more or less uniform and about one inch shorter than pan. Lay in greased pan. Repeat with remaining 3 pieces. Now take sharp knife and slash each loaf 4 or 5 times (long diagonal). Brush beaten egg white over loaves with pastry brush, painting top and sides. Place pans back in warm place again. Let loaves raise until they fill the pans and center stands well above the edge. Bake in 450 degree oven for 15 minutes. Then turn oven down to 350 degrees and continue baking for another 30 minutes.

Mrs. Jack Campbell (Toni)

GOLDEN SESAME BRAID

1½ cups milk, scalded
¼ cup vegetable shortening
¼ cup sugar
1 tablespoon salt
1 package active dry yeast
½ cup lukewarm water

3 eggs
7½ cups sifted all purpose flour
1 egg, beaten
1 tablespoon water
2 tablespoons sesame seeds

Preheat oven to 350 degrees. Combine scalded milk, shortening, sugar and salt. Cool to lukewarm. Sprinkle yeast on lukewarm water and stir to dissolve. Add yeast, 3 eggs and 2 cups flour to milk mixture. Beat with wooden spoon or with electric mixer at medium speed until smooth, scraping bowl occasionally. Gradually add enough remaining flour to make a soft dough that leaves the sides of the bowl. Turn to grease top. Cover and let rise in warm place until doubled, about 1 hour. After dividing dough into 6 parts, roll each into a 12 inch strip. Braid 3 strips together to form loaf, tucking ends under. Place on 2 greased baking sheets. Cover and let rise until doubled, about 45 minutes. Brush braids with glaze made with 1 beaten egg and 1 tablespoon water. Sprinkle with sesame seeds. Bake for 30 minutes or until loaves sound hollow when tapped. Remove from baking sheets and cool on racks. Makes 2 loaves. Freezes well.

Mrs. Thomas Mobley (Sue)

HONEY ALMOND CRANBERRY BREAD

6 cups Biscuit Mix
1 teaspoon ground allspice
2 cups fresh cranberries,
  rinsed and drained
Grated rind of 1 orange
1 cup chopped blanched
  almonds

2 eggs, well beaten
1 cup honey
½ cup milk
½ cup orange juice

Preheat oven to 350 degrees. Combine biscuit mix, allspice, cranberries, orange rind, and almonds. Add eggs, honey, milk, and orange juice. Beat until well blended. Spoon mix into 2 (9x5x3) loaf pans. Bake for 50-55 minutes or until top springs back when touched. Unmold and cool thoroughly. Slice thinly to make sandwiches.

Fillings: cream cheese, deviled ham and thinly sliced apple.

Mrs. John Pace (Rachel)

BLUEBERRY QUICK BREAD

5 cups all purpose flour
1½ cups sugar
2 tablespoons baking powder
1 teaspoon ground cinnamon
1 teaspoon salt
¾ cup butter
1½ cups chopped walnuts
1 teaspoon lemon peel

4 eggs
2 cups milk
2 teaspoons vanilla
juice of 1 lemon
3 cups fresh or frozen
   blueberries (if frozen,
   do not thaw)

Preheat oven to 350 degrees. Grease and flour pan(s) 1 bundt pan, 2 9x5x3 loaf pans, or 4 5x3 loaf pans. Mix dry ingredients. Cut in butter until mixture resembles fine crumbs. Stir in nuts and lemon peel. Beat eggs. Stir in milk, vanilla, and lemon juice. Mix well. Blend in to flour mixture until moistened. Gently stir in blueberries. Spoon evenly into pan(s) and bake until toothpick inserted in center comes out clean. About 80-90 minutes. Cool 10 minutes. Remove from pan(s). Serve warm or cool. Wrap and store in refrigerator.

Mrs. G. Terry Stewart (Susan)

CRANBERRY-SWEET POTATO BREAD

¾ cup light or dark brown
   sugar
¼ cup butter or margarine
   melted
¾ cup mashed cooked sweet
   potatoes
3 eggs, slightly beaten
⅓ cup orange juice
2½ cups all purpose flour

½ teaspoon baking powder
½ teaspoon baking soda
¼ teaspoon ground cinnamon
¼ teaspoon ground nutmeg
⅛ teaspoon ground mace
1 cup coarsely chopped fresh
   cranberries
½ cup nuts

Preheat oven to 350 degrees. Grease a 9x5x3 loaf pan or two smaller pans. Combine sugar, butter, potatoes, eggs, and orange juice. In separate bowl, sift dry ingredients. Add sweet potato mixture and mix. Fold in cranberries and nuts; turn into loaf pan. Bake 60-70 minutes or until cake tester is clean. Cool in pan 10-15 minutes, then remove to wire rack and cool.

Mrs. William P. Parker (Connie)

PUMPKIN BREAD WITH CREAM CHEESE ICING

3 cups sugar
1 cup salad oil
4 eggs
2 teaspoons vanilla
3⅓ cups unsifted flour
2 teaspoons soda
2½ teaspoons salt

1 teaspoon baking powder
1 teaspoon nutmeg
1 teaspoon cinnamon
2 teaspoons pumpkin spice
⅔ cup water
2 cups pumpkin-pureed
1 cup chopped pecans

Frosting:
4 tablespoons butter or
   margarine
1 (8 ounce) package cream
   cheese

1½ teaspoons vanilla
1½ cups confectioner's sugar
Dash of salt
½ cup finely chopped pecans

Preheat oven to 325 degrees. Combine sugar and oil in large bowl. Add eggs one at a time, beating after each addition. Add vanilla. Sift dry ingredients together. Add dry ingredients alternately with water. Add pumpkin and nuts. Stir until well mixed. Pour into 3 well greased and floured 9x5x3 inch loaf pans. Bake at 325 degrees for 1 hour. Frost when cool.

Frosting: Cream butter or margarine with package cream cheese. Add vanilla. Sift together confectioner's sugar and a dash of salt. Add to creamed cheese mixture. Fold in ½ cup finely chopped pecans.

Mrs. Darrell Tackett (Peggy)

HOLIDAY DATE NUT LOAF

½ package of pitted dates, cut
   into thirds (put dates in a cup
   and fill cup with boiling water
   and 1 teaspoon soda. Let
   stand while mixing
   ingredients below)
½ cup sugar

½ cup walnut pieces
4 tablespoons butter
1 egg
1½ cups plain flour (level)
pinch of salt
¼ teaspoon mace

Mix sugar, walnuts, butter, egg, flour, salt and mace in a bowl. Add date and water mixture. Mix well and pour into a well greased loaf pan. Top with candied fruits and walnuts. Bake at 300 degrees for 1 hour. Makes 1 loaf.

Mrs. David P. Thomas (Ginny)

QUICK AND EASY MORNING BREAD

½ cup butter, melted
2 teaspoons cinnamon
½ cup sugar
½ cup nuts

¼ cup raisins
1 or 2 packages refrigerator
   biscuits

Preheat oven to 350 degrees. Dip individual biscuits in butter, then in cinnamon and sugar mixture. Place in round cake pan with sides touching. Sprinkle with nuts and raisins. Bake in 350 degree oven according to package directions.

Mrs. Jack Campbell (Toni)

ANGEL BISCUITS

1 package dry yeast
2 tablespoons lukewarm
  water
5 cups unsifted flour
1 teaspoon salt

1 teaspoon soda
3 tablespoons baking powder
5 tablespoons sugar
2 cups buttermilk
1 cup shortening

Dissolve yeast in water. Mix dry ingredients and cut in shortening. Add yeast mixture and buttermilk and mix well. Roll to desired thickness and cut. Bake in lightly greased pan at 400 degrees for 20 minutes. The dough will keep for a week in the refrigerator if it is kept tightly covered.

Mrs. Henry P. Singletary (Gorda)

MAMOO'S FAMOUS ROLLS

1 cup lard or shortening
¾ cup sugar
1 cup boiling water
2 packages yeast (or cakes)
1 cup lukewarm water

2 eggs (beaten)
1 teaspoon salt
6 cups flour
½ teaspoon soda
1 teaspoon baking powder

Preheat oven to 400 degrees. Cream lard and sugar. Dissolve in boiling water. Cool. Soak yeast in lukewarm water. Add beaten eggs to lard mixture. Add yeast, salt. Beat in flour, soda and baking powder. Let rise 2 hours. Add more flour, if needed. Make into rolls and let rise 2 hours. Bake for 20 minutes.

Mrs. E. Tilghman Poole (Jean)

YEAST ROLLS

1 cup hot water
1 teaspoon salt
6 tablespoons shortening
  (Crisco)
¼ cup granulated sugar

1 package yeast
2 tablespoons lukewarm water
1 egg, well beaten
3½-4 cups sifted self-rising
  flour

Preheat oven to 400 degrees. Combine hot water (boiling), shortening, sugar and salt in a bowl (large enough to allow for some rising during storage). When above ingredients have almost melted in bowl, let cool. Add the yeast in the 2 tablespoons of lukewarm water, mix; add to the bowl of mixture. Add the egg, half the flour and beat well. Stir in more of the flour to make the dough easily handled. Grease top of dough. Cover and refrigerate if not going to use (note: easier to handle after it has been refrigerated). Roll out and cut with cookie cutter. Fold rolls over in half. Brush with melted butter. Let rise 2 hours covered with clean towel. Bake until brown, about 10 minutes.

Mrs. David Bunn, Jr. (Dana)

WHOLE WHEAT PARKER HOUSE ROLLS

¼ cup shortening
2 tablespoons sugar
¾ teaspoon salt
½ cup boiling water
1 package dry yeast
1 teaspoon sugar

½ cup warm water
  (105-115 degrees)
1 egg, slightly beaten
1½ cups all-purpose flour
1 cup whole wheat flour
½ cup graham cracker crumbs

Preheat oven to 350 degrees. Combine shortening, sugar, salt and boiling water; cool to lukewarm. Dissolve yeast and 1 teaspoon sugar in ½ cup warm water. Add yeast mixture and egg to shortening mixture. Stir in flour and cracker crumbs, blending well. Place in a greased bowl, turning to grease top. Cover and let rise in a warm place until doubled in bulk. Roll dough to ¼ inch thickness; cut into 2½ inch rounds with a biscuit cutter. With dull edge of knife, make a crease just off center on each round; brush with melted butter. Fold rounds over so top overlaps slightly; press edges together. Place on greased baking sheets. Let rise in a warm place until doubled. Bake for 15 to 20 minutes. Yield: 2 dozen.

Mrs. Ralph C. McCoy (Emily)

HUSH PUPPIES

1 cup Autry cornmeal
1 cup self-rising flour
1½ teaspoons sugar

a pinch of salt
1½ cups water (or about that
   for right consistency)

Combine dry ingredients. Add water until the right consistency. Drop by spoonfuls into deep hot fat - 375 degrees. Fry until brown. Will make about 6 servings.

Sandfiddlers Restaurant
Highway 211
Southport, N.C.

SPOON BREAD

1 cup boiling water
½ cup cornmeal
½ cup milk
2 eggs

½ teaspoon salt
1½ teaspoons baking powder
2 tablespoons melted butter

Preheat oven to 350 degrees. Pour boiling water over cornmeal. Add milk, eggs, salt, baking powder and melted butter. Pour into greased 1½ quart casserole. Bake at 350 degrees for 30-35 minutes. Serves 6.

Mrs. Fred Butler (Ann)

LAURA'S CORNY CORNBREAD

1 box (12 ounce) Flako
   corn muffin mix
1 teaspoon salt
3 eggs, beaten
½ cup corn oil

½ pint sour cream
1 (17 ounce) can creamed corn
1 (17 ounce) can whole kernel
   corn, drained

Preheat oven to 350 degrees. Stir together corn muffin mix, salt, beaten eggs, corn oil and sour cream. Stir until smooth. Fold in creamed corn and whole kernel corn. Pour into greased 9x13x2 inch pan (or two 8x8x2 inch pans). Bake for 30 minutes.

Mrs. Wilbur P. Matthews (Katherine)

SPECIAL CORNBREAD

1 cup self rising corn meal
8 ounces sour cream
8 ounces creamed corn

1 teaspoon salt
½ cup cooking oil
2 eggs, beaten

Mix corn meal, sour cream, creamed corn, salt, oil and eggs. Pour into 8 to 10 inch skillet or 9 inch Pyrex pie pan. Bake at 450 degrees for 30 minutes. Serves 4 to 6.

Mrs. Landon B. Anderson (Connie)

CORN FRITTERS

2 eggs
½ cup milk
1 cup corn (about 3 cobs)
1 cup flour, sifted

1 teaspoon baking powder
1 teaspoon salt
1 teaspoon sugar
1 teaspoon oil

Beat 2 eggs. Stir in ½ cup milk. Add corn. Beat in flour, baking powder, salt, sugar and oil. Drop by spoonfuls into hot oil (375 degrees). Turn to brown, drain. Serve hot with maple syrup or sprinkle with powder sugar. Canned corn may be used, but fresh off the cob is far better. Makes 12.

Mrs. Donald D. Getz (Judy)

FAVORITE OATMEAL MUFFINS

1 cup quick cooking oats
1 cup sour milk
1 egg
½ cup brown sugar
½ cup shortening, melted

1 cup flour
½ teaspoon salt
1 teaspoon baking powder
½ teaspoon soda

Preheat oven to 400 degrees. Soak oatmeal in sour milk for 1 hour. Add egg and beat well. Add sugar and mix. Add cooled shortening. Add sifted mixture of flour, salt and baking powder and soda. Bake in greased muffin pans for about 15-20 minutes. Makes 1 dozen.

Mrs. Oliver Raymond Hunt, Jr. (Eleanor)

BLENDER BLUEBERRY MUFFINS

2⅔ cups flour
1½ cups sugar
4 teaspoons baking powder
¼ teaspoon salt
2 eggs

½ cup butter or margarine,
   melted
1 cup milk
2 cups blueberries

Preheat oven to 350 degrees. Sift dry ingredients together into large bowl. Place eggs and milk in blender, add melted butter and blend. Stir into dry ingredients. Do not overmix, will be a stiff batter. Fold in blueberries. Fill paper lined muffin tins ½ full. Bake for 30-40 minutes.

Mrs. Donald D. Getz (Judy)

MISS MARGARET'S BRAN MUFFINS

1 cup Bran Buds
⅔ cup flour
⅔ teaspoon baking powder
¼ teaspoon baking soda
1 cup 40% Bran Flakes
½ cup brown sugar

2 tablespoons margarine
½ cup hot water
1 egg
¼ teaspoon vanilla
1 cup buttermilk
¼ cup raisins

Mix together Bran Buds, flour, baking powder, soda, Bran Flakes and brown sugar in a large mixing bowl. Add margarine and hot water. Let stand for 5 minutes. At moderate speed, with electric mixer, blend in 1 egg, vanilla and buttermilk. Beat until mixture is smooth. Fold in raisins. Grease muffin pan. Fill muffin cups ¾ full. Bake in 350 degree oven for 20 minutes or until done. Makes 12 muffins.

Margaret Hamilton
"The Sandwich Factory"
Wilmington, N.C.

BRAN MUFFINS

2½ cups sugar
1 cup plus 3 tablespoons
  shortening
4 eggs
2 cups boiling water
2 cups 100% Bran

1 quart buttermilk
4 cups Kellogg's All Bran
6 cups flour
2 teaspoons salt
5 teaspoons soda

Preheat oven to 400 degrees. Cream shortening and sugar. Add eggs, one at a time. Pour boiling water over Bran. Add buttermilk and All Bran to water and Bran mixture. Sift dry ingredients and stir all ingredients together. Put ¼ cup mixture in greased muffin tins. Bake at 400 degrees for 20 minutes. Makes 4-5 dozen. These can be kept in refrigerator for weeks and used as needed. They also freeze very well.

Mrs. James O. Hundley (Linda)

GRANOLA

4-6 cups oats (old fashioned)
2 cups coconut (unsweetened,
  if possible)
2 cups flaked wheat or rye
2 cups wheat germ
¼-1 cup sunflower seeds
  (hulled)

¼-1 cup sesame seeds (hulled)
1 cup chopped nuts
¾ cup raw honey
⅓ cup brown sugar
1 cup safflower oil
2 teaspoons vanilla

Dissolve sugar in honey. Add oil and vanilla and heat gently. Add remaining ingredients and bake at 225 degrees for 2-3 hours stirring occasionally.

Mrs. James D. Hundley (Linda)

SUNDAY MORNING WAFFLES

2 cups sifted cake flour
4 teaspoons baking powder
¼ teaspoon salt

2½ cups milk
2 eggs, separated
8 tablespoons melted butter

Mix flour baking powder and salt. Add the milk and beat until smooth. Separate eggs, add beaten egg yolks. Fold in stiffly beaten egg whites and melted butter. Bake in a hot waffle iron until golden brown and crisp. Makes 8 medium size waffles.

Mrs. William H. Weinel, Jr. (Robbie)

BELGIAN WAFFLES

4 eggs, separated
½ teaspoon vanilla
3 tablespoons butter, melted

1 cup flour
½ teaspoon salt
1 cup milk

Preheat waffler until it reads bake. Beat egg yolks until very light. Add vanilla and butter. Combine flour and salt; add with milk to egg mixture. Beat well. Beat egg whites until stiff and fold into batter. Bake on hot waffler. Bake about 30-45 seconds; turn Belgian waffler to other side and continue baking until steaming stops or golden brown. Garnish with melted butter. Spread fresh whipped cream and North Carolina strawberries on top or a syrup made with fresh blueberries.

Mrs. Thomas H. Maloy (Jane)

FAVORITE BUTTERMILK PANCAKES

2 cups sifted all-purpose flour
1 teaspoon baking soda
1 teaspoon salt
2 tablespoons sugar

2 eggs, slightly beaten
2 cups buttermilk
2 tablespoons melted butter

Sift flour, baking soda, salt and sugar into mixing bowl. Combine eggs, buttermilk and melted butter. Stir into flour mixture just to moisten flour. Do not overmix. The batter will have a few lumps. Bake on a hot, lightly greased griddle or in an electric skillet heated to 375 degrees. Dip batter with a ¼ cup measure to get pancakes of uniform size. Turn cakes when bubbles appear and break over top and around the edges; turn only once. Serve hot with butter or margarine and syrup. Serves 4-6.

Variations: Note: fold additions in just before you bake pancakes.
Banana Pancakes: Add ⅔ cup diced bananas to batter for favorite banana pancakes. Bake. Sift confectioners sugar over top of pancakes. Serve with honey and butter.
Blueberry pancakes: Drain canned blueberries well. Add ⅔ cup to batter for favorite blueberry pancakes. Bake. Sift confectioners sugar on top of pancakes. Serve with butter or maple syrup. You may use ⅔ cup fresh blueberries instead of canned blueberries.

Mrs. Howard L. Armistead (Linda)

Desserts & Pies

Sailing—either on a sunfish or under spinnaker—a contagious sport of coastal North Carolina.

QUICK AND EASY BLUEBERRY COBBLER

1 stick butter
1 cup sugar
¾ cups self-rising flour

½ cup milk
1 can blueberries

Preheat oven to 375 degrees. Melt butter in an 8x10 inch square baking dish. Mix together 1 cup sugar, ¾ cup self-rising flour and ½ cup milk. Pour this batter over the melted butter. Pour 1 can of blueberries over above ingredients. *Do not mix.* Bake in oven for 40-45 minutes. Good served warm or cold. Serve with vanilla ice cream on top of each serving.

Mrs. Horace G. Moore, Jr. (Sally)

BLUEBERRY PUDDING

4 cups fresh or frozen
  blueberries
½ cup white sugar
1 tablespoon lemon juice
⅓ cup flour
½ teaspoon cinnamon

⅓ cup brown sugar, packed into
  cup
4 tablespoons butter or
  margarine
¾ cup oatmeal

Preheat oven to 350 degrees. Place berries in deep ½ quart greased casserole. Sprinkle the white sugar and lemon juice over them. Mix flour, cinnamon and brown sugar together in mixing bowl. Cut the butter into flour mixture with a pastry blender. When mixture resembles fine bread crumbs, mix in oatmeal. Spread on top of berries. Bake 35-40 minutes or until top is nicely browned, berries soft, and juice bubbling. Serves 6-8.

Mrs. Robert L. Morrison (Marion)

APPLES A LA GRECQUE

6 large apples
2 tablespoons seedless raisins
2 tablespoons almonds,
  blanched and slivered
¼ teaspoon cinnamon

¼ cup sugar
¼ cup brandy (optional)
Dash nutmeg
1 cup water
Whipped cream

Core apples and carefully scoop out the pulp. Chop pulp and mix well with raisins, almonds, cinnamon, sugar, and brandy. Stuff apple shells, sprinkle lightly with nutmeg, place in a baking pan with 1 cup water, cover pan with aluminum foil and bake at 350 degrees for 20 minutes. Garnish with a dollop of whipped cream and serve hot or cold. Serves 6.

Peter G. Zack, M.D.

BANANA EGG ROLL

4 egg roll skins
2 bananas
1 can jack fruit (Oriental
  food store)

4 teaspoons sugar
½ teaspoon sugar
Dash ginger powder

Mix sugar with cinnamon well. Take banana, divide into quarters. Put banana on egg roll skin, then add 2 pieces of jack fruit to top of banana. Sprinkle 1 teaspoon of sugar mix on fruit and roll up skin as you would for regular egg roll. Seal the corner with water tightly. Deep fry egg roll in hot oil 350 degrees for 10 minutes. Serve with vanilla ice cream. Serves 4.

The Egg Roll Factory
Wrightsville Beach, N.C.

ELSA'S GRAPE DESSERT

1 16 ounce carton sour cream
2 cups seedless green grapes,
  washed, drained dry

4 tablespoons brown sugar

Preheat oven to broil. Into 4 one cup custard cups put ½ cup sour cream. Push ½ cup grapes into each custard cup, submerge grapes into the sour cream. (Fingers work best for this job.) Sprinkle 1 tablespoon brown sugar over the top of each dessert. Run under broiler, watch carefully, a minute or two will be about right, brown sugar will first melt and then begin to caramelize. Remove from oven and serve at once. Serves 4.

Mrs. W. P. Matthews (Katherine)

CHRISTMAS WINE JELLY

4 envelopes Knox unflavored
  gelatin
1½ cups cold water
2 cups sugar

Juice of 2 lemons
3 cups boiling water
3 cups medium sherry (do not
  use pale dry or sweet)

In a large bowl, soften gelatin with 1½ cups cold water. Add sugar and lemon juice. Add 3 cups boiling water and stir until gelatin and sugar are dissolved and mixture is lukewarm. Stir in 3 cups sherry. Pour into sherbet glasses. Top with whipped cream just before serving. Serve with fruitcake or cookies. Serves 12.

Mrs. Fletcher Rieman (Harriet)

CHERRY PUDDING

Batter:

½ cup of butter or vegetable
   shortening
1 cup sugar
1 large egg
1½ cups all purpose flour

2 teaspoons baking powder
¼ teaspoon salt
1 teaspoon vanilla extract
1 cup milk

Sauce:

1 cup sugar
1 one pound can red, sour,
   pitted cherries (1½ cups
   pitted, fresh, sour cherries
   and ½ cup water)

½ cup water

Preheat oven to 350 degrees. In small bowl of mixer combine butter, sugar, egg, flour, baking powder, salt, vanilla and half of the milk. Mix at slow speed for 2 minutes. Beat at medium speed for 2 minutes. Add remaining milk, mix at slow speed and beat at medium speed for 2 minutes. Pour into a greased 9 inch square baking pan. Heat sugar, cherries, cherry juice and water (liquid equal to one cup) in saucepan to boiling. Spoon hot cherries and liquid over the batter. Bake for about 40 minutes or until the pudding pulls away from the sides of the pan and the top is golden brown. (When the pudding is done the cherries and sauce will be on the bottom of the baking pan.) Serve hot or cold. Serves 6 to 8.

Mrs. Robert L. Morrison (Marion)

PÊCHES CARDINAL

2 (1 pound) cans peach halves,
   chilled and drained
1 (10 ounce) package frozen
   raspberries, defrosted and
   drained

1 tablespoon sugar
1½ teaspoon kirsch
½ cup heavy cream, whipped
1½ tablespoons sugar
2 teaspoons vanilla extract

With the back of a heavy spoon, purée the raspberries through a sieve into a small bowl. Stir 1 tablespoon sugar and 1½ teaspoons kirsch into purée. Refrigerate tightly covered. Whip cream, adding 1½ tablespoons sugar and 2 teaspoons vanilla until cream holds soft peaks. Chill six dessert bowls. Place 2 peach halves in each bowl. Cover with raspberry sauce and decorate with whipped cream. Serves 6.

Mrs. John Codington (Betsy)

FRESH BLUEBERRY CRUMB CAKE

2 cups all purpose flour
2 teaspoons baking powder
½ teaspoon salt
¼ cup butter or margarine

¾ cup sugar
1 large egg
½ cup milk
2 cups fresh blueberries

Streusel Topping:
½ cup firmly packed light
   brown sugar
3 tablespoons flour
2 teaspoons cinnamon

3 tablespoons butter or
   margarine
½ cup finely chopped nuts

Preheat oven to 375 degrees. Stir together the flour, baking powder and salt. Cream the butter and sugar; beat in the egg. Add the flour mixture and the milk. Stir only until the flour mixture is moistened. Fold in the blueberries. Turn into a greased and floured 9 inch springform pan. Sprinkle with streusel topping which has been prepared in the following manner: stir together brown sugar, flour and cinnamon; cut in butter until fine; stir in nuts. Bake for 45-50 minutes. If streusel gets very brown before cake has baked, place a sheet of foil over the top. Cool on wire rack for about 5 minutes; loosen edges and remove the springform band. Serve warm. Serves 6-8.

Mrs. Wilbur P. Matthews (Katherine)

MARLBOROUGH PUDDING I

2 lemons, rind only, thinly
   pared
1½ cups water
7 medium cooking apples
½ cup butter

2 tablespoons heavy cream
7 eggs, beaten
7 tablespoons sugar
½ nutmeg, freshly grated

Simmer the lemon rind in the water for 30 minutes. Strain it and reserve the water. Peel, core and chop the apples. Put them into a saucepan with the lemon water and simmer, covered, for 15 minutes. Rub them through a sieve. Beat in the butter, cut into small pieces, add the cream, eggs, sugar and nutmeg. Pour the mixture into a lightly buttered, 8 cup, ovenproof dish and bake the pudding in a preheated oven at 350 degrees for 50 minutes until it is set and golden.

Whistler's Mother's Cook Book

Reprinted with permission from G.P. Putnam's and Son.

PEARS ELEGANTE

1 lemon
1 orange
1 (1 pound 13 ounce) can
pear halves in heavy syrup
(7 pears)

⅓ cup sugar
¼ cup whipping cream
1 pint vanilla ice cream
3 squares sweet chocolate,
grated

Grate lemon and orange rind and squeeze juice from fruit. Mix the rind and juice with the juice from the pears and the sugar. Boil 15 minutes. Allow to cool slightly and pour over the pears. Cover and refrigerate for 10 hours. Just before serving whip the cream. Place a pear half in a stemmed sherbet. Pour some sauce over the pear then about ¼ cup of ice cream. Top with a generous teaspoon of whipped cream and sprinkle with 1 teaspoon of grated chocolate. Serves 7.

Note: Pears in sauce can be prepared the night before or in the morning to serve at dinner.

Mrs. Oliver Raymond Hunt, Jr. (Eleanor)

STRAWBERRY CHIFFON PARFAIT

6 cups fresh strawberries
washed and capped
¼ cup Grand Marnier
⅓ cup granulated sugar
1 can Eagle Brand sweetened
condensed milk

1 (6-ounce) can frozen
lemonade
1 (6-ounce) can frozen limeade
12 ounces Cool Whip

Marinate strawberries in Grand Marnier and sugar and set aside. Whip together Eagle Brand condensed milk, lemonade, limeade and Cool Whip until smooth. In parfait glasses layer strawberries and chiffon mixture until full. Sprinkle grated lemon and lime rind on top. Refrigerate remainder of chiffon mixture and use with fresh fruit for another dessert. Makes 8 large parfaits.

Jerry Rouse
Figure 8 Yacht Club
Wilmington, N.C.

FRESH STRAWBERRY MOUSSE

1 pint strawberries
2 (3 ounce) packages
  strawberry flavor gelatin

¼ cup sugar
1 pint whipping cream

Crush the strawberries and drain the juice, reserve. Add enough water to the juice to make 1½ cups. Bring the juice to a boil and stir in gelatin; dissolve and cool. Add strawberries and sugar. Whip cream until it stands in soft peaks and fold into strawberry mixture. Pour mixture into a 2-quart ring mold or 1½-quart soufflé dish with a 2 inch collar. Chill several hours or overnight.

Note: Two (10 ounce) packages of frozen strawberries can be substituted for the fresh strawberries. Omit sugar if frozen berries are used.

Mrs. James L. Kesler (Jana)

ALMOND ICE BOX DESSERT

¾ pound butter
2½ cups unsifted confectioners'
  sugar
7 eggs
2½ teaspoons instant coffee
½ teaspoon vanilla
½ teaspoon almond flavoring

Angel or other fine textured
  cake (about ½-¾ of cake)
Whipped cream
Almonds (slivered)
Alternative: rum flavoring and
  pecans in place of almond
  flavoring and almonds)

Cream butter thoroughly. Add sugar gradually. Add eggs one at a time, beating thoroughly. Add instant coffee and flavorings. Line a flat bottomed bowl, casserole or soufflé dish, bottom and sides with the cake cut in ¾-1 inch slices. Pour in the mixture covering the cake completely. Refrigerate for several hours or overnight. The cake will be absorbed. Garnish with whipped cream and nuts. (The mixture is not cooked.)

Mrs. Albert B. Brown (Margaret)

ICE CREAM MOLD

2 cups chocolate ice cream
2 cups vanilla ice cream
2 cups pistachio ice cream
2½ cups whipping cream
¼ cup sugar

½ cup finely chopped toasted
nuts (pecans, peanuts or a
mixture of both)
Chocolate sauce (optional)

Coat the inside of a round 2 quart bowl evenly with the chocolate ice cream and freeze until it is very firm. Next, spread an even layer of vanilla ice cream over the chocolate and freeze it in place. Spread the pistachio over the vanilla ice cream and freeze it. Whip 1 cup of whipping cream until stiff and sweeten with 2 tablespoons of the sugar. Fold the chopped nuts into the whipped cream and fill the center of the ice cream with it. Cover the bowl with plastic wrap and freeze for 2 hours. Unmold onto a chilled serving platter. Whip the remaining cream until stiff and sweeten with the remaining sugar. Spread the cream evenly over the mold and freeze for 2 hours longer. Serve cut into wedges to provide 8 to 10 servings. This is very good served with chocolate sauce drizzled over the top.

Mrs. Thomas Mobley (Sue)

HEATH BAR TORTE

6 egg whites, room temperature
⅛ teaspoon cream of tartar
1¾ cup sugar
1 teaspoon vanilla
1 pint whipping cream

1 teaspoon vanilla
3 tablespoons sugar
12 Heath candy bars, frozen,
then chopped

Preheat oven to 300 degrees. Line large cookie sheet with foil. Beat egg whites and cream of tartar until stiff, then gradually add sugar and vanilla. Make two large flat circles of meringue on cookie sheet. Bake for 40-60 minutes. Cool. Whip cream, then add sugar and vanilla. Fold in frozen chopped candy bars. Spread on the cooled meringues and stack. Freeze overnight. Allow to soften slightly before serving.

Mrs. Stephen Kash (Ann)

NUTORTE

½ cup sugar, granulated
½ cup butter
4 egg yolks, beaten
1 teaspoon vanilla
¾ cup sifted flour
1 teaspoon baking powder
4 tablespoons milk

4 egg whites
1 cup sugar, granulated
¾ cup chopped walnuts
1 pint whipping cream
2 tablespoons sugar, granulated
1 teaspoon vanilla

Preheat oven to 300 degrees. Cream butter and ½ cup sugar until light. Add beaten egg yolks and vanilla. Sift together the flour and baking powder. Add the flour mixture first and then the milk alternately, beginning and ending with flour. Grease two 8 or 9 inch cake pans and then cut wax paper circles to line them. Spread the yellow cake mixture in the two lined pans. Make meringue by beating the 4 egg whites with 1 cup of sugar until stiff. Spread the egg whites over the cake mixture. Sprinkle with the ¾ cup walnuts. Bake for one hour. While the cooked layers are cooling, whip one pint of whipping cream with the 2 tablespoons of sugar and 1 teaspoon of vanilla. Remove the layers from the pans and place one layer on the serving plate. Spread the whipping cream mixture on this layer and then top with the additional layer. Serves 10.

Mrs. Britton E. Taylor (Harriette)

SM

CHERRIES JUBILEE

1 can (1 pound 13 ounce) peach halves in heavy syrup
2 cans (1 pound) pitted bing cherries
3 teaspoons vanilla

1 jar (10 ounce) currant jelly
1 cup brandy
Ice cream (vanilla)

Strain juice from peaches and cherries into a saucepan. Add vanilla. Cook this mixture down until thick. Add currant jelly, cherries and peaches. Let it get very hot. Put in a chafing dish. Warm brandy and ignite. Pour into cherry and peach mixture and stir carefully. Put flaming fruit over ice cream. Serve immediately. Serves 8.

Mrs. Michael Donahue (Teri)

BANANAS FOSTER

2 tablespoons brown sugar
1 tablespoon butter
1 ripe banana, peeled and
 sliced lengthwise

Dash cinnamon
½ ounce banana liqueur
1 ounce white rum
1 large scoop vanilla ice cream

Melt brown sugar and butter in flat chafing dish. Add banana and sauté until tender. Sprinkle with cinnamon. Pour in banana liqueur and rum all over and flame. Baste with warm liquid until flame burns out. Serve immediately over ice cream. Serves 1.

Mrs. Landon B. Anderson (Connie)

CHOCOLATE DREAM DESSERT

Pastry:
1 cup flour, all purpose
1 stick butter

1 cup pecans, chopped

Layer One:
1 (8 ounce) cream cheese
1 cup confectioners' sugar

1 cup Cool Whip

Layer Two:
1 (3⅝ ounce) instant vanilla
 pudding
1 (3⅝ ounce) instant chocolate
 pudding

2 cups milk

Layer Three:
Cool Whip - the remainder of an
 8 ounce carton

1 Hershey candy bar, grated (for
 topping garnish)

Preheat oven to 350 degrees. Mix the flour, butter and pecans together and spread into a 9x13 inch pan. Bake for 20 minutes. Cool. Mix the cream cheese, confectioners' sugar and 1 cup of the Cool Whip together and then spread over the pastry. Combine vanilla pudding and chocolate pudding with the milk. Blend well. Spread pudding mixture over layer 1. Cover with the remainder of the Cool Whip. Sprinkle top with a grated Hershey candy bar. Serves 10-12.

Poplar Grove Plantation
Scott's Hill, North Carolina

MOCHA ROLL WITH RUM CREAM

2 egg yolks
¼ cup sugar
2 tablespoons unsweetened
  cocoa
1½ teaspoons instant espresso
  powder (coffee)
⅓ cup ground hazelnuts
  (Filberts)

3 tablespoons flour
1 teaspoon double-acting
  baking powder
3 egg whites
pinch of cream of tartar
¼ cup sugar

Rum Cream:
1 cup heavy cream
1 tablespoon rum
1 tablespoon coffee liqueur
  (Kahlua)

2 tablespoons confectioners'
  sugar

Preheat oven to 350 degrees. Line a buttered 11½x7½ inch jelly roll pan with wax paper and butter and lightly flour the paper. In a bowl beat the egg yolks until they are thick and lemon colored, beat in gradually the ¼ cup sugar sifted with the 2 tablespoons cocoa and the 1½ teaspoons instant coffee powder, and beat the mixture for 2-3 minutes or until it ribbons when beater is lifted. Stir in the ⅓ cup ground nuts and the 3 tablespoons flour sifted with baking powder (if batter gets too stiff and clogs the beaters, sprinkle in a little water). In another bowl beat the egg whites with cream of tartar until they hold soft peaks, beat in ¼ cup sugar, 1 tablespoon at a time, and continue to beat the whites until they hold stiff peaks. Stir ¼ of the whites into the yolk mixture and fold in the remaining whites gently but thoroughly. Pour the mixture into the jelly-roll pan, spread it evenly and bake the cake for 10 minutes or until it shrinks from the sides of the pan. Loosen the wax paper from the pan and invert the cake onto a tea towel sprinkled with sifted confectioners' sugar. Roll cake lengthwise while warm. Let the cake cool and peel off the paper. In a chilled bowl beat 1 cup heavy cream until it thickens, beat in 2 tablespoons confectioners' sugar and the rum and coffee liqueur; continue to beat the cream until it holds stiff peaks. Spread the cream over the cake to within ¼ inch of the edge, roll up the cake tightly lengthwise, lifting it with the towel and finishing with the seam side down and chill it for 1 hour. Transfer the roll to a platter and sift confectioners' sugar over it.

Mrs. John Parkinson (Vicki)

CREAMY MINCEMEAT TARTS

1 (3 ounce) package instant
  vanilla pudding mix
¾ cup milk
½ cup sour cream

1 cup prepared mincemeat
Tiny tart shells (about 4 to 5
  dozen)

Stir pudding mix into milk. Add sour cream; blend thoroughly. Stir in mincemeat. Chill. Spoon into tart shells.

Mrs. Ralph McCoy (Emily)

APPLE PIE

Crust:
2 cups all purpose flour, sifted
1 teaspoon baking powder
¾ teaspoon salt

1 cup vegetable shortening
3-6 tablespoons water

Filling:
1 quart canned sliced apples,
  drained
1 cup juice from apples
½ cup sugar
2 tablespoons corn starch

½ tablespoon lemon juice
3 tablespoons butter
⅛ teaspoon cinnamon
⅛ teaspoon mace
1 light dash nutmeg

Preheat oven to 450 degrees. To make the crust, sift together flour, salt and baking powder. Add the shortening, cutting into flour mixture until evenly distributed. Gradually sprinkle water a few tablespoons at the time. Mix thoroughly, add more water as necessary to hold all ingredients together. Roll out ⅛ inch thick on lightly floured board.

For the filling, combine sugar and cornstarch and add fruit juice gradually in a saucepan over low heat. Cook until thick and clear. Remember to stir constantly to keep smooth. Stir in drained, sliced apples, lemon juice, butter, cinnamon, mace and nutmeg and continue to cook for 10 minutes. Cover a 9 inch pie pan with the crust. Pour in hot apple mixture. Roll out remainder of pie crust, cut into ½ inch strips and place over the apple filling in lattice work fashion. Bake in 450 degree oven for 20 minutes. Serves 6-8.

King Neptune Restaurant
Wrightsville Beach, North Carolina

HOLLY'S APPLE PIE

1 (20 ounce) can apple pie
   filling
2 tablespoons sugar
1 tablespoon cinnamon
¾ cup butter, room temperature
1 cup sugar

Pinch of salt
1 cup flour
1 egg
1 cup chopped pecans
1 teaspoon vanilla

Preheat oven to 350 degrees. Spread apple pie filling in buttered pie plate. Sprinkle 2 tablespoons of sugar and 1 tablespoon cinnamon over apples. Make a batter by creaming together butter, 1 cup sugar and salt, then add flour, egg, pecans and vanilla, mixing well. Spread evenly over apples. Bake for 1 hour or until top is golden brown.

Mrs. James L. Kesler (Jana)

FRESH BLUEBERRY PIE

1 baked 9 inch pie shell
4 cups blueberries
1 cup sugar
3 tablespoons cornstarch

¼ teaspoon salt
¼ cup water
1 tablespoon butter

Line cooked pie shell with 2 cups of the blueberries. Sauce: Cook 2 cups blueberries with sugar, cornstarch, salt and water over medium heat until thick, stirring often while cooking. Remove from heat and add butter. Cool. Pour over blueberries in shell. Chill before serving. Serve with ice cream or Cool Whip.

Mrs. Henry Singletary (Gorda)

STRAWBERRY PIE

Graham cracker pie shell
1 quart vanilla ice cream
1 cup sugar

3 tablespoons cornstarch
½ teaspoon baking powder
2 cups sliced strawberries

Line crust with vanilla ice cream. Freeze. Combine sugar, cornstarch, baking powder and strawberries in saucepan. Cook over medium heat for ten minutes. Cool. Then pour over pie shell. Freeze. Serves 6-8.

Mrs. Stephen Kash (Ann)

GRAPE PIE

5½ cups thick skin grapes
1¼ cups sugar
4 tablespoons flour
2 teaspoons lemon juice
Dash salt

½ teaspoon cinnamon
 (optional)
2 tablespoons butter
Pastry for 9 inch two crust pie

Preheat oven to 375 degrees. Remove and reserve grape skins. Place grape pulp and juice in a sauce pan over low heat. Slowly bring to a rolling boil so as not to scorch. Stirring now and then will keep grape pulp from sticking to the bottom of pan. Pour grape pulp and juice into a strainer and rub pulp through to remove seeds. Mix strained grape pulp and juice with reserved grape skins. Mix sugar, flour, lemon juice, salt and cinnamon together and stir into grape mixture. Pour grape and flour mixture into a pie pan lined with uncooked pastry and dot with butter. Cover with a top crust, either solid or lattice. Bake for 45 minutes. Serve cool or warm.

Mrs. Robert L. Morrison (Marion)

ICE CREAM PIE

Crust:
½ cup nuts
1 cup graham cracker crumbs

¼ cup sugar
¼ cup softened butter

Filling:
1 quart ice cream, softened

Meringue:
1 (7½ ounce) jar marshmallow
 cream
2 egg whites, stiffly beaten

¼ cup sugar
¼ teaspoon salt

Preheat oven to 375 degrees. Pat crumb mixture into a 9 inch pie plate and bake for 8 minutes in a 375 degree oven. Cool. Put softened ice cream into crust. Fold the egg whites which have been beaten stiff with the sugar and salt into the marshmallow cream. Cover pie with the meringue and brown in a 450 degree oven, then freeze at least six hours before serving.

Mrs. E. Thomas Marshburn, Jr. (Pat)

ICE CREAM PIE

2 tablespoons butter
2 squares unsweetened
  chocolate
1 cup sugar
⅔ cup evaporated milk
1 teaspoon vanilla
1 quart favorite ice cream,
  softened

1 (9 inch) pie shell, baked and
  cooled
3 egg whites, room temperature
½ teaspoon vanilla
¼ teaspoon cream of tartar
6 tablespoons sugar

Make fudge sauce: mix butter, chocolate, sugar, and evaporated milk in heavy saucepan. Cook and stir over low heat until thick and smooth. Remove from heat and add vanilla. Cool. Spread half of the ice cream in shell and cover with half the fudge sauce. Freeze firm. Spread the other half of the ice cream and cover with the other half of the fudge sauce. Freeze firm. Preheat oven to 400 degrees. Beat egg whites with vanilla and cream of tartar until frothy. Add sugar gradually and beat until stiff peaks form. Spread on ice cream pie sealing meringue to edges of pastry. Bake 6-8 minutes or until browned. Return immediately to freezer unless serving at once.

Note: Keeps well in freezer for one month if covered.

Mrs. Kenny J. Morris (Carolyn)

CHOCOLATE CHESS PIE

1 cup brown sugar
½ cup white sugar
1 teaspoon flour
⅛ teaspoon salt
2 eggs
½ eggshell milk

1 teaspoon vanilla
1 stick butter
2 squares unsweetened
  chocolate
1 9 inch pie shell, unbaked

Preheat oven to 325 degrees. Mix sugars, flour, salt, eggs, vanilla and milk. Melt butter and chocolate together, and pour into other mixture. Stir well, and pour into unbaked shell. Bake for 35-40 minutes. Delicious with ice cream.

Mrs. Daniel Gottovi (Karen)

FROZEN CHOCOLATE PECAN PIE

Crust:

2 cups finely chopped toasted pecans

5 tablespoons plus 1 teaspoon firmly packed brown sugar

5 tablespoons butter, chilled and cut into small pieces

2 teaspoons dark rum

Chocolate filling:

6 ounces semisweet chocolate

½ teaspoon instant coffee powder

4 eggs, room temperature

1 teaspoon vanilla

1 tablespoon dark rum

1½ cups whipping cream

4 tablespoons shaved semisweet chocolate

Combine pecans, brown sugar, butter and 2 teaspoons dark rum until mixture holds together. Press into the bottom and sides of a 9 inch pie plate. Freeze for a least 1 hour. To make the filling, melt the chocolate with the coffee in the top of a double boiler over hot water. Remove from heat and whisk in eggs, vanilla and rum until smooth. Let cool for five minutes. Whip 1 cup cream until stiff. Gently fold the whipped cream into the chocolate mixture and blend well. Pour into crust and freeze. Transfer the pie from the freezer to the refrigerator about 1 hour before serving. Whip remaining ½ cup cream and pipe over pie. Sprinkle with chocolate shavings. Serves 6-8. This pie may be frozen for up to 3 months.

Mrs.Thomas B. Mobley (Sue)

FRENCH SILK CHOCOLATE PIE

½ cup butter

¾ cup sugar

2 squares semi-sweet chocolate, melted and cooled

1 teaspoon vanilla

2 eggs

1 baked graham cracker crust - 8 inch or 9 inch

1 pint whipping cream

2 tablespoons sugar

1 teaspoon vanilla or almond flavoring

Chocolate curls

Cream butter and sugar; blend in chocolate. Add vanilla. Add eggs one at a time, beating for 5 minutes after each addition. Pour into baked pie shell. Chill thoroughly. Whip whipping cream with sugar and flavoring and spread on top of chilled chocolate. Sprinkle chocolate curls made from sweet milk chocolate on top.

Mrs. Britton E. Taylor (Harriette)

FRENCH CHOCOLATE PIE

3 egg whites
½ teaspoon cream of tartar
1 cup sugar
1 tablespoon cocoa
12 saltine crackers, crushed

½ cup pecans, crushed
1 teaspoon vanilla
1 cup (½ pint) heavy cream, whipped
1 tablespoon cocoa

Preheat oven to 325 degrees. Beat egg whites with cream of tartar until frothy. Gradually add sugar, 1 tablespoon cocoa, crushed saltine crackers, crushed nuts and vanilla. Place in a buttered 9 inch pie plate and bake for 30 minutes. Cool completely. Whip heavy cream and add 1 tablespoon cocoa. Spread mixture over cooled pie. Refrigerate at least six hours before serving.

Mrs. David B. Sloan, Jr. (Emily)

HOT FUDGE PIE

2 squares bitter chocolate
  (unsweetened)
¼ pound margarine
1 cup sugar

¼ cup flour
2 teaspoons vanilla
2 eggs
Pinch of salt

Preheat oven to 350 degrees. Melt together chocolate and margarine over low heat. Mix together all other ingredients. Stir in melted chocolate and margarine. Pour in greased 8 inch pie pan. Bake for 20 minutes. Serve hot with ice cream. Serves 6.

Mrs. Donald MacQueen (Lynn)

CHESS PIE

½ cup butter or margarine
1½ cups sugar
3 eggs, beaten
1 tablespoon cider vinegar

1 tablespoon vanilla
¼ teaspoon salt
1 (8-inch) pie shell, unbaked

Preheat oven to 300 degrees. Combine butter and sugar in a saucepan. Cook over medium heat, stirring constantly until very smooth. Remove from heat. Add eggs. Mix thoroughly. Stir in vinegar, vanilla and salt. Beat to blend ingredients. Pour into pie shell. Bake 50 minutes. Yield: 6 servings.

Minnie Pearl
Nashville, Tennessee
Azalea Festival - 1981

BOB HOPE'S FAVORITE LEMON PIE

1 cup sugar
3 tablespoons cornstarch
1 cup water, boiling
4 eggs, separated
2 tablespoons butter

Rind of 1 lemon, grated
4 tablespoons lemon juice
Pinch of salt
2 tablespoons sugar
1 (9-inch) pie shell, baked

Combine in saucepan cornstarch and sugar. Add water slowly, stirring constantly, until thick and smooth. Add slightly beaten egg yolks, butter, lemon rind, juice and salt. Cook 2 or 3 minutes. Pour into baked pie shell. Cover with meringue made from 3 egg whites, beaten stiff with 2 tablespoons sugar. Bake in slow oven 15 minutes or until light brown.

Bob Hope
North Hollywood, California
Participated in Azalea Festival - 1981

AUNT DESSIE'S LEMON PIE

3 egg yolks
1 cup sugar
5 tablespoons cornstarch
juice of 3 lemons
2 cups water, boiling

¼ teaspoon salt
2 tablespoons butter
1 (9-inch) pie shell, baked
3 egg whites
6 tablespoons sugar

Preheat oven to 400 degrees. In top of double boiler, beat egg yolks. Combine 1 cup sugar and cornstarch. Add to egg yolks. Gradually add lemon juice, water, and salt. Cook until thick, stirring occasionally. Remove from heat and add butter. Pour cooled filling into cooled pie shell. Beat egg whites. Add 6 tablespoons sugar to egg whites and beat until stiff. Put on top of filling. Bake until brown. Yield: 6 servings.

Charlie Daniels
Popular musician - Wilmington native

SOUTHERN PECAN PIE

½ recipe plain pastry
¼ cup butter
⅔ cup firmly packed brown
  sugar
Dash of salt

¾ cup dark corn syrup
3 eggs, well beaten
1 cup pecan halves
1 teaspoon vanilla

Preheat oven to 450 degrees. Prepare pastry; line 8-inch pie plate with pastry. Cream together butter, brown sugar and salt; stir in remaining ingredients. Turn into pastry-lined plate and bake at 450 degrees for 10 minutes; then reduce heat to 350 degrees and bake 30 to 35 minutes longer, or until knife inserted comes out clean; cool. Serve with whipped cream, if desired.

Mrs. H. M. Pickard (Doris)

KEY LIME PIE

1 (14-ounce) can sweetened
  condensed milk
1 (12-ounce) can frozen limeade
2 (8-ounce) containers frozen
  whipped topping (Cool Whip)

Green food coloring as needed
2 (9-inch) graham cracker
  crusts
Red cherry or lime slices for
  each slice of pie

Combine sweetened condensed milk with limeade. Mix well. Add whipped topping and fold in well. Add green food coloring mixing well. Spoon into pie crust, top with lime slices or red cherries. Refrigerate several hours. Makes two 9-inch pies.

Tuesday's 1865 Eating Establishment
Wilmington, N.C.

PUMPKIN PECAN PIE

4 eggs, slightly beaten
2 cups canned or mashed
  cooked pumpkin
1 cup sugar
½ cup dark corn syrup

1 teaspoon vanilla
½ teaspoon cinnamon
¼ teaspoon salt
1 (9-inch) pie shell, unbaked
1 cup pecans, chopped

Preheat oven to 350 degrees. Combine eggs, pumpkin, sugar, corn syrup, vanilla, cinnamon and salt. Pour into pie shell, top with pecans. Bake 40 minutes or until set.

Nancy Reagan
Washington, D.C.
Participated in Azalea Festival—1969 (Ronald Reagan)

Cakes, Cookies, Candy

Historic Wilmington—The stately Governor Dudley Mansion and a peek at the outside kitchen of the Burgwin-Wright House.

PILOT HOUSE CHEESE CAKE

Crust:
¼ cup butter melted
2 cups vanilla wafers—ground
   or crushed

Filling:
3 8-ounce packages cream
   cheese
¾ cup sugar

Juice of one lemon
1 teaspoon vanilla

Topping:
3 cups sour cream
1 teaspoon vanilla

¾ cup sugar

Mix the melted butter and vanilla wafers, then mold into the bottom of a cheese cake pan. Cream together the cream cheese and the first ¾ cup sugar. Add the lemon juice and vanilla until you have a smooth mixture. Pour into the crust layer. Bake at 350 degrees for 35 minutes. Cool to room temperature. Blend the topping ingredients: sour cream, vanilla and sugar. Spread over the cooled cheese cake. Bake again at 350 degrees for 30 minutes. Makes 12 small slices.

Pilot House - Chandler's Wharf
Wilmington, N.C.

PETITE CHEESECAKES

Vanilla Wafer crumbs
2 eggs
½ cup sugar
2 teaspoons vanilla
1½ cups sour cream

2 (8 ounce) packages softened
   cream cheese cut into pieces
2 tablespoons melted butter
Cherry pie filling

Preheat oven to 350 degrees. Using the smallest cupcake tins and petit-fours paper cups, sprinkle bottoms with crumbs. Place eggs, sugar, vanilla and sour cream in blender; mix well. Add cheese gradually while mixing; add butter. Pour petit-fours cups approximately ⅔ full. Bake for 35 minutes or until set in center. If cakes sink in center, don't worry. Chill. Just before serving, top with one cherry from a can of cherry pie filling. Yield: 7 dozen.

Mrs. James L. Cathell (Drukie)

CHEESE CAKE

Crust:
1⅔ cups graham cracker
  crumbs

¼ cup sugar
½ stick margarine, melted

Second Layer:
⅓ cup butter
⅓ cup brown sugar
1 cup flour

½ cup chopped nuts
  (walnuts, filberts, pecans)

Cheese Filling:
½ cup sugar
1 teaspoon grated lemon peel
2 tablespoons lemon juice
1 teaspoon vanilla
16 ounces cream cheese

5 egg yolks
2 cups sour cream
5 egg whites
½ cup sugar

Preheat oven to 350 degrees. Combine graham cracker crumbs, sugar and margarine. Press into bottom and sides of a well-buttered 10-inch spring-form pan.

Cream butter, brown sugar, and flour; then add nuts. Press over the graham cracker crust and bake for 10 minutes at 350 degrees.

Reduce oven temperature to 325 degrees. In a separate bowl beat sugar, lemon peel, lemon juice, vanilla and cream cheese. Mix egg yolks and sour cream and blend into the cream cheese mixture.

Beat egg whites until stiff and gradually add sugar. Fold cheese mixture into whites. Pour over crust and bake at 325 degrees for 1 hour 15 minutes.

Serve with fresh strawberries or pineapple flavored with cognac.

Catherine H. Kassens, M.D.

NEW YORK CHEESE CAKE

1 cup sifted flour
¼ cup sugar
1 stick butter, not softened
1 slightly beaten egg yolk
¼ teaspoon vanilla
3 (8-ounce) packages cream
  cheese

¾ cup sugar
½ teaspoon vanilla
3 eggs
⅛ teaspoon nutmeg

Preheat oven to 400 degrees. Combine flour and ¼ cup sugar. Cut in butter until mixture is crumbly. Add egg yolk and vanilla and blend. Pat one-third of the dough onto bottom of 9-inch springform pan with sides removed. Bake for 6 minutes and cool thoroughly. Butter sides of pan and attach to bottom. Pat remaining dough evenly onto sides to a height of approximately two inches. Cream cream cheese and ¾ cup sugar. Add vanilla and 3 eggs, one at a time. Sprinkle one-half of the nutmeg into the mixture. Blend thoroughly. Pour mixture into crust (Remember, sides are unbaked). Sprinkle the remaining nutmeg on the top of mixture. Bake for 40 minutes. Cool cake for 15 minutes. Remove sides.

Mrs. David Bunn (Dana)

PLUM CAKE

2 cups self-rising flour
2 cups sugar
1 teaspoon cinnamon
1 teaspoon ground cloves
3 eggs

2 small jars baby food plums
1 cup pecans, chopped
1 cup confectioners' sugar
Juice of 1 lemon

Preheat oven to 350 degrees. By hand, mix flour, sugar, cinnamon, ground cloves, oil, eggs, and plums in a large bowl. Stir in pecans. Pour batter into a greased and floured tube or Bundt pan. Bake for 1 hour. Cool in pan for 15 minutes. Turn out and drizzle with glaze made by mixing the confectioners' sugar and lemon juice.

Mrs. Ralph McCoy (Emily)

BEVERLY'S CHOCOLATE SHEET CAKE

Cake:

2 cups plain flour
2 cups sugar
½ teaspoon salt
6 tablespoons cocoa
1 cup water
½ cup oil

1 stick margarine
½ cup buttermilk
1 teaspoon baking soda
2 eggs
1 teaspoon vanilla flavoring

Icing:

1 stick margarine
3 tablespoons cocoa
1 teaspoon vanilla

1 (1-pound) box confectioners' sugar

Mix the flour, sugar, and salt together in a bowl and set aside. In a saucepan combine cocoa, water, oil, and 1 stick margarine. Bring to a boil and boil for one minute. Combine the already mixed dry ingredients with the boiled mixture. Now add the buttermilk, soda, eggs, and vanilla. Bake in a 9x13 cake pan in a moderate oven (350 degrees) about 20 minutes or until the sides begin to turn loose from the pan. Mix all the icing ingredients and bring to a boil on the stove. While the cake is still warm, frost with the icing.

Causey's Deli
Long Beach, N.C.

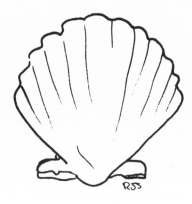

CHOCOLATE CHIP CAKE

1 (8-ounce) package cream
  cheese
½ cup sugar
1 egg
⅛ teaspoon salt
1 (6 ounce) package chocolate
  chips
1½ cups unsifted flour

¼ cup unsweetened cocoa
½ teaspoon salt
½ cup oil
1 teaspoon vanilla extract
1 teaspoon baking soda
1 cup water
1 cup sugar
1 tablespoon vinegar

Preheat oven to 350 degrees. Combine cream cheese, ½ cup sugar, egg, and ⅛ teaspoon salt. Beat until well blended. Add chocolate chips. Set aside. Combine flour, cocoa, ½ teaspoon salt, oil, vanilla, baking soda, water, 1 cup sugar, and vinegar. Batter will be quite thin. Pour into greased 8 inch square pan. Drop cream cheese mixture over batter and swirl mixture into batter. Bake 50-60 minutes. Cool before cutting. Very rich and moist.

Mrs. James Wortman (Martha)

UPSIDE DOWN CHOCOLATE CAKE

2 cups flour
½ teaspoon salt
1½ cups sugar
3 tablespoons cocoa

2 teaspoons baking powder
1 cup milk
4 tablespoons melted butter
2 teaspoons vanilla

Topping:
1 cup white sugar
1 cup brown sugar

5 tablespoons cocoa
2 cups water, boiling

Preheat oven to 350 degrees. Sift together flour, salt, 1½ cups sugar, 3 tablespoons cocoa, and baking powder. Add milk, melted butter, and vanilla. Mix well and pour into 2 quart ungreased baking dish. Mix together 1 cup sugar, brown sugar, 5 tablespoons cocoa, and water. Pour over cake batter. Bake for 30-35 minutes. Serve warm with vanilla icecream. Very rich!

Mrs. Ellis A. Tinsley (Betty)

MAMOO'S SMALL CHOCOLATE TEA CAKES

1 stick margarine or butter
1½ squares unsweetened
 Baker's chocolate
1 cup sugar

1 teaspoon vanilla
⅔ cup flour, sifted
2 eggs
½ cup black walnuts, chopped

Icing:
2 tablespoons margarine
1 square unsweetened
 chocolate

½ box confectioners' sugar
Hot black coffee

Preheat oven to 350 degrees. Melt margarine and chocolate together. Mix sugar, flour, vanilla and eggs together. Pour melted chocolate and margarine over sugar and flour mixture. Stir. Add nuts. Pour batter into bite-sized cup cake papers in smallest sized cup cake tins. Fill each paper ½-⅔ full. Bake for 12 minutes. Cool 5 minutes and ice. These will rise up like little cakes and fall back down. If you bake them longer than 12 minutes, they will be tough. The first time you won't think they are done.

Icing
Melt margarine and chocolate. Add sugar. Stir, adding enough black coffee to mixture until it has the consistency of icing. Ice the tea cakes while warm.

Mrs. E. Tilghman Poole (Jean)

GERMAN APPLE CAKE

½ cup shortening
1 stick butter
2 cups sugar
4 eggs
3½ cups flour
1 teaspoon cinnamon
1 teaspoon nutmeg
1 teaspoon allspice
1 teaspoon baking powder

¼ teaspoon salt
1 teaspoon soda
1 cup cold water
2½ cups chopped apples
1 (8-ounce) package chopped dates
1½ cups chopped walnuts
¼ cup brandy or bourbon

Preheat oven to 350 degrees. Cream shortening, butter, and sugar in large bowl. Add eggs, one at a time, beating well after each addition. Sift flour, cinnamon, nutmeg, allspice, baking powder, salt and soda together. Add to the creamed mixture, alternating with the water and brandy or bourbon. Stir in apples, dates, nuts, and mix thoroughly. Pour batter into a greased 9-inch tube pan. Bake for 1 hour 15 minutes. Cool, turn out of pan, and sprinkle with confectioners' sugar.

Mrs. Ralph B. Moore, Jr. (Vickie)

HARVEY WALLBANGER CAKE

6 ounces orange juice
1 ounce vodka
½ ounce Galliano
1 Duncan Hines orange cake mix

1 (3¾ ounce) package vanilla instant pudding
4 eggs, at room temperature
½ cup Crisco oil
½ cup Galliano

Glaze:
1 cup confectioners' sugar
1 tablespoon vodka

1 tablespoon Galliano

Preheat oven to 350 degrees. Mix in glass, the orange juice, vodka and ½ ounce Galliano. Pour into large mixing bowl and add cake mix, instant pudding, eggs, oil, and ½ cup Galliano. Mix thoroughly with electric mixer until batter is very smooth. Pour into greased and lightly floured 10 inch tube pan. Bake at 350 degrees for 45 minutes. Cool cake for 10 minutes in pan before removing. Mix confectioners' sugar, vodka and Galliano until smooth. Pour glaze over top of cake. Serves 12-16.

Mrs. Stephen Kash (Ann)

GOOEY BUTTER CAKE

1 yellow Duncan Hines II cake
  mix
1 stick margarine, softened
1 egg
½ box confectioners' sugar

1 (8 ounce) package cream
  cheese, softened
2 eggs
small amount confectioners'
  sugar

Preheat oven to 325 degrees. Grease a 13x9 inch glass pan. In a large mixing bowl, pour cake mix, margarine, and egg. Mix until well blended. Spread in pan. In medium mixing bowl, mix confectioners' sugar, cream cheese, and two eggs. Beat for 3 minutes. Pour over cake batter. Bake for 40 minutes. Sprinkle cake with confectioners' sugar while hot.

Mrs. Stephen Kash (Ann)

ROMAN'S NATURAL ENERGY CAKE

½ cup butter
1 to 1½ cups uncooked,
  unfiltered honey
2 eggs
1½ medium (9 ounce) cans
  crushed pineapple in own
  juice

1 tablespoon lemon juice
½ tablespoon sea salt
1 teaspoon baking soda
1 teaspoon vanilla
2 to 3 cups whole wheat flour
1 cup raisins
1 cup walnuts

Preheat oven to 350 degrees. Melt butter and honey in skillet. Beat, by hand, eggs in mixing bowl. Add butter and honey. Beat in pineapple and its juice. Add lemon juice, salt, soda and vanilla. Mix in wheat flour until you get a good consistency. Add raisins and walnuts. Pour into well oiled regular sized bundt pan. Bake at 350 degrees for 40-60 minutes. Top of cake should be firm. Yield: 10 to 12 servings.

Roman Gabriel
Pomona, California
Football player—Wilmington native

PRUNE SPICE CAKE WITH SEA FOAM ICING

2 cups all purpose flour
½ teaspoon salt
1 teaspoon soda
½ teaspoon baking powder
1½ teaspoons cinnamon
1 teaspoon nutmeg
1 teaspoon allspice

½ cup shortening
1½ cups sugar
3 eggs
1 cup cooked prunes, pitted
 and drained
1 cup buttermilk

Icing:
2 egg whites
1½ cups brown sugar
5 tablespoons cold water
⅛ teaspoon salt

1½ teaspoons dark corn syrup
1 teaspoon vanilla
Chopped pecans for garnish

Preheat oven to 350 degrees. Grease two 9-inch cake pans. Sift together flour, salt, soda, baking powder, cinnamon, nutmeg, and allspice. Set aside. In a large bowl, cream shortening and sugar. Add eggs and beat well. Add prunes. Then add sifted flour mixture alternately with the buttermilk. Scrape sides of the bowl while beating and beat only enough to blend. Pour the batter into prepared pans. Bake approximately 35 minutes. Put egg whites, brown sugar, cold water, and salt and dark corn syrup into the top of a double boiler. Place over boiling water. Beat at low speed of mixer until blended. Cook mixture, beating constantly at high speed until mixture stands in peaks. Remove from heat. Add vanilla and continue beating until mixture is spreading consistency. Frost cooled cake. Garnish with chopped pecans.

Mrs. Thomas H. Maloy (Jane)

HEAVENLY ORANGE-PINEAPPLE CAKE

1 yellow cake mix
4 beaten eggs
½ cup oil
1 (11-ounce) can Mandarin
  oranges
1 (20-ounce) can crushed
  pineapple

1 (3-ounce) package vanilla
  instant pudding
1 (9-ounce) container whipped
  topping

Preheat oven to 350 degrees. Grease and flour 3 9-inch cake pans. Mix thoroughly cake mix, eggs, oil and undrained Mandarin oranges. Divide mixture among pans and bake 15-20 minutes. Cool layers thoroughly. Combine undrained pineapple, instant pudding, and whipped topping. Frost cake. Refrigerate.

Mrs. James E. Wortman (Martha)

FRENCH ORANGE CAKE

1 (8-ounce) package dates,
  chopped
1 cup pecans, chopped
1 teaspoon baking soda
1 cup water, boiling
1 stick butter or margarine

1 cup sugar
1 egg
Rind of one orange, grated
2 cups flour, sifted
1 cup sugar
1 cup fresh orange juice

Preheat oven to 350 degrees. Generously grease and flour a 13x9 inch pan. Mix dates and nuts. Sprinkle with baking soda. Pour boiling water over mixture. Set aside. Cream one stick of butter and 1 cup of sugar. Add one egg and mix well. Add grated orange rind and 2 cups of flour. Add date and nut mixture. Turn batter into prepared pan. Bake for 30 minutes. Dissolve 1 cup sugar in 1 cup orange juice. Pour mixture gradually over hot cake. Cut into squares and top with whipped cream and a cherry.

Mrs. J. J. Pence, Jr. (Joan)

HUMMINGBIRD CAKE

2 cups sugar
1½ cups Crisco oil
3 large eggs
2 cups ripe bananas, diced
1 small can crushed pineapple,
    drained and reserve juice

3 cups all purpose flour
1 teaspoon baking soda
1 teaspoon salt
2 teaspoons cinnamon
1 cup chopped pecans
    (optional)

Icing:
1 box confectioners' sugar
1 stick margarine, softened
1 (8-ounce) package cream
    cheese

1 teaspoon vanilla

Preheat oven to 350 degrees. Grease and flour a 12 cup bundt pan. Cream sugar and oil. Add eggs, bananas, and pineapple. In a separate bowl, mix flour, soda, salt, and cinnamon. Blend into the sugar and oil mixture, the dry ingredients alternately with the banana and pineapple mixture. *Mix only until all are blended together.* Add chopped pecans at this point if desired and blend. Pour into pan and bake for 80-90 minutes. Cool cake thoroughly before icing.

Mix confectioners' sugar, margarine, cream cheese, and vanilla together and blend. If icing is too thick to spread, add a small smount of pineapple juice until consistency is correct. Ice cooled cake.

Mrs. Howard L. Armistead (Linda)

PECAN FRUITCAKE

1 pound pecan halves (4 cups)
½ pound diced candied
   pineapple (1 cup)
½ pound halved candied
   cherries (1 cup)
¾ cup flour

¾ cup sugar
½ teaspoon baking powder
½ teaspoon salt
3 eggs, beaten
1 teaspoon vanilla

Preheat oven to 300 degrees. Combine nuts and fruit in large bowl. Sift flour and sugar, baking powder and salt. Add to fruit and nuts. Toss with hands to coat fruit evenly. Beat eggs with vanilla; pour over fruit mixture and mix thoroughly (will be very stiff). Press into well-greased 9x5x3 loaf pan that has been lined with brown paper and again well greased. Bake 1 hour and 45 minutes. Cool, put in foil, and refrigerate.

Mrs. William F. Credle (Jean)

PUMPKIN-COCONUT BARS

1 (3½ ounce) can flaked
   coconut
1 cup graham cracker crumbs
1 cup chopped walnuts
¼ cup butter or margarine,
   melted
2 cups cooked pumpkin

1 (14 ounce) can Eagle Brand
   milk
2 eggs
2 teaspoons pumpkin pie spice
   or cinnamon, nutmeg, and
   cloves to taste
½ teaspoon salt

Preheat oven to 375 degrees. Combine coconut, graham cracker crumbs, walnuts, and butter; mix well. Pat ⅔ of the mixture into an ungreased 9x13x2 baking pan. Combine pumpkin, milk, eggs, spices, and salt, stirring well. Spoon mixture evenly over mixture in pan, then sprinkle with remaining coconut mix. Bake for 35 minutes or until knife inserted in center comes out clean. Cool, and chill. Cut into 2 inch by 3 inch bars. Makes 2-3 dozen bars.

Mrs. William P. Parker (Connie)

BUTTER PECAN BARS

2 eggs
1 cup brown sugar
1 cup sugar
1½ sticks butter, melted

1¼ cups flour
1 cup chopped pecans
1 teaspoon vanilla

Preheat oven to 350 degrees. Beat eggs, add sugar and brown sugar, and beat well. Add butter, flour, pecans, and vanilla and beat after each one. Pour into greased 9x9 pan. Bake at 350 degrees for 35 to 45 minutes.

Lloyd Roberts, M.D.

MOTHER'S TOFFEE NUT BARS

Bottom Layer:
½ cup butter or margarine
½ cup brown sugar

1 cup sifted flour

Top Layer:
2 eggs
1 cup brown sugar
1 teaspoon vanilla
2 tablespoons flour
½ teaspoon salt

1 teaspoon baking soda
1 cup coconut
1 cup chopped nuts
Confectioners' sugar

Preheat oven to 350 degrees.

To make the bottom layer: Cream butter, add brown sugar gradually and cream thoroughly. Add flour slowly to creamed mixture. With hands, work mixture into smooth dough. Pat dough into bottom of ungreased 9-inch pan. Bake 10 minutes. Remove from oven and allow to cool slightly.

To make top layer: Beat eggs until light. Stir in brown sugar and mix well. Blend in vanilla. In separate bowl, sift the flour, salt, and baking soda together and stir into the brown sugar mixture. Beat until smooth. Add coconut and nuts. Spread the topping over the baked, slightly cooled bottom layer. Bake 25 minutes. Cut into bars when cool. Remove each bar when cold and roll in confectioners' sugar.

Mrs. John Cashman (Diane)

REBEL SPICE BARS

1 cup flour
½ teaspoon soda
½ teaspoon cinnamon
½ teaspoon nutmeg
¼ teaspoon cloves
⅛ teaspoon salt

½ cup water
½ cup raisins
1 stick margarine
⅔ cup sugar
1 egg

Preheat oven to 350 degrees. Sift flour with soda, cinnamon, nutmeg, cloves, and salt. Set aside. Simmer raisins in water until soft. Drain, reserving 2 tablespoons of liquid. Melt margarine in heavy saucepan. Remove from heat and add sugar, 2 tablespoons liquid from raisins, and sifted flour mixture. Add egg and raisins. Mix thoroughly. Pour into a 9-inch square pan. Bake for 30 minutes. Cut into squares when cool.

Mrs. Heber W. Johnson (Betty)

LUSCIOUS SQUARES

1 cup flour
2 tablespoons sugar
1 stick butter (no substitute)
3 eggs
1½ cups brown sugar

2 tablespoons flour
1 teaspoon baking powder
1 cup chopped pecans
½ cup flaked coconut
1 teaspoon vanilla extract

Frosting:
2 tablespoons melted butter
1½ cups confectioners' sugar
   (add more if needed)

2 tablespoons light cream

Preheat oven to 325 degrees. Sift together 1 cup flour and sugar. Blend in butter with hands until dough is smooth. Pat into bottom of a greased 9-inch square baking dish or pan. Bake for 10-15 minutes. Meanwhile, in a mixing bowl, beat eggs together with brown sugar, 2 tablespoons flour, and baking powder. Stir in pecans, coconut, and vanilla. Pour over baked crust. Return to oven for 25 minutes. Let remain in pan to cool. Then frost and cut into squares. Remove from pan carefully to avoid breaking bottom crust. Freezes well. Yield: 36-1 to 1½ inch squares.

Mrs. Lucien Wilkins (Freda)

FUDGIE SCOTCH SQUARES

1 (6-ounce) package
  butterscotch chips
1 (6-ounce) package chocolate
  chips
1½ cups graham cracker
  crumbs
1 can Eagle Brand milk
½ cup chopped nuts

Preheat oven to 350 degrees. Grease a 9-inch square pan. Mix together butterscotch chips, chocolate chips, graham cracker crumbs, Eagle Brand milk, and nuts. Pour into pan and bake for 30 minutes. Cool and cut into squares.

Mrs. James D. Hundley (Linda)

CHOCOLATE BARS

3 squares unsweetened
  chocolate
1½ sticks butter
3 eggs
1½ cups sugar
¾ cup flour
¾ cup chopped pecans

Preheat oven to 350 degrees. Melt chocolate and butter over very low heat. Cool. Beat eggs and sugar together and add to chocolate mixture. Add flour and nuts. Mix well. Spread into a 9x13 pan and bake 20 minutes, no more. Cool.

Icing:
6 tablespoons butter, softened
3 cups powdered sugar
3 tablespoons evaporated milk
1 teaspoon vanilla

Mix butter, sugar, milk, and vanilla. Spread over cool cake.

Glaze:
1 square unsweetened
  chocolate
1 tablespoon vanilla

Melt chocolate. Add vanilla. Drizzle over cake. Refrigerate. Makes 15 squares.

Mrs. Terry Stewart (Susan)

CRANBERRY BARS

1 stick butter or margarine
1 cup granulated sugar
¾ cup brown sugar, firmly
  packed
¼ cup milk
2 tablespoons orange juice
1 egg, beaten

3 cups flour
1 teaspoon baking powder
¼ teaspoon baking soda
½ teaspoon salt
¾ cup chopped nuts
2½ cups chopped fresh
  cranberries

Preheat oven to 350 degrees. Cream butter and sugars together. Beat in milk, orange juice, and egg. Sift together flour, baking powder, baking soda, and salt. Combine dry ingredients with creamed mixture and blend well. Stir in chopped nuts and cranberries. Spread mixture in greased jelly roll pan. Bake 25-30 minutes. Cut into bars. (Can also be dropped by teaspoonfuls. Makes 12 dozen cookies. Bake cookies for 10-15 minutes.)

Mrs Ralph B. Moore, Jr. (Vickie)

ST. TIMOTHY'S COFFEE CAKE

2 sticks butter
2 cups sugar
½ teaspoon vanilla extract
2 eggs
2 cups unsifted flour
1 teaspoon baking powder
1 teaspoon cinnamon

¼ teaspoon salt
1 cup chopped nuts
½ cup golden raisins
1 cup sour cream
1-2 teaspoons cinnamon and
  sugar (mixed)

Preheat oven to 350 degrees. Grease and flour a 12 cup bundt pan or a 10-inch tube pan. Mix butter and sugar. Add vanilla and eggs. Combine in a separate bowl flour, baking powder, cinnamon, and salt. Add nuts and raisins and coat well. Add to first mixture alternately with sour cream. Blend well (batter looks like honey). Spoon into prepared pan. Sprinkle with cinnamon and sugar. Bake one hour. Cool on rack one hour. Serves 16.

Mrs. Thomas H. Maloy (Jane)

ORANGE COFFEE CAKE

2 cups Bisquick or Jiffy Mix
½ cup sugar
¾ cup orange juice
1 egg
2 tablespoons oil

½ cup brown sugar
1 teaspoon cinnamon
2 tablespoons margarine,
  softened
2 teaspoons grated orange rind

Preheat oven to 400 degrees. Grease a 9-inch square pan. Mix together Bisquick or Jiffy Mix, sugar, orange juice, egg, and oil. Pour batter into prepared pan. Mix together brown sugar, cinnamon, margarine, and orange rind. Sprinkle over batter in pan. Bake 20-25 minutes. Serve warm.

Mrs. James W. Markworth (Ruthe)

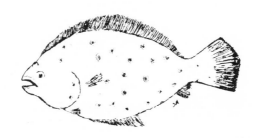

CREAM CHEESE COOKIES

1 cup flour
¼ cup brown sugar
1 cup chopped pecans
1 stick butter
2 (8 ounce) packages of cream
  cheese

1 cup sugar
1 teaspoon vanilla
3 eggs
1 pint sour cream
6 tablespoons sugar
1 teaspoon vanilla

Preheat oven to 350 degrees. Mix 1 cup flour, ¼ cup brown sugar, 1 cup chopped pecans and 1 stick of butter and press in 9x13 pan. Bake 10 minutes. Mix 2 (8 ounce) packages of cream cheese with 1 cup sugar, 1 teaspoon vanilla add three eggs. Beat well. Pour over pastry and bake for 20 minutes. Mix 1 pint sour cream, 6 tablespoons of sugar, 1 teaspoon of vanilla and pour over filling. Bake for 3 minutes and cool.

Mrs. Britton E. Taylor (Harriette)

HOLLY WREATH COOKIES

1 cup butter, softened
1 3-ounce package cream
   cheese, softened
½ cup sugar

1 teaspoon vanilla
2 cups flour
Cookie press

Preheat oven to 375 degrees. Cream butter and cream cheese. Add sugar and cream thoroughly. Beat in vanilla. Gradually blend in flour. Fill cookie press. Form cookies with star tip in the shape of a wreath on an ungreased cookie sheet. Bake 8 to 10 minutes or until set—not browned. Remove at once to cooling racks. Makes 4 dozen.

Mrs. Michael Donahue (Teri)

STRUDEL COOKIES

1 cup butter or margarine
1¾ cups all purpose flour
1¼ cups uncooked oatmeal,
   processed in blender for
   1 minute
1 cup dairy sour cream
1 cup shredded or flaked
   coconut

¾ cup chopped pecans
½ cup wheat germ
1 teaspoon cinnamon
¼ teaspoon nutmeg
12 ounces fruit jam or
   marmalade
Confectioners' sugar

Preheat oven to 350 degrees. To make cookie dough, soften butter and beat until fluffy. Blend in all purpose flour, oatmeal, and sour cream, mixing well. Cover and chill dough until it is very firm to the touch. Divide dough into thirds and roll out one third at a time on a well-floured surface to form a rectangle approximately 10 by 12 inches. Do not roll dough too thin as it will split while baking. Keep remaining dough chilled until ready to roll out. For the filling, combine the coconut, pecans, wheat germ, cinnamon, and nutmeg and mix. Spread the rectangle of dough with one third of the jam or marmalade to within one half inch of the edge. Sprinkle one third of the coconut and pecan mixture over the jam. Beginning at the wide side of the rectangle, roll up dough and filling. Place seam side down on an ungreased cookie sheet. Across the top of each roll, cut one half inch slashes an inch apart. Bake for 45 minutes or until golden brown. Remove to a wire rack and cool. Slice, sprinkle with confectioners' sugar, and serve.

Mrs. Robert L. Morrison (Marion)

BANANA OATMEAL COOKIES

2 cups sifted flour
1 teaspoon cinnamon
¼ teaspoon nutmeg
1½ teaspoons salt
1 teaspoon baking powder
¼ teaspoon soda
1 cup sugar

1 cup softened shortening
1 cup mashed bananas
  (2-3 bananas)
2 eggs
2 cups Quaker Oats (Quick or
  Old Fashioned, uncooked)

Preheat oven to 375 degrees. Sift together flour, cinnamon, nutmeg, salt, baking powder, soda, and sugar. Add shortening, mashed bananas, and eggs. Beat until smooth, about two minutes. Fold in rolled oats. Drop by teaspoons onto a well greased cookie sheet. Bake 10 to 12 minutes. Nuts may be added. Makes 4 dozen cookies.

Mrs. Robert J. Andrews (Mary Leila)

BROWN SUGAR-PECAN WAFERS

¾ cup flour, sifted
1 teaspoon baking powder
½ teaspoon salt
1 stick butter or margarine
1 cup light brown sugar,
  firmly packed

¾ teaspoon vanilla
1 egg
½ cup finely chopped pecans

Preheat oven to 400 degrees. Sift together flour, baking powder, and salt. Cream butter, brown sugar, and vanilla. Beat in egg. Stir in sifted flour mixture until well blended. Add pecans. Drop by slightly rounded teaspoonfuls onto ungreased cookie sheet about 3 inches apart. Bake about 5 minutes or until well browned around edges. Cool in pan 30 seconds. Remove at once with spatula to wire racks to cool. Makes 2 dozen.

Mrs. Oliver Raymond Hunt, Jr. (Eleanor)

HALLIE'S PRALINE CRACKERS

1 stick butter or margarine,
  softened
1 cup brown sugar

1 cup chopped pecans
1 (16-ounce) box Butter Thin
  or Ritz crackers

Preheat oven to 300 degrees. Mix softened butter, sugar and pecans. Place ½ teaspoon of mixture on a cracker. Bake for 10 minutes. Store in a tight tin. Easy, but delicious!

Mrs. Charles A. Wilkinson (Ann)

WHIPPED SHORTBREAD

1 pound softened butter
1 cup confectioners' sugar

3 cups flour
½ cup cornstarch

Preheat oven to 275 degrees. Whip butter in large bowl of mixer. Sift together sugar, flour, and cornstarch. Add gradually to butter and mix well. Chill in refrigerator for at least one hour. Roll on floured board and cut into desired shapes with cookie cutters. Decorate as desired or leave plain. Bake for approximately 20 minutes.

Mrs. Albert B. Brown (Margaret)

WALNUT CRESCENTS

1 cup butter
¼ cup confectioners' sugar
1½ teaspoons water

1 teaspoon vanilla
2 cups flour
1 cup chopped walnuts

Cream butter and ¼ cup confectioners' sugar. Add all the remaining ingredients and mix well. Shape into rolls about ½ inch in diameter and cut in 1 inch pieces. Place on cookie sheet and pull ends down slightly to form crescents. Bake in 375 degree oven for about 15 minutes. While warm, roll in confectioners' sugar. Roll *again* when cool. Makes about 6 dozen.

Ann-Marie Clifton
The Sandwich Factory
Wilmington, N.C.

KENTUCKY BOURBON BALLS

1 can Eagle Brand Milk
1 stick margarine, melted
⅓ cup bourbon
3 boxes confectioners' sugar

1 cup pecans, chopped
1 (12-ounce) package chocolate
  chips
⅓ bar paraffin

In a large mixing bowl, combine the Eagle Brand Milk, margarine, and bourbon. Gradually add sugar and pecans. Refrigerate mixture overnight. Roll candy into small balls and place on trays in refrigerator. Melt chocolate chips and paraffin in a large pyrex cup over boiling water. Using a toothpick, dip refrigerated balls into chocolate mixture. Return to trays and refrigerate. After cooling, candy can be stored in air tight container in refrigerator.

Mrs. Stephen Kash (Ann)

SUGARPLUMS

½ cup dried apricots
½ cup pecans
¼ cup plus 1 tablespoon
  grated sweet coconut

¼ cup raisins
¼ cup dried apples
2 tablespoons kirsch
3 tablespoons sugar

In a food processor fitted with the steel blade, chop finely the apricots, pecans, coconut, raisins, and apples. With the motor running, add 2 tablespoons kirsch and blend the mixture for 5 seconds. Form the mixture into ¾ inch balls, pressing candy firmly into shape. In a shallow bowl sprinkle balls with 3 tablespoons sugar. Roll the sugarplums in sugar to coat evenly. Sugarplums will keep up to two weeks in an airtight container or may be frozen. Makes approximately 36.

Mrs. Landon B. Anderson (Connie)

NO-FAIL FUDGE

2 cups sugar
½ cup evaporated milk
4 tablespoons white Karo syrup
⅛ teaspoon salt
⅓ stick butter or margarine

1 teaspoon vanilla
2 squares unsweetened
   chocolate
1 cup pecans or walnuts

Combine sugar, milk, Karo syrup, salt, and butter in heavy saucepan and bring to a rapid boil, stirring constantly. Drop in chocolate and continue to boil, stirring constantly, for 2 minutes by the clock. Remove from heat and place saucepan in sink of cold water. Beat for 1 minute, then add vanilla and beat 1 more minute. Add pecans, stir until mixed, and pour immediately into well greased pan. (1½ quart size pan is excellent). Cool and eat!

Note: This recipe has never failed to harden. However, if a larger batch is desired, make 2 batches separately. Do not double recipe!

Mrs. Robert H. Hutchins (Seldie)

MELTING MOMENTS

1 cup flour
¾ cup cornstarch
½ teaspoon almond flavoring

2 sticks margarine
⅓ cup confectioners' sugar

Icing:
½ stick margarine
¾ pound confectioners' sugar

¼ cup milk

Preheat oven to 375 degrees. Combine flour, cornstarch, almond flavoring, two sticks margarine. and sugar until stiff. Roll into balls and bake on ungreased cookie sheet 10-15 minutes. Cool. For icing, combine ½ stick margarine and milk. Add confectioners' sugar gradually until desired consistency has been reached. Beat until smooth. Ice cookies. Makes 3 dozen.

Mrs. Thomas H. Maloy (Jane)

CHOCOLATE-DIPPED CHERRIES

3 tablespoons butter
  (use real butter)
3 tablespoons light corn syrup
¼ teaspoon salt
2 cups powdered sugar, sifted
1½ pound chocolate
  (2 8-ounce) packages
  semi-sweet chocolate and
  1 (8-ounce) package
  unsweetened chocolate)

60 maraschino cherries with
  stems (approximately 3 (10-
  ounce) jars)

Drain cherries and spread on paper towels for approximately one hour for surface drying. Combine softened butter, syrup, and salt. Gradually stir in powdered sugar. Knead until smooth, then chill dough in refrigerator until dough is not sticky (approximately 30-45 minutes). Pinch marble-sized pieces of dough and shape around each cherry. Cover cherry completely and do not squeeze juice into dough. Should the dough become gummy when shaping, rechill the dough. Have damp paper towels available to keep fingers freshly wiped. Place wrapped cherries on wax paper and chill until dough is hard. In top of double boiler, melt chocolate for coating, stirring frequently. Do not add any other liquid. Holding the cherry stem, quickly dip the cherry into the chocolate. Place on wax paper. Chill in refrigerator to harden and then store in a covered container. Place in cool area.

Note: These can be eaten immediately but are better when stored and allowed to ripen and liquefy (7-10 days).

Mrs. William P. Parker, Jr. (Connie)

TAFFY CRUNCH POPCORN

12 quarts popped popcorn
1 pound salted Spanish peanuts
4 sticks butter or margarine
2 (1 pound) boxes brown sugar

½ cup dark corn syrup
½ cup molasses
1 teaspoon salt
2 teaspoons vanilla

Preheat oven to 250 degrees. Place popcorn in a very large bowl. Stir peanuts in. In a 4 quart sauce pan, melt butter. Stir in brown sugar, corn syrup, molasses, and salt. Bring to boil over medium heat. Boil, stirring occasionally, for 5 minutes. Remove from heat. Stir in vanilla. Gradually pour mixture over popcorn and peanuts and mix. Turn popcorn into 2 very large shallow pans or 4 smaller shallow pans. Bake in oven for 1 hour. Stir every 15 minutes. Remove from oven and cool completely. Break apart and pack in plastic bags or tightly covered containers. Crunch keeps perfectly fresh when sealed.

Mrs. Thomas H. Maloy (Jane)

GLAZED NUTS

1 cup sugar
½ teaspoon cinnamon
⅛ teaspoon cream of tartar

¼ cup boiling water
3 cups pecan halves

Mix together sugar, cinnamon, and cream of tartar. Add boiling water to mixture just to thread stage. Place pecan halves in a bowl. Pour sugar mixture over nuts. Mix until glaze begins to harden on the nuts. Spread pecan halves on waxed paper and separate. Remove nuts from waxed paper when they are completely hardened.

Mrs. John Pace (Rachel)

preserves,
Pickles,
Sauces

Sea oats, shells, and solitude—natural resources of Figure Eight Island.

FRENCH VINAIGRETTE SALAD DRESSING

1 teaspoon salt
1 teaspoon white pepper
½ teaspoon cracked black
  pepper
¼ teaspoon sugar
½ teaspoon dry mustard
1 tablespoon fresh lemon juice

1 clove garlic, pressed
5 tablespoons tarragon vinegar
½ cup vegetable oil
2 tablespoons olive oil
1 egg, lightly beaten
½ cup light cream

Combine salt, white pepper, black pepper, sugar, mustard, lemon juice, garlic, vinegar, vegetable oil, olive oil, egg and cream in a jar with a tightly fitting lid. Shake vigorously to blend, and store in refrigerator. This will keep for several weeks. It does miracles to a simple head of lettuce or any cold vegetable.

Mrs. Charles Graham (Jean)

CREAMY OIL AND VINEGAR SALAD DRESSING

¾ cup wine vinegar
2 quarts salad oil
¾ cup wine vinegar
1 egg
1½ tablespoons salt
1 tablespoon mustard powder

1 tablespoon coarse ground
  pepper
1 tablespoon monosodium
  glutamate
2 tablespoons sugar

Refrigerate oil and vinegar 8 hours before using. Bring egg to room temperature. Place egg in mixing bowl. Whip on high speed until very fluffy. Add all dry ingredients and lower speed to medium. Add first ¾ cup wine vinegar very slowly. Slowly add salad oil. Whip 2 minutes. Add second ¾ cup wine vinegar. Whip 6 minutes. Refrigerate and serve chilled. Makes ¾ gallon.

The Bridge Tender
Wrightsville Beach, N.C.

PRIZE SALAD DRESSING

½ cup vinegar
½ cup sugar
½ cup catsup
1 teaspoon salt
⅓ teaspoon ground cloves

Dash of paprika
2 tablespoons Worcestershire
  sauce
1 cup salad oil
1 small onion, grated fine

Boil vinegar, sugar, catsup, salt, cloves, paprika and Worcestershire sauce for 3 minutes. Cool, and beat in oil and onion. This keeps well in the refrigerator.

Mrs. Charles Graham (Jean)

HOMEMADE FRENCH DRESSING

½ cup chili sauce
1 cup mayonnaise or
  salad dressing
Salt to taste
Pepper to taste
¾ cup sugar

1 (10½ ounce) can tomato soup
2 teaspoons prepared mustard
¼ cup vinegar
½ cup catsup
½ cup salad oil
Garlic salt to taste

Blend chili sauce, mayonnaise, salt, pepper, sugar, tomato soup, mustard, vinegar, catsup, salad oil and garlic salt, until well mixed. Refrigerate.

Mrs. Durwood Almkuist (Gloria)

HOUSE DRESSING FOR GREEN SALADS

1 cup sugar
1 cup white vinegar
1 cup vegetable oil
1 medium green sweet pepper
1 medium onion
1 (2 ounce) jar pimiento

3 tablespoons prepared
  mustard
3 tablespoons coarse salt
3 tablespoons Worcestershire
  sauce

Stir sugar, vinegar and oil until sugar dissolves. Pureé pepper, onion and pimientos in blender. Mix sugar mixture with pureé. Stir in mustard, salt and Worcestershire sauce. Let stand 3 hours before using. Keeps well in refrigerator. Makes 1 quart.

Mrs. Frederick Butler, Jr. (Ann)

CHILI SAUCE

15 tomatoes, peeled and cut small (may use food processor)
2 cups onions, cut small
2 cups celery, cut small
2 cups apples, cut small
2 green peppers, cut small
2 red peppers, cut small
2 tablespoons salt
½ teaspoon nutmeg
½ teaspoon cinnamon
3 cups vinegar
3 cups sugar
1 can tomato paste

In large pan, place tomatoes, onions, celery, apples, green peppers, red peppers, salt, nutmeg, cinnamon, vinegar and sugar. Cook for ½ hour. Add the tomato paste and cook 1 hour more. Fill sterilized jars and seal. Makes 7 or 8 pints.

Mrs. David P. Thomas (Ginny)

CHILI SAUCE

1 hot pepper
6 green peppers
12 onions
36 tomatoes, peeled
3 cups vinegar
3 tablespoons salt
1 tablespoon black pepper
Dash allspice
1 cup sugar

Chop peppers, onions and tomatoes. Mix together peppers, onions, tomatoes, vinegar, salt, black pepper, allspice and sugar. Cook over low heat 4 to 5 hours. Boil canning jars and lids. Fill with the chili sauce and put on lids. Let cool until lids pop.

Note: One hot pepper makes the sauce moderately hot. Add 1 or 2 more if you like it really hot!

Mrs. Clifford Lewis (Libby)

CUCUMBER MAYONNAISE

1 cup Hellman's mayonnaise
3 tablespoons lemon juice
Dash Tabasco

¼ teaspoon curry powder
½ cup cucumber, finely
  chopped

Blend mayonnaise, lemon juice, Tabasco and curry powder. Drain cucumber and add to mayonnaise mixture. Chill several hours before serving. Good with cold fish salad.

Mrs. John Codington (Betsy)

SPICED TOMATO SAUCE

3 large onions
6 medium carrots
3 cloves garlic
⅓ cup oil

6 (28 ounce) cans tomatoes
1 tablespoon sugar
1 tablespoon salt
⅛ teaspoon pepper

Place onions, quartered, in blender container; add enough water to cover. Cover and blend until chopped; drain and set aside. Repeat with cleaned carrots, cut in chunks. In kettle, cook onion, carrot and garlic, minced, in oil until tender, but not brown. Place tomatoes, one can at a time, in blender; blend until chopped. Add to kettle with sugar, salt and pepper. Boil gently, uncovered, for 1¼-1½ hours, stirring toward the end of cooking time; cool. Press through food mill. Refrigerate or freeze. Makes 12 cups. Can be used for base for spaghetti sauce or barbecue sauce.

Mrs. Ralph McCoy (Emily)

TARTAR SAUCE

3 stalks celery, blend or chop, drain
1 large onion, blend or chop, drain

2 cups mayonnaise
6 tablespoons horseradish
6 tablespoons red pickle relish

Drain chopped celery and onion, Add the mayonnaise, the horseradish, and the red pickle relish. Refrigerate well before using.

Iris and Jim Smith
"Waterway"
Southport, N.C.

LOUISVILLE MEAT SAUCE

1 (12 ounce) bottle chili sauce
1 (14 ounce) bottle tomato catsup
1 (11 ounce) bottle A-1 sauce, or your favorite equivalent

1 (10 ounce) bottle Worcestershire sauce
1 (8 ounce) jar chutney
Tabasco sauce to taste

Mix chili sauce, catsup, A-1 sauce, Worcestershire sauce, chutney and Tabasco sauce together. If fruit pieces in the chutney are large, chop into small pieces. Wash out the bottles you have used and fill with this delicious sauce. Refrigerate. This meat sauce is a zestful addition to meat. It was first concocted by Henry Bain, chef at the Pendennis Club in Louisville, Kentucky.

Mrs John Cashman (Diane)

BLUE CHEESE DRESSING

¾ pound blue cheese crumbled
12 ounces sour cream

2½ cups mayonnaise
1 quart buttermilk

Mix together all ingredients. Refrigerate before serving.

Cape Fear Country Club
Wilmington, N.C.

SEAFOOD SAUCE

2 cups catsup
6 tablespoons horseradish
Juice of ½ lemon
1½ tablespoons Worcestershire
  sauce

1 tablespoon celery salt
Dash of Texas Pete (increase or
  eliminate according to taste)

Blend all of the ingredients. Refrigerate well for some time.

Iris and Jim Smith
"Waterway"
Southport, N.C.

HOT PEPPER JELLY

¼ cup chopped hot green
  pepper
1½ cups chopped green bell
  pepper (core and remove
  inside membrane)

6½ cups sugar
1½ cups white vinegar
1 bottle (2 pouches) of Certo
  fruit pectin

Chop peppers (in food processor for speed), and place in blender with vinegar. Blend well and strain liquid into bowl. Discard pepper residue for clear jelly. (If flecked jelly is preferred, add 2 or 3 teaspoons of chopped pepper to liquid.) Pour pepper-vinegar liquid into sugar, bring to a boil and stir frequently while continuing to boil for 10 minutes. Add Certo and boil 5 minutes. Skim foam with metal spoon. Pour into hot jars and seal. Makes six ½ pint jars.

Mrs. William P. Parker, Jr. (Connie)

BARBECUE SAUCE

2 cups tomato catsup
¾ cup Worcestershire sauce
½ cup cider vinegar
1 teaspoon salt

2 tablespoons oil
2 cloves garlic, minced
1 dash cayenne pepper

Mix together catsup, Worcestershire sauce, vinegar, salt, oil, garlic and cayenne pepper. Bring to a boil over medium heat. Cook slowly for 20 minutes. Very good sauce for cooking barbecued chicken. Sauce may be refrigerated and kept for several weeks.

Mrs. Bertram Williams, Jr. (Ellen)

CHEF'S SALT

1 cup table salt
1 tablespoon paprika
1 teaspoon ground black
  pepper

¼ teaspoon ground white
  pepper
¼ teaspoon celery salt
¼ teaspoon garlic salt

Mix table salt, paprika, black pepper, white pepper, celery salt and garlic salt well. Use in soups, stews, meat dishes, etc., instead of plain salt.

Mrs. John Morse (Jane)

HORSERADISH MOLD

1 (3 ounce) package lemon
  Jello
½ cup boiling water
1 envelope Knox gelatin

¼ cup cold water
1 (8 ounce) carton sour cream
1 (5 ounce) jar horseradish
¾ cup mayonnaise

Dissolve Jello in boiling water. Dissolve gelatin in cold water. Mix together and add sour cream, horseradish and mayonnaise. Pour into a greased mold , and set aside until firm. Serve with beef and ham.

Mrs. Thomas Maloy

EMMET'S STEAK SAUCE

½ cup butter
½ cup catsup
½ cup soy sauce

½ cup dry vermouth
1 (4 ounce) can mushrooms,
  drained

Mix together butter, catsup, soy sauce, vermouth and mushrooms and heat for 5-10 minutes. This is excellent on steaks.

Mrs. Frank Reynolds (Marguerite)

LEMON BUTTER SAUCE FOR DIPPING VEGETABLES

3 tablespoons butter
1 tablespoon fresh lemon juice
¼ teaspoon salt

⅛ teaspoon black pepper
Dash of paprika

Barely melt butter over very low heat. Beat in lemon juice, salt, pepper and paprika with a fork. Serve in small heated bowls for dipping artichokes, asparagus, broccoli or cauliflower.

Mrs. John Codington (Betsy)

DARK CHOCOLATE SUNDAE SAUCE

2 squares bitter chocolate
2 tablespoons butter
⅔ cup sugar
½ cup evaporated milk,
  undiluted

1 teaspoon vanilla
¼ cup sherry (optional)

Melt chocolate and butter over low heat. Stir in sugar and milk. Cook over low heat until sugar is dissolved and sauce thickened. Add vanilla and sherry. This keeps well in the refrigerator.

Mrs. Oliver Raymond Hunt (Eleanor)

HOT BLUEBERRIES WITH SOUR CREAM SAUCE FOR SPONGE CAKE

1 pint sour cream
2 teaspoons pure vanilla
2 tablespoons sugar
2 cups fresh or frozen
blueberries

½ cup sugar
1 tablespoon lemon juice
1 teaspoon cornstarch
1 cup water

Mix sour cream, vanilla and 2 tablespoons sugar with a fork. Chill. In a saucepan, heat blueberries with ½ cup sugar, lemon juice and ½ cup water. Bring to a boil and cook 2 minutes. (If this is too watery, let it cook a further 4 or 5 minutes.) Dissolve cornstarch in ½ cup cold water, add to berries, and boil another minute. Spoon sour cream sauce over sponge cake, then hot blueberries. Pound cake may be substituted for sponge cake.

Mrs. Charles Graham (Jean)

BRANDIED FIGS

4 pounds figs
4 pounds sugar
2 cups water

2 inches vanilla bean
Brandy

Rinse figs. Make a syrup by boiling together the sugar and water. When the sugar is dissolved, add the figs and cook until transparent. Set aside for 24 hours; then drain off the liquid. Add vanilla bean to liquid. Boil the liquid down until very thick. When cold, remove the vanilla. Measure the liquid and add an equal quantity of good brandy. Put the figs in jars. Fill to overflowing with the syrup and seal at once.

Mrs. James Cathell (Drukie)
Wrightsville Beach, North Carolina

RUM RAISIN SAUCE

½ cup dark rum
½ cup seedless raisins
½ cup sugar
¼ cup water
1 cinnamon stick, broken in half

½ teaspoon vanilla extract
1 tablespoon grated lemon rind
1 tablespoon grated orange rind
½ cup chopped pecans

Pour rum over raisins to plump. Set aside. In heavy saucepan, mix sugar and water. Add cinnamon stick. Bring to a boil and boil hard for 2 minutes. Add raisins and rum and cook for 5 minutes more. Add vanilla, lemon rind, orange rind and pecans. Spoon in sterilized jar and seal. or store covered in refrigerator. Marvelous on ice cream or pound cake.

Mrs. Charles Graham (Jean)

MRS. HILL'S PEACH CHUTNEY

1 (29 ounce can) peaches, drained and chopped (reserve juice)
1 cup sugar
¾ cup vinegar
1 cup raisins
¼ cup crystallized ginger, chopped

1 clove garlic (optional), finely minced
½ teaspoon curry powder
½ teaspoon ground cloves
¼ cup pecans, chopped

Set aside drained peaches. Put juice in heavy saucepan. Add sugar, vinegar, ginger, garlic, curry powder, cinnamon and ground cloves. Bring to a slow boil. When boiling point is reached, add peaches and raisins. Cook over medium-low heat in open pan for 45 minutes or until thickened. Add nuts. Put into hot sterilized jars leaving ⅛ inch space in top of jar. Seal jars. Makes five ½ pints.

Note: This may be served with cheese and crackers as an appetizer or as a side dish with meat.

Mrs. Wilbur Matthews (Katherine)

CRANBERRY-ORANGE CHUTNEY

1 cup fresh orange sections
¼ cup orange juice
4 cups fresh cranberries
2 cups sugar
1 cup apple, chopped and
  unpeeled

½ cup raisins
¼ cup walnuts, chopped
1 tablespoon vinegar
½ teaspoon ground ginger
½ teaspoon cinnamon

Combine orange sections, orange juice, cranberries, sugar, apple, raisins, walnuts, vinegar, ground ginger and cinnamon in a large saucepan. Bring to a boil. Reduce heat and simmer 5 minutes until berries begin to burst. Chill before serving. Makes about 5 cups.

Note: Store in refrigerator.

Mrs. Charles A. Wilkinson (Ann)

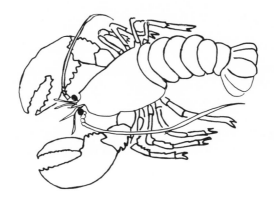

CRANBERRY RELISH

1 pound fresh cranberries
2 cups sugar
4 apples

3 oranges
1 cup pecans

Wash and drain cranberries. Grind coarsely. Add sugar and mix. Let stand at least overnight in the refrigerator. Grind coarsely (or hand chop finely) the apples with peel, the oranges (using peeling of one), and the pecans. Add cranberry and sugar mixture to this. Mix well and serve.

Mrs. James B. Sloan (Blair)

CAULIFLOWER RELISH

2 tablespoons flour
1 teaspoon dry mustard
¼ teaspoon turmeric
1 cup cold water
¼ cup sugar
2 teaspoons salt
⅓ cup cider vinegar
⅛ teaspoon black pepper

½ teaspoon celery seed
⅛ teaspoon garlic powder
1 teaspoon mustard seed
2 cups raw cauliflower florets
½ cup onion rings
Pimento strips for color
Whole red peppers to taste

Combine in 2 quart saucepan the flour, mustard and turmeric. Add water slowly to make a paste. Add sugar, salt, vinegar, pepper, celery seed, garlic powder and mustard seed. Mix well. Stir in cauliflower and onions and bring to a boil. Cook 2 minutes. Add pimentos and red peppers and stir. Let stand overnight before serving cold with ham, turkey or chicken.

Note: This may be sealed in sterile jars to keep indefinitely.

Mrs. Ellis Tinsley (Betty)

SQUASH PICKLES

8 cups sliced yellow squash
   or zucchini
2 cups sliced onions
3 bell peppers, sliced in
   lengthwise strips
Salt

2¾ cups sugar
2 cups white vinegar
2 teaspoons mustard seed
2 teaspoons celery seed
2 teaspoons turmeric

Place squash, onions and peppers in mixing bowl and sprinkle with salt. Gently combine. Let stand 1 hour and then drain. Heat sugar, vinegar, mustard seed, celery seed and turmeric. Pour over squash. Check for salt to see if there is enough. Bring to a boil. Place in hot sterile jars and seal. Serve cold.

Mrs. Charles Graham (Jean)

SPICED PEACHES

2 (1 pound 13 ounce) cans
  cling peach halves
1⅓ cups sugar

1 cup cider vinegar
4 cinnamon sticks
3 teaspoons whole cloves

Drain peaches, reserving syrup. Combine peach syrup, sugar, vinegar, cinnamon sticks and cloves in a saucepan. Bring mixture to a boil; simmer for 10 minutes. Pour hot syrup over peach halves. Let cool. Chill thoroughly before serving. Store in refrigerator. Makes about 4 pints.

Mrs. Michael Donahue (Teri)

MRS. HAMME'S DILL PICKLES

2 pints cucumbers or green
  cocktail tomatoes
1½ cups water
½ cup white vinegar

1 tablespoon salt
Garlic
Dill
Dill seed

Bring water, vinegar and salt to a boil. Pack sterilized jars with cucumbers or tomatoes. Put 1 clove garlic, 1 piece dill (stem, leaves and flower if possible) and a few dill seeds in each jar. Fill with boiling vinegar mixture and seal. Makes 2 pints.

Mrs. Charles Graham (Jean)

BECKIE'S TIRED CUCUMBER PICKLE

5 pounds cucumbers, peeled,
  cut-up and seeded
3 cups lime
½ cup powdered alum
½ cup ground ginger

3 pints vinegar
5 pounds sugar
2 tablespoons pickling spice
Red or green food coloring

Use the large yellow cucumbers usually left in the field at the end of the season. Soak cut-up cucumbers in 3 gallons of water mixed with lime for 24 hours. Drain and wash thoroughly in 3 waters. Soak for 3 hours in 2 gallons of water mixed with alum. Drain. Soak 6½ hours in 1 gallon of water mixed with ginger. Drain. Cook 1 hour in 3 pints of water mixed with vinegar, sugar and pickling spice. Add red or green food coloring for desired effect. Bottle and seal.

Mrs. Charles Graham (Jean)

PEAR CONSERVE

6 cups finely chopped pears,
cored and seeded
Pulp and juice of 3 oranges
Pulp and juice of 2 lemons

1 pound pecans, finely chopped
1 pound raisins
5 cups sugar

Combine pears, oranges, lemons, pecans, raisins and sugar. Cook over medium heat until thick, approximately 15 to 20 minutes. Use as spread on bread with cream cheese.

Mrs. Ellis A. Tinsley (Betty)

STRAWBERRY FIG PRESERVES

8 cups figs
6 cups sugar
2 large or 4 small boxes
strawberry Jello

½ bottle Certo or 1 box
jelling agent

Mix figs, sugar and Jello the night before cooking so sugar will be completely melted. Boil mixture slowly for 20 minutes. Add jelling agent and boil two minutes longer. Put in jars and seal. Makes approximately 4 pints.

Mrs. James Cathell (Drukie)
Wrightsville Beach, North Carolina

BLUEBERRY MARMALADE

1 medium orange
1 medium lemon
3 cups fresh blueberries,
crushed

¾ cup water
5 cups sugar
3 ounces of liquid fruit pectin

Carefully remove peel from orange and lemon. Scrape white from peel and cut peel into fine shreds. Place peel and water in large pan. Bring to boil. Reduce heat and simmer, covered for 10 minutes. Chop pulp of lemon and orange. Add to cooked peel along with blueberries. Cover and simmer 12 minutes. Add sugar. Bring to rolling boil for 1 minute, stirring constantly. Remove from heat and stir in pectin. Skim off top foam. Stir and skim for 7 minutes. Ladle into scalded glasses. Seal at once. Makes six ½ pints.

Mrs. Charles A. Wilkinson (Ann)

Special Diets

Within the same building—columned City Hall and the oldest theater in the U.S.—Thalian Hall.

SPECIAL DIETS

The American public seems to be obsessed with being thin. In its quest for youth, beauty and good health many are vulnerable and easily exploited. There are numerous fad diets touted in magazines, books and by word of mouth, but tragically, they are not all nutritionally sound. There are a number of problems affected by diet. Any problem or deviation from normal health should be consulted or supervised by your physician.

Some of the health problems which require a special diet are hypertension (high blood pressure), diabetes, congestive heart failure, food allergies, diverticulitis, gall bladder disease, arteriosclerosis and peptic ulcers.

We have not included a large number of recipes in this section but have dealt mainly with low fat, low salt, low cholesterol and low calorie. These problems have an enormous effect on a large number of people.

The U. S. Government puts out a pamphlet on dietary goals, which helps the public understand the importance of a nutritionally sound and sensibly balanced diet. The secret of success is to start early in your family's growth and development years to establish sensible eating patterns of nutritionally balanced and satisfying foods.

HEALTH SPA SALAD

2 carrots, coarsely grated
2 apples, coarsely grated
(not peeled)
10 radishes, grated
2 cups red cabbage, shredded
4 ribs celery, chopped or thinly
sliced

½ cup parsley, chopped
½ cup raisins
3 tablespoons chopped peanuts
(or sunflower seeds)
8 leaves romaine lettuce

Dressing:
½ cup corn oil
⅓ cup lemon juice

1 teaspoon honey
½ teaspoon salt

Using food processor: *grate*—carrots, apples with peeling, radishes, and red cabbage. Use *steel blade*—to chop celery, then parsley. Stir together grated carrots, apples, radishes, and red cabbage. Add chopped celery and parsley. Toss in raisins. Refrigerate until ready to serve. Then top with chopped peanuts or sunflower seeds. Serve on romaine lettuce base. Top with honey-lemon dressing.

Dressing: Blend together corn oil, lemon juice, honey, and salt. Refrigerate until used. Keeps well. 8 servings. 90 calories each.

Mrs. Wilbur P. Matthews (Katherine)

FAVORITE LOW CALORIE SALAD DRESSING

2 tablespoons flour
1 cup water
½ cup vinegar
¼ cup catsup
¾ teaspoon liquid non-calorie
sweetener

½ teaspoon salt
1 clove garlic
1 teaspoon dry mustard powder
1 teaspoon prepared
horseradish

Mix flour and water to a smooth paste. Add vinegar, catsup, sweetener, salt, garlic, dry mustard and horseradish. Leave at room temperature for 6 hours, shaking jar occasionally, to blend flavors. Refrigerate.

Note: Also good tossed with crabmeat which has been sprinkled with celery seed or chopped celery. (Low calorie)

Mrs. Fletcher Rieman (Harriet)

NANCY'S MAYONNAISE

1 tablespoon plus 2 teaspoons
  white wine vinegar
3 tablespoons Second Nature
  imitation eggs
1 teaspoon sugar

1 teaspoon dry mustard
¼ teaspoon white pepper
Dash of cayenne pepper
1 cup vegetable oil

In small mixing bowl, beat vinegar, imitation eggs, sugar, mustard, pepper and cayenne pepper until blended. Continue beating, adding oil by the teaspoon; as the mixture thickens, increase amounts of oil. Store in tightly covered container in refrigerator. Yields 1½ cups. 2 teaspoons equal 55 calories. (Low salt, low cholesterol)

Mrs. Ellis A. Tinsley (Betty)

TUNA-ORANGE SANDWICH

7 ounces canned, water packed
  tuna, drained and pressed dry
1 large seedless orange, peeled
  and diced
1 celery rib, diced
2 hard cooked eggs, diced

2 tablespoons low calorie
  mayonnaise
1 tablespoon frozen orange
  juice concentrate
6 slices grain bread
6 lettuce leaves, clean and dry

Put drained tuna, diced orange, diced celery, diced eggs, mayonnaise and orange juice concentrate into large mixing bowl. Mix together well. Store in air tight container in refrigerator until ready to serve. To serve, place one lettuce leaf on one slice of bread. Arrange a spoonful of tuna mixture on top of lettuce. Repeat for each sandwich. Serves 6. 170 calories per serving, with one slice of bread. (Low fat)

Mrs. John Morse (Jane)

BROCCOLI VINAIGRETTE

½ cup corn oil
⅓ cup vinegar or lemon juice
½ to 1 teaspoon sugar (may
  substitute Sweet 'N Low)
¾ teaspoon salt
¾ teaspoon dry mustard
¾ teaspoon paprika
½ teaspoon dried basil, crushed

1 pound fresh broccoli
⅓ cup dill pickle, finely
  chopped
⅓ cup green pepper, finely
  chopped
3 tablespoons snipped parsley
1 hard-boiled egg, finely
  chopped

In a screw-top jar combine corn oil, vinegar or lemon juice, sugar, salt, dry mustard, paprika, and basil. Cover and shake well to mix. Chill. (Makes ¾ cup.) Cut fresh broccoli stalks lengthwise into uniform spears. Place broccoli in steamer basket over boiling water. Cover and steam about 10 minutes till crisp-tender. Meanwhile, add dill pickle, green pepper, and parsley to oil-vinegar mixture. Set aside. Arrange broccoli spears on serving plate. Top with finely chopped eggs. Shake vinaigrette dressing and pour over broccoli. Chill. Pour off excess dressing before serving. Makes 8 servings. 97 calories per serving (Low calorie)

Mrs. Michael Donahue (Teri)

CHINESE FRIED RICE

1 cup raw rice (brown or white)
1 bunch green onions (4 or 5),
  thinly sliced
3 tablespoons corn oil
6 strips Morningstar Breakfast
  Strips

½ carton (4.2 ounces)
  Fleishmann's Egg Beaters
3 tablespoons soy sauce
Ground black pepper, to taste

Cook rice your favorite way. Mine is to place 1 cup raw rice in top of double boiler with 1¼ cups water and 1 tablespoon oil. Cook over boiling water without removing top for 45 minutes. Flake with fork and set aside when cooked. Wash green onion and thinly slice both white and green parts. Place oil in frying pan and cook Morningstar Strips until crisp. Drain on paper towel, but leave oil in pan. Reheat oil and add Egg Beaters and stir quickly with a fork until they are crumbly and dry looking. Add cooked rice, green sliced onions, crumbled strips, soy sauce and ground pepper. Toss with a fork. Serves 4. (Low cholesterol, low fat poly-unsaturated)

Note: This may be made ahead and reheated in oven or double boiler. Very good for vegetarian meal with stir-fry vegetables.

Mrs. Emile E. Werk (Dottie)

FRESH CORN PUDDING

8 ears of corn (grated) or 1 pint
of grated fresh corn
½ carton Fleischmann's Egg
Beaters
2 cups skim milk

¼ cup melted corn oil
margarine
1 tablespoon sugar
1 teaspoon salt

Heat oven to 350 degrees. Grease a 1½ quart casserole. Place grated corn in bowl, add Eggbeaters, milk, melted margarine, sugar, and salt. Stir well and pour into greased casserole. Bake for 45 minutes or until set. Serves 4. (Low cholesterol)

Mrs. Emile E. Werk (Dottie)

GARDEN VEGETABLE STIR-FRY

2 medium carrots, cut into
thirds
2 cups green beans, bias sliced
into one inch lengths
2 cups cauliflower, sliced
2 tablespoons cold water
1½ teaspoons corn starch
2 tablespoons soy sauce

1 tablespoon dry sherry
2 teaspoons sugar
Dash pepper
2 tablespoons cooking oil
1 medium onion, cut in thin
wedges
1 cup zucchini, sliced

Prepare vegetables. In covered saucepan cook carrots and green beans in boiling salted water for 3 minutes. Add cauliflower. Cover and cook 2 minutes more; drain well. In small bowl blend water into corn starch; stir in soy sauce, dry sherry, sugar, and pepper. Set aside. Preheat wok or large skillet over high heat; add cooking oil. Stir-fry onion in hot oil for 1 minute. Add carrots, green beans, cauliflower, and zucchini; stir-fry for 2 minutes or till vegetables are crisp-tender. Stir soy mixture, add to vegetables. Cook and stir till bubbly. Serve at once. 6 servings. 95 calories per serving.

Mrs. Michael Donahue (Teri)

SCALLOPED EGGPLANT

Medium eggplant
½ cup boiling water
1 small onion, chopped fine
1 tablespoon oleo or salt free
butter
½ cup skim milk
2 eggs, well beaten
Black pepper, to taste

3 tablespoons oleo or salt free
butter
¾ cup cracker crumbs (low
sodium crackers), or ½ cup
bread crumbs
⅛ teaspoon paprika
Diet cheese, cut in thin strips

Pare and dice eggplant. Simmer until tender in ½ cup boiling water. Drain well. Chop onion. Melt butter. Sauté onion until tender in butter. Add to eggplant with ½ cup milk and 2 well beaten eggs. Add black pepper to taste. Melt 3 tablespoons butter, stir in crumbs. Place layers of eggplant and layers of crumbs in baking dish, finishing with layer of crumbs. Sprinkle with paprika, and top with thin strips of diet cheese. Bake at 375 degrees for 25 minutes. (Low salt)

Mrs. Conway H. Ficklen (Rose)

SPINACH SOUFFLÉ

2 tablespoons margarine
2 tablespoons flour
½ teaspoon salt
½ cup skim milk
½ package frozen spinach
(⅔ cup), cooked, chopped,
and drained

1 tablespoon onion, finely
chopped
¾ cup Egg Beaters

Preheat oven to 325 degrees. Melt margarine. Blend in flour and salt. Cook over low heat, stirring until mixture is smooth and bubbly. Remove from heat and gradually stir in milk. Return to heat and bring mixture to a boil, stirring constantly. Cook 1 minute longer. Remove from heat. Stir in spinach and onion. Beat Egg Beaters at high speed for 5 minutes. Fold in spinach mixture. Grease bottom of 2 cup casserole; pour in spinach mixture. Bake for 50 minutes. Serve immediately. (Low cholesterol, low fat)

Mrs. William F. Credle (Jean)

VEGETABLE QUICHE

1 9-inch whole wheat pastry shell, partially baked (recipe below)
1 (8 ounce) box of fresh mushrooms, sliced
1 medium onion, coarsely chopped
2 tablespoons corn oil margarine
Salt to taste
Pepper to taste
2 medium zucchini, cut in ¼-inch slices
Kraft Golden Image Imitation Cheddar Cheese—six medium slices
1 (8.5 ounce) carton Fleischmann's Egg Beaters, defrosted
Tabasco to taste

Heat oven to 350 degrees. Wash mushrooms and slice. Coarsely chop onion. Melt margarine in skillet, and sauté mushrooms and onion until onion is transparent. Lightly sprinkle with salt and pepper. Set aside. Wash and slice zucchini, cook in boiling water for 5 minutes. Drain well. Place zucchini in pie shell. Cut 6 medium slices of the Imitation Cheese and arrange over zucchini. Spoon sautéed mushrooms and onions over cheese. Pour carton of Egg Beater over all. Sprinkle top with dashes of tabasco. Bake on lowest shelf in oven for 30 minutes or until set. Serves 4. (Low cholesterol)

Note: Fresh broccoli or spinach may be substituted for zucchini.

Mrs. Emile Werk (Dottie)

WHOLE WHEAT PIE CRUST

1½ cups whole wheat flour
½ teaspoon salt
⅓ cup corn oil
4 tablespoons ice water

Preheat oven to 400 degrees. Prepare 9 inch pie pan by *brushing bottom and sides with oil.* (Important step.) Then sift dry ingredients into a bowl. Mix oil and ice water. Add liquid to dry ingredients using a fork. Stir until a ball is formed. Press into prepared pie pan or roll out between sheets of plastic wrap and place in pan, making a high edge around outside. Prick sides and bottom with fork to keep pastry flat while baking. Bake in 400 degree oven for 10-12 minutes.

Note: If using frozen, prepared shell for quiche bake only for 6-8 minutes, then fill and continue recipe directions for baking. (Low cholesterol, Low fat)

Mrs. Emile Werk (Dottie)

DIET DELIGHT CHICKEN

1 cup diet catsup (no salt)
1 small onion, minced
½ pound fresh mushrooms
½ cup red wine
1 tablespoon maple syrup or
  cane syrup
Black pepper to taste

1 teaspoon cooking oil
½ teaspoon dry mustard
½ teaspoon curry powder
1 frying chicken, or 4 chicken
  breasts, skinned
1 cup white seedless grapes

In medium size mixing bowl, mix catsup, onion, mushrooms, wine, syrup, pepper, oil, mustard, and curry. Put skinned chicken into marinade for 2-3 hours, turning to cover each piece. Preheat oven to 350 degrees. Put chicken in skillet or pan, pour sauce over all. Bake for 25 minutes, spooning sauce over chicken frequently. Garnish with white grapes. Serves 4. (Low cholesterol, low fat, low salt)

Mrs. Conway H. Ficklen (Rose)

HERBED CHICKEN BREASTS

3 whole chicken breasts,
  boned and skinned
2 tablespoons melted butter
½ teaspoon oregano
Salt and pepper to taste

1 lemon, juiced
½ cup white wine
2 tablespoons fresh parsley,
  chopped

Preheat oven to 350 degrees. Brush chicken breasts with melted butter. Sprinkle with oregano, salt and pepper. Pour juice of one lemon and white wine over all in sauté pan. Cover and bake 30 minutes or until juice is absorbed. Slice diagonally and sprinkle with parsley. Pour juice from pan over chicken before serving. Serves 6. 250 calories per serving. (Low calorie)

Mrs. Wesley W. Hall (Anne)

LEMON SHRIMP ORIENTAL

2 tablespoons corn starch
1 teaspoon sugar
1 teaspoon salt
1 teaspoon instant chicken
  bouillon granules
⅛ teaspoon pepper
1 cup water
½ teaspoon lemon peel,
  finely shredded
3 tablespoons lemon juice

2 tablespoons cooking oil
1 medium green pepper,
  cut in strips
1½ cups celery, bias cut
¼ cup green onions, sliced
2 cups fresh mushrooms, sliced
1 6-ounce package frozen pea
  pods
1 pound fresh shrimp, shelled

Combine corn starch, sugar, salt, bouillon, and pepper; blend in water, lemon peel and juice. Set aside. Heat wok or large skillet over high heat; add oil. Add green pepper, celery, and onion; stir-fry for 3 minutes. Add mushrooms and pea pods; stir-fry for 2 minutes more till tender-crisp. Remove vegetables. (Add more oil to wok, if needed.) Stir-fry shrimp 7-8 minutes or till done. Stir lemon mixture; add to wok. Cook and stir till bubbly. Stir in vegetables. Cover; cook 1 minute or till heated through. Makes 6 servings. 174 calories per serving. (Low calorie)

Mrs. Michael Donahue (Teri)

VEGETARIAN CHILI

1 cup Vita-burger mix
1 cup hot water
1 large onion, chopped
3 large pods garlic, chopped
¼ cup corn oil
1 (6 ounce) can tomato paste
1 (32 ounce) can tomatoes
3 (15 ounce) cans kidney beans
½ teaspoon cinnamon

1½ teaspoons oregano
3 tablespoons chili powder
1 tablespoon ground cumin
1 teaspoon salt
1 cup water
Toppings—grated Kraft
  Imitation Golden Image
  Cheddar Cheese,
  chopped onion

Place one cup dried Vita-burger mix into bowl and add one cup hot water, set aside for 15 minutes. Add onion and garlic pods to ¼ cup oil in large pot, and sauté until onion is transparent. Break up tomatoes with spoon and add with tomato paste to onion and garlic mixture. Add kidney beans, cinnamon, oregano, chili powder, cumin, salt, one cup water; then add Vita-burger—water mixture. Simmer covered, 45 minutes, stirring occasionally. If mixture becomes too thick add more water. Serve in bowls with chopped onion and grated Kraft Imitation cheese sprinkled over top of chili. (Low cholesterol, low fat)

Mrs. Emile E. Werk (Dottie)

TOFU LASAGNA

1 package whole wheat lasagna noodles
2-2½ cups spaghetti sauce
2 cups (½ pound) mozzarella, swiss or monterey jack cheese, grated
½ pound sautéed mushrooms
¼ cup parsley, chopped
1 cup Tofu, mashed (or Tofu slices for a layer effect)
¼ cup grated parmesan cheese
Garlic clove, crushed or garlic powder to taste

Cook lasagna noodles, then douse with cold water and set aside. Have sauce, grated cheese, mushrooms and parsley ready for assembly. Mix Tofu, parmesan cheese and garlic. Line the bottom of an oiled 8½ by 11 inch pan with a layer of noodles. Save those noodles in the best shape for the top layer. Sprinkle with about half of the mashed Tofu mixture, half of the mushrooms, half of the parsley, about ½ cup of the sauce, and some of the cheese. Now add another layer of noodles, and repeat the procedure with each of the fillings. Place the best noodles on top, sprinkle with the remaining grated cheese and top with the remaining tomato sauce. Bake at 350 degrees for about 45 minutes or until nicely browned and blended throughout.

Note: Use your own spaghetti sauce recipe. An interesting variation uses two layers of slightly cooked spinach, chopped and drained well. This recipe makes a dish that tastes as if you used ricotta, but is much lighter than the standard lasagna. (Vegetarian diet)

Mrs. John G. Daley (Pat)

LIVER DIVINE

1½ pound calves' liver
1 tablespoon butter
1½ cups onion, thinly sliced
1 teaspoon salt or seasoned salt
¼ teaspoon pepper, freshly ground
¼ cup white wine
2 tablespoons parsley, finely chopped

Purchase or cut liver in thin slices. Cut into strips 1 to 2 inches long. Melt butter in skillet; add onion, cover and cook over very low heat for 15 minutes. Add liver and cook over high heat for 3 minutes. Season with salt and pepper. Transfer liver and onions to a hot platter. Stir wine and parsley into skillet; bring to a boil and pour over liver. Serves 4. 242 calories per serving.

Mrs. William R. Weinel, Jr. (Robbie)

NANCY'S STIR 'N ROLL BISCUITS

2 cups all purpose flour
1 tablespoon plus 1½
    teaspoons low-sodium baking
    powder

⅓ cup vegetable oil
⅔ cup skim milk
unsalted margarine

Heat oven to 450 degrees. Measure flour and baking powder into bowl. Pour oil and milk into measuring cup. Do not stir. Pour into flour mixture. Stir well. Work until mixture cleans side of bowl and forms a ball. Knead until dough is smooth. Roll dough ½ inch thick; cut with unfloured 2 inch biscuit cutter. Place on ungreased baking sheet. Bake 10-12 minutes. Makes 16 biscuits. 110 calories per serving (Low salt)

Note: Spread with unsalted margarine.

Mrs. Ellis A. Tinsley (Betty)

NANCY'S OIL PASTRY

One Crust Pie:
1 cup, plus 2 tablespoons,
    all-purpose flour

⅓ cup vegetable oil
2 to 3 tablespoons cold water

Two Crust Pie:
1¾ cup all-purpose flour
½ cup vegetable oil

3 to 4 tablespoons cold water

Measure all-purpose flour into mixing bowl. Blend oil and water with flour. Stir lightly, with fork, until particles stick together and form dough that clings to fork. With cupped hand, lightly form dough into smooth ball. Divide into 2 balls if making two crusts, wrap in waxed paper, Saran or aluminum foil and refrigerate to ½ hour before rolling. 205 calories per serving. (Low salt)

Mrs. Ellis A. Tinsley (Betty)

NANCY'S CRÊPES

1½ cups all purpose flour
1 tablespoon sugar
¾ teaspoon low-sodium baking powder
2 cups skim milk

⅓ cup Second Nature imitation eggs
½ teaspoon vanilla
2 tablespoons unsalted margarine, melted

Measure all ingredients into bowl; beat with rotary beater until smooth. Lightly grease 7 or 8 inch skillet with margarine; heat until margarine is bubbly. For each crêpe pour scant ¼ cup batter into skillet. Immediately rotate skillet until batter covers bottom. Cook until light brown, loosen around edge with wide spatula, turn and cook other side until light brown. Stack crêpes placing waxed paper or paper towel between them. Keep crêpes covered to prevent drying out. 1 serving (3 crêpes) 100 calories. (Low salt)

Note: May use canned, spiced applesauce, strawberries or variety jams on each crêpe. Roll and sprinkle with powdered sugar.

Mrs. Ellis A. Tinsley (Betty)

CAROB SYRUP

1 cup carob powder
1 tablespoon cornstarch
½ teaspoon salt

¼ cup brown sugar
2 cups water
2 teaspoons vanilla

Combine powder, cornstarch, salt, and sugar. Gradually add water, bring to a boil, and boil gently for 5 minutes, stirring frequently. Remove from heat, cool 5 minutes, add vanilla. Store in refrigerator.

Note: Use over ice cream, puddings, and fruit. Makes 2 cups.

Mrs. Howard L. Armistead (Linda)

CARIBBEAN JUMBLE

1 banana, sliced
1 package (10 ounces) frozen
  sliced strawberries, or 2 cups
  sliced strawberries

1 can (8½ ounces) crushed
  pineapple
1 ounce dark rum

Mix sliced banana, sliced strawberries and crushed pineapple with dark rum. Cover and refrigerate until ready to serve. Serves 6. 110 calories per serving. (Low fat)

Mrs. Ellis A. Tinsley (Betty)

BAKED APPLES

6 small baking apples

1 bottle (16 ounce) sugar-free
  carbonated beverage
  (strawberry or raspberry
  flavor)

Heat oven to 350 degrees. Wash apples and cut in half. Remove core of apples; do not peel. Place cut side down in baking dish. Pour the flavored beverage into dish. Bake about one hour or until tender. 1 small apple equals 40 calories. Serves 6. (Low salt, Low calorie)

Note: Before serving, fresh grated nutmeg may be added to each apple.

Mrs. Howard L. Armistead (Linda)

CHOCOLATE PIE

1 envelope Dream Whip
½ teaspoon vanilla
½ cup cold skim milk
1 (4½ ounce) package instant
  chocolate pudding

1¾ cups skim milk
1 baked 9 inch pie shell

Combine Dream Whip, vanilla and add ½ cup milk. Beat at high speed, 2 minutes, until light and fluffy. Add pudding and 1¾ cups of milk, beat until all is well mixed. Pour into pie shell and refrigerate. Serves 6. (Low cholesterol, low fat, low salt)

Mrs. William F. Credle (Jean)

LEMON CHESS PIE

1½ cups sugar
2 tablespoons corn meal
1 tablespoon flour
1 container, (8 fluid ounces) Egg Beaters

⅓ cup lemon juice
¼ cup margarine
¼ cup skim milk
1 unbaked, 9 inch, pie crust

Combine sugar, meal and flour. Mix well. Add Egg Beaters gradually, beating continuously. Add lemon juice, margarine, milk and mix well. Pour this mixture into unbaked pie shell and bake at 325 degrees for 45 minutes or until top is light brown. Serves 6. (Low calorie, low cholesterol, low fat)

Mrs. William F. Credle (Jean)

SUPER FUDGE

1 cup honey
1 cup peanut butter
1 cup carob powder

1 cup sesame seeds
1 cup coconut, grated
½ cup dates

Heat honey and peanut butter. Add carob powder and then all the seeds, coconut and dates. Pour into a buttered square pan and refrigerate to set.

Mrs. Howard L. Armistead (Linda)

Index

Index

251

253

A COOK'S TOUR OF THE AZALEA COAST
236 Beach Road North
Wilmington, North Carolina 28405

Please send me _____ copies of A Cook's Tour of the Azalea Coast at
$8.95 per copy plus $1.55 for postage and handling.

Enclosed you will find my check or money order for $_____.

Name_____

Address_____

City_____State_____Zip_____

North Carolina Residents please add 4% sales tax.

A COOK'S TOUR OF THE AZALEA COAST
236 Beach Road North
Wilmington, North Carolina 28405

Please send me _____ copies of A Cook's Tour of the Azalea Coast at
$8.95 per copy plus $1.55 for postage and handling.

Enclosed you will find my check or money order for $_____.

Name_____

Address_____

City_____State_____Zip_____

North Carolina Residents please add 4% sales tax.

A COOK'S TOUR OF THE AZALEA COAST
236 Beach Road North
Wilmington, North Carolina 28405

Please send me _____ copies of A Cook's Tour of the Azalea Coast at
$8.95 per copy plus $1.55 for postage and handling.

Enclosed you will find my check or money order for $_____.

Name_____

Address_____

City_____State_____Zip_____

North Carolina Residents please add 4% sales tax.

Re-Order Additional Copies